Footprint Handbook

Cape Town &
Garden Route

This is
Cape Town &
Garden Route

Described by Sir Francis Drake as "the fairest Cape in all the circumference of the earth", the southwestern tip of South Africa has attracted seafarers since the 16th century. Today few people fail to recognize the iconic images of cloud drifting across the flat top of Table Mountain, whales leaping dramatically out of the Atlantic Ocean, or sweeping wild beaches backed by towering mountains and verdant forests. South Africa is also home to a fascinating mix of cultures and its history is compelling too, from the early hunter-gatherers to the arrival of the Europeans, the Boer War and the more recent breakdown of Apartheid. This is reflected in colonial architecture, lively townships, moving memorials and contemporary museums. Cape Town, one of the world's favourite cities, features historic monuments, the botanical gardens of Kirstenbosch, the famous Constantia wine estates, and has some of the best eating and shopping opportunities on the African continent.

Beyond Cape Town, the Winelands' old towns of Stellenbosch, Franschhoek and Paarl nestle in a range of low mountains and scenic valleys covered by the vineyards of historic wine estates which have been cultivating grapes for some 300 years. The southern coast claims to have the best land-based whale watching in the world; in season, sightings are almost guaranteed from the clifftops in Hermanus, while further south the waters around Gansbaai are home to seals, penguins and great white sharks.

To the east, the famous Garden Route is a 200-km stretch of rugged coast backed by mountains, with long expanses of sand, nature reserves, leafy forests and seaside towns. The larger resorts are highly developed for tourism while other areas offer stunning uncrowded beaches, pretty wildernesses and wonderful hikes, and there are various attractions hugging the N2 coast road to distract the motorist.

Lizzie Williams

Best of
Cape Town &
Garden Route

top things to do and see

❶ Table Mountain

Ride the dizzying aerial cableway or hike to the stunning table-top of South Africa's most iconic landmark. Its forested slopes and scenic paths offer an instant escape from city life and there are outstanding views from the summit across Table Bay and the mountainous spine of the Cape Peninsula. Pages 26 and 86.

❷ Victoria and Alfred Waterfront

Cape Town's original Victorian harbour has been developed into a vast entertainment attraction that draws millions of visitors each year. Take a boat cruise around the harbour or beyond, visit the excellent Two Oceans Aquarium, enjoy exclusive shops and fine-dining restaurants, all in a teeming maritime environment. Page 42.

❸ Robben Island

Offshore from Cape Town in Table Bay, and reached by ferry from the V&A Waterfront, this former maximum security prison was where Nelson Mandela was incarcerated. Today it's a fascinating and moving museum and a World Heritage Site for the significance of its place in South African history. Page 47.

❹ Kirstenbosch National Botanical Garden

Set against the eastern slopes of Table Mountain, South Africa's most beautiful formal gardens were laid out in 1913 to showcase the country's indigenous flora. Enjoy the glorious flowers and giant trees, duck ponds and waterfalls, picnic spots and tea rooms, and in summer, outdoor concerts on the lawns. Page 51.

❺ Cape Point

Dramatic mountain scenery, pretty villages, quaint fishing harbours, penguins and seals are attractions around the Cape Peninsula. But it is Cape Point that is the highlight—the most southwesterly tip of Africa features breathtaking bays and beaches and rolling green hills and valleys covered in endemic fynbos. Page 87.

❻ Atlantic Seaboard

Dazzling beaches, palm-fringed promenades, vibrant nightlife and swish restaurants are what make the Atlantic Seaboard suburbs the most desirable places to live and play in Cape Town. Sunbathe with the beautiful people at Clifton, stroll along the Sea Point Promenade, or enjoy sunset and cocktails at Camps Bay. Page 79.

❼ Stellenbosch

South Africa's second oldest town after Cape Town has streets lines with Cape Dutch, Georgian, Regency and Victorian architecture and magnificent old oak trees. The highlight is sampling world-class wines and gourmet food next to the vines at the more than 200 wineries on the Stellenbosch Wine Route. Page 109.

❽ Hermanus

The principle town on the Whale Coast is one of the world's best land-based whale-watching spots, and the Hermanus clifftops are the perfect vantage point. The drive there from Cape Town goes along an exhilarating coastline backed by wildflower- and fynbos-covered mountains, which plunge down to wave-swept beaches and the stormy Atlantic. Page 138.

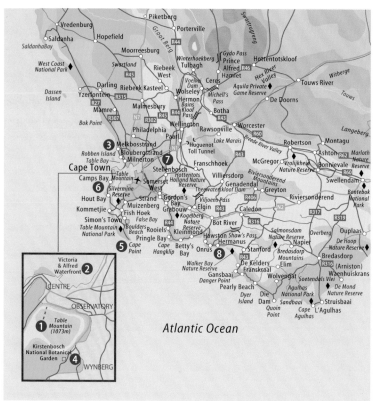

❾ Knysna

A summer playground for the wealthy, this attractive seaside town lies in the heart of the Garden Route – a journey along South Africa's most celebrated stretch of coastline which is sandwiched between majestic mountains and the warm Indian Ocean. With a year-round mild climate, it offers sandy beaches, indigenous forests and peaceful lagoons. Page 178.

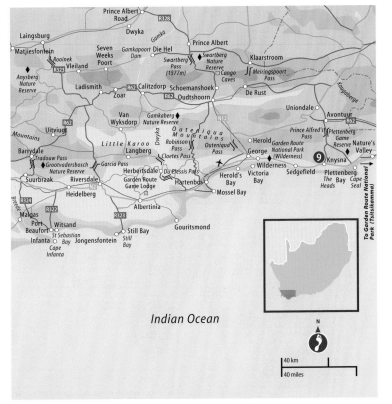

Indian Ocean

40 km

40 miles

African penguin, Boulders Beach

Route planner

Allow two to three weeks to fully explore the beauty and diversity of Cape Town and the Garden Route. The 'mother city', as **Cape Town** affectionately called, is home to historic buildings, museums, the botanical gardens of Kirstenbosch and the famous Constantia wine estates. Climbing or riding the cable car to the top of Table Mountain should definitely be on the agenda, while organized and thought-provoking tours to Robben Island and the townships on the Cape Flats offer a glimpse of South Africa's fragile past.

An additional seasonal activity is spotting southern right whales along the **Whale Coast** from July to November. An easy day's drive from Cape Town, the cliff tops at Hermanus, overlooking Walker Bay, are considered to be one of the best places in the world for land-based whale watching.

Allow at least a day for a tour to Cape Point via the spectacular **Cape Peninsula** with its spine of mountains, fishing villages, golden beaches and beautiful bays. On the way include visits to the seal colony offshore from Hout Bay and the African penguin colony at Boulders Beach, while there are numerous opportunities to eat at a seafood restaurant or shop in the craft markets.

Another excursion is warranted to explore the beautiful historic estates in the **Cape Winelands**, where the scenic valleys linking the historical towns of Stellenbosch, Paarl and Franschhoek are dotted with vineyards. These are open to the public for winetasting alfresco under oak trees or underground in the cool cellars, and many offer superb country restaurants or the chance to stay overnight in a Cape Dutch manor house.

After sightseeing, Cape Town offers a number of relaxing social endeavours from sipping sundowners on the impossibly trendy Camps Bay strip of bars, to a fine gourmet meal at the V&A Waterfront overlooking the working harbour, or a night at the theatre, ballet or opera.

Head further east to join the **Garden Route** at Mossel Bay, stopping off along the way at pretty Swellendam, the third oldest town in South Africa, and also one of its most picturesque. With its appealing, quiet atmosphere, you can visit the museums and historical buildings and sample traditional South African cuisine in one of the many fine restaurants.

Well geared up for local tourism, the Garden Route is the most celebrated region of South Africa, featuring numerous wildlife attractions and outdoor activities, from bungee jumping and mountain biking to surfing and sunbathing. There's an excellent choice of accommodation, restaurants and shopping in the tourist-friendly towns like Knysna or Plettenberg Bay, while the beautiful Wilderness and Tsitsikamma sections of the Garden Route National Park are worth spending time in for hiking through the coastal forests.

When to go

South Africa's Western Cape has a moderate Mediterranean-type climate with long sunny days for most of the year. During summer, from mid-October to mid-February, daytime temperatures seldom dip below 25°C and it rarely gets hotter than 30°C. At this time of year the coast around Cape Town and the Garden Route is at its best, and in the evening there are lingering sunsets over the ocean when the sun sets as late as 2100. However, January and February are the season for a southeasterly wind, which many Capetonians refer to as the 'Cape Doctor' as it blows the pollution off the city. It can get fairly strong and is irritating, so if you're heading to the coast consider the most sheltered beaches.

It is still warm enough to consider a beach holiday until about Easter and during the autumn months of March to June the Winelands look their best as the vines turn an array of gold and brown colours. Most of the rain falls in the winter months of July and August and there are often very heavy storms. It can get cold at night in Cape Town when temperatures rarely top 15°C on a sunny day and fall to around 7°C at night and the interior mountains sometimes get frosts and snowfalls. However, winter is the best time for hiking, avoiding the summer's high temperatures and frequent thunderstorms, and July to November are the best months for whale watching. Nowhere in South Africa is more spectacular than the Western Cape during the spring months of September and October when the grey winter is forgotten and the landscape is covered in an iridescent carpet of wild flowers.

Weather Cape Town

January	February	March	April	May	June
28°C	29°C	27°C	25°C	22°C	19°C
16°C	16°C	15°C	12°C	10°C	8°C
9mm	15mm	15mm	63mm	64mm	79mm

July	August	September	October	November	December
19°C	19°C	21°C	23°C	25°C	27°C
7°C	8°C	9°C	1°C	13°C	15°C
94mm	88mm	44mm	37mm	24mm	17mm

December and January, followed by Easter, are by far the busiest periods for South African domestic tourism in the region. Despite being cooler, July and August are also popular with overseas visitors as they coincide with the European school holidays. Be sure to book your car hire and accommodation well in advance during these times. For further advice on when to go to South Africa, visit www.weathersa.co.za.

Cape Town also has an exciting and vibrant calendar of events throughout the year, which includes food, wine and film festivals, the **Cape Town International Jazz Festival**, the **Kirstenbosch Summer Concerts**, the **Cape Town Carnival**, the **Two Oceans Marathon** and the **Cape Town Cycle Tour** (the largest timed cycle race in the world). These and more festivals are detailed in the listings sections throughout the book. Public holidays are listed on page 211.

What to do

from birdwatching to wine tasting

Birdwatching

With about 850 species of bird, and its incredibly diverse ecosystems ranging from semi-desert to rainforest, seashore and open oceans, birdwatching is a popular pastime in South Africa. Looking for typical bush and savannah birds is easily combined with game viewing in the interior of the country, while endemic, fynbos specials and pelagic birds can be seen when exploring the coast of the Western Cape. **BirdLife South Africa** (www.birdlife.org.za) is an excellent resource and lists the region's birding hotspots and has extensive bird lists. It also recommends tour operators for specialist bird tours, community bird guides, birder-friendly accommodation and self-drive itineraries.

Bungee jumping

Face Adrenalin (T042-281 1458, www.faceadrenalin.com) operate the exhilarating Bloukrans Bungee off the Bloukrans River Bridge, on the Garden Route, and with a drop of 216 m it's the highest in the world.

Canoeing and kayaking

There are plenty of opportunities for canoeing on the Western Cape's rivers, from a gentle few hours' paddle with a picnic on the Breede River to a day's exploration of the lakes in the Garden Route National Park. Along the coast, there are several opportunities to go sea kayaking, which provide an excellent vantage point for seal, dolphin, penguin and whale watching.

Diving

The Agulhas current sweeps warm water down from the subtropical Indian Ocean into the the cold nutrient-rich waters of the Atlantic. This mixing of water temperatures and convergence of two major ocean environments provides the South African coast with a particularly rich and diverse marine flora and fauna. The best time of year to dive the east and southern coast is during the South African winter, April-October, when visibility is generally good and the waters calm. Summer, October-March, is the best time to brave the icy waters of the Atlantic for some incredible wreck and kelp dives. All major diving organizations' qualifications are recognized in South Africa and good-quality dive gear is easily hired. One of South Africa's most popular underwater excursions is cage-diving to see great white sharks around Dyer Island off

Gansbaai (see box, page 146), and you can also dive in the tanks of the Two Oceans Aquarium at Cape Town's V&A Waterfront.

Elephant riding

Lumbering through the bush on the back of an elephant is an unforgettable experience, and there are a couple of places on the Garden Route where you can ride an elephant including the Elephant Sanctuary near Plettenberg Bay and the Knysna Elephant Park. Some private reserves, such as Botlierskop Private Game Reserve, also offer this excursion. As well as riding the elephants, a strong emphasis is placed on the elephant experience and guests are encouraged to interact with them, and an elephant presentation is given, detailing their lifestyles and history.

Fishing

With over 3000 km of coastline and numerous dams and rivers, South Africa has plenty to offer the fishing enthusiast. The unique marine coastal environment offers a wide variety of species including larger game fish like shark, barracuda, sailfish and tuna. There are numerous fishing charter companies on the Cape Peninsula and in the towns along the Garden Route that can organize a day's deep-sea fishing, even for beginners. Fly-fishing, especially for trout, is also popular in the nature reserves and at farm dams.

Golf

One of the world's most renowned golf destinations, South Africa has hundreds of world-class courses, many of which have been designed (or at the very least

played on) by legendary South African golfer Gary Player. With splendid natural surrounds, cool ocean breezes and rolling hills, the Western Cape makes for the perfect setting for a good game of golf and most clubs welcome visitors and hire out clubs, caddies and golf carts. For details of courses visit **www. golfinsouthafrica.com**.

Hiking

The Western Cape has an enormous number of well-developed hiking trails, many passing through spectacular areas of natural beauty. These range from pleasant afternoon strolls through nature reserves to challenging multi-day hikes in wilderness areas. Hiking opportunities begin in Cape Town on Table Mountain and the coastal trails around Cape Point, with a number of longer trails along the Garden Route. For information about hiking trails visit **www.sahikes.co.za**.

Horse riding

Horse riding is popular all over South Africa, and there are opportunities for both the galloping professional and apprehensive beginner. The choice includes a canter along a sandy beach, a leisurely trot through the lush vineyards in the Winelands, and a horseback game-watching safari in one of the private game reserves.

Safaris

One of South Africa's biggest draws is the opportunity to go on safari, and while not quite on the scale of Kruger, the Western Cape has numerous conservation and wildlife-watching areas, some owned by the government (such as Bontebok National Park) while others are in the private sector (including Botlierskop Private Game Reserve and Garden Route Game Lodge). These offer visitors the chance to enjoy some splendid African scenery and spot wildlife including the Big Five: elephant, buffalo, rhinoceros, lion and leopard, along with countless others and innumerable bird species.

Surfing

South Africa has some of the best waves in the world. There are, however, two drawbacks to surfing in the Western Cape. Firstly, as it's on the Atlantic side of the country, the water is cold and full-length wetsuits are generally essential. Secondly, there is a small risk of shark attack – but remember that attacks on surfers are very rare. Wherever you surf, be sure to listen to local advice, vital not just for safety but also for learning about the best surf spots.

Cape Town has a vibrant surf scene with some excellent, reliable breaks on the Atlantic Seaboard and False Bay beaches– Kommetjie, Noordhoek, Llandudno, Kalk Bay, Muizenberg and Bloubergstrand are some of the best. There are equally good exposed waves and sheltered bays along the Garden Route.

There are numerous surf schools which also rent out boards to experienced surfers. For more information visit **www.wavescape.co.za**, which has everything you need to know about surfing in South Africa including weather reports and the low-down on local wave action.

Whale watching

The Whale Coast, along Walker Bay near Cape Town, trumpets itself as the world's best land-based whale-watching spot and with good reason. Between July and November southern right and humpback whales congregate in impressive numbers in the bay to calve. Whales can also be seen in the sheltered bays from Elands Bay on the West Coast all the way round to Mossel Bay and even Ttsitsikamma on the South Coast. For information about whale migration routes and explanations of breaching, blowing, lobtailing and spy hopping, go to **www.whale-watching.co.za**. Also see the box on page 139.

Wine tasting

The Winelands, near Cape Town, is South Africa's oldest and most beautiful wine-producing area and the most popular tourist destination in the province after Cape Town itself. There are several wine routes criss-crossing the valleys, visiting hundreds of wine estates, which open their doors for tastings, cellar tours and sales. For details of all the routes, visit www.wine.co.za.

Where to stay

from the ultra-luxurious s to B&Bs and everything in between

South Africa offers a wide variety of accommodation from top-of-the-range five-star hotels, game lodges and tented camps that charge R3000-8000 or more per couple per day, to mid-range safari lodges and hotels with air-conditioned double rooms for R1500-3000, to guesthouse or B&Bs that charge R500-1500 and dormitory beds or camping for under R200 a day. Generally, there are reasonable discounts for children and most places offer family accommodation. Comprehensive accommodation information can be found on the regional tourism websites listed in each area. All accommodation in South Africa is graded a star value by the **Tourism Grading Council of South Africa**, www.tourismgrading.co.za, and the website has comprehensive lists in all categories. There are numerous resources for independently booking accommodation in South Africa; exploring the websites of **AA Travel Guides**, www.aatravel.co.za, **SA-Venues**, www.sa-venues.com, and **Sleeping Out**, www.sleeping-out.co.za, is a good start.

Hotels

There are some delightful family-run and country hotels, boutique hotels with stylish interiors in the cities and towns and, for those who enjoy the anonymity of a large hotel, chains like **Tsogo Sun**, **Protea** and **City Lodge**. Many of the more upmarket hotels offer additional facilities like spas, golf courses and fine restaurants, which are almost always open to non-guests. Every small town has at least one hotel of two- or three-star standard, and although some tend to be aimed at local business travellers and may be characterless buildings with restaurants serving bland food, they nevertheless represent good value.

Guesthouses

Guesthouses can offer some of the most characterful accommodation in South Africa, with interesting places springing up in both cities and small towns. Standards obviously vary enormously; much of what you'll get has to do with the character of the owners and the location of the homes. Some are simple practical overnight rooms, while at the more luxurious end, rooms may be in historic homes filled with antiques. For listings look at the websites of the **Guest House Association of Southern Africa**, www.ghasa.co.za, or the **Portfolio Collection**, www.portfoliocollection.com.

Backpacker hostels

Apart from camping, backpacker hostels are the cheapest form of accommodation, and a bed in a dormitory will cost as little as R120 a night. Some also have budget double rooms with or without bathrooms, while others have space to pitch a tent in the garden. You can usually expect a self-catering kitchen, hot showers, a TV/DVD room and internet access. Many hostels also have bars and offer meals or nightly braais, plus a garden and a swimming pool. Most hostels are a good source of travel information and many act as booking agents for bus companies, budget safari tours and car hire. The **Baz Bus** (see page 207) caters for backpackers and links most hostels along the coast between Cape Town and Durban. **Coast to Coast**, www.coasttocoast.co.za, publishes a free annual backpackers' accommodation guide and is available in all the hostels.

Camping and caravan parks

Every town has a municipal campsite, many of which also have simple self-catering chalets. As camping is very popular with South Africans, sites tend to have very good facilities, although they may be fully booked months in advance, especially during the school holidays. Even the most basic site will have a clean washblock with hot water, electric points, lighting and braai facilities. Some sites also have kitchen blocks. At the most popular tourist spots, campsites are more like holiday resorts with shops, swimming pools and a restaurant; these can get very busy and are best avoided in peak season.

Price codes

Where to stay	Restaurants
$$$$ over US$350	$$$ over US$30
$$$ US$150-350	$$ US$15-30
$$ US$75-150	$ under US$15
$ under US$75	

Price of a double room in high season, not including service charge or meals unless otherwise stated.

Prices for a two-course meal for one person, including a soft drink, beer or glass of wine.
See page 211 for exchange rates.

Camping equipment is widely available in South Africa if you don't want to bring your own. Lightweight tents, sleeping bags, ground mats, gas lights, stoves and cooking equipment, etc, can be bought at good prices in all the major cities, and some car hire companies rent out equipment. **Cape Union Mart**, www.capeunionmart.co.za, is a quality outdoor adventure shop for gear, as well as outdoor clothing, and branches can be found in the larger shopping malls across the country.

Self-catering

Self-catering chalets, cottages or apartments are particularly popular with South African holidaymakers. The choice is enormous, especially along the coast, and accommodation in national parks and nature reserves is generally self-catering. The quality and facilities vary, from basic rondavels with bunks, to chalets with a couple of bedrooms and fully equipped kitchens. They can be excellent value and the cost could be as little as R100-200 per person per day and are ideal for families or a group of friends on a budget.

National parks across South Africa are under the jurisdiction of **South African National Parks (SANParks)**, central reservations T012-428 9111, www.sanparks. org, which also has a drop-in office at the tourist office on the corner of Burg and Castle streets in central Cape Town, T021-487 6800. The smaller nature and game reserves in the Western Cape are managed by **Cape Nature**, T021-659 3500, www.capenature.co.za. Both offer online reservations and are good sources of information.

Food & drink

South African food tends to be fairly regional, although a ubiquitous love of meat unites the country. In and around Cape Town visitors will find many restaurants offering Cape Malay cuisine, a blend of sweet and spicy curries and meat dishes cooked with dried fruit. Seafood along the coast is excellent and usually very good value. Portuguese influences, thanks to neighbouring Mozambique, are strong – spicy peri-peri chicken or Mozambiquan prawns are widespread. Meat, however, is universal and, as well as quality steak and Karoo lamb, South Africa offers plenty of opportunities to try an assortment of game such as popular ostrich or springbok. One of the first local terms you are likely to learn will be braai, which quite simply means barbecue. The braai is incredibly popular, part of the South African way of life, and every campsite, back garden and picnic spot has one. Given the excellent range of meat available, learning how to cook good food on a braai is an art that needs to be mastered quickly, especially if you are self-catering. A local meat product which travellers invariably come across is biltong – a heavily salted and spiced sun-dried meat, usually made from beef but sometimes from game.

Supermarkets have a similar selection of groceries to that found in Europe. There are several large supermarket chains and the larger ones also feature extensive counters for takeaway hot meals, pizzas and sandwiches (in some, even sushi). The region's numerous farmers' markets and roadside *padstalls*, are great for picking up tasty home-made goodies, organic vegetables, wine and olives.

Drink

South Africa is a major player in the international market and produces a wide range of excellent wines. The Winelands in the Western Cape have the best-known labels (see pages 102-131) but there are a number of other wine regions dotted around the country. South Africa also produces a range of good beer. Major names include Black Label, Castle and Amstel. Bitter is harder to come by, although a good local variety is brewed at Mitchell's Brewery in Knysna and can be found at outlets in Cape Town and along the Garden Route.

The standard shop selling alcohol is known as a bottle store, usually open Monday-Friday 0800-1800, Saturday 0830-1600. Supermarkets do not sell beer or spirits, stop selling wine at 2000, and not all sell alcohol on Sundays. They do however usually have a bottle store attached or nearby.

Soft drinks Tap water in South Africa is safe to drink. Bottled mineral water and a good range of fruit juices are available at most outlets – the Ceres and Liquifruit brands are the best. Another popular drink is Rooibos (or red bush) tea – a caffeine-free tea with a smoky flavour, usually served with sugar or honey, that is grown in the Cederberg Mountains in the Western Cape.

Eating out

South Africa has an excellent variety of restaurants that represent every kind of international cuisine as well as a good choice of quality South African dishes. Eating out is fairly good value and a two-course evening meal with wine in a reasonable restaurant will cost under R400 for two people, and you can be pretty assured of good food and large portions. For the budget traveller there are plenty of fast-food outlets, and almost every supermarket has a superb deli counter. A great starting point for choosing a restaurant is the *Eat Out* website, www.eatout.co.za, which features South Africa's best selection of restaurants, or you can buy the latest edition of their magazine, available at CNA and Exclusive Books. *Dining Out*, www.dining-out.co.za.is another excellent resource that provides hundreds of reviews and contact details for restaurants throughout the country.

South African dishes

Bobotie A Cape Malay dish similar to shepherd's pie but with a savoury custard topping instead of mashed potatoes, and the mince stew is mixed with fruit. Some consider it South Africa's national dish.

Boerewors A coarse, thick sausage made from beef or game meat and usually cooked in a spiral on the braai. The word is a combination of 'farmer' and 'sausage' in Afrikaans.

Bredie The Afrikaans word for 'stew' this is usually made with mutton, cinnamon, chilli and cloves and is cooked for a very long time and is traditionally served with saffron rice.

Waterblommetjie bredie Meat cooked with the flower of the Cape pondweed (tastes a bit like green beans).

Cape brandy pudding Also known as tipsy tart, this warming winter pudding was probably concocted soon after brandy was distilled in the Cape in 1672. Dates and nuts are added to this syrupy dish.

Frikkadels Beef or lamb meatballs, usually made with nutmeg and coriander and baked or deep fried.

Koeksisters A popular sweet snack, which is (sometimes) plaited, made of deep-fried sugary dough and then coated in honey and cinnamon.

Malva pudding A traditional caramelized dessert made with apricot jam and sponge and usually served with custard. Many restaurants have this on the menu, and a twist is to soak the sponge in dessert wine.

Melktart A variation of a baked custard tart, with a biscuit shell and dusted with cinnamon. Popular at braais (after all the meat) and often served in cafés.

Potbrood A traditional yeasty bread cooked with honey in a cast-iron covered pot over the coals. Another accompaniment to a braai.

Potjieko Stew cooked over coals in three-legged cast-iron pots of the same name, and thought to originate from the Voortrekkers who hooked the pots under their wagons and then heated them up again over the fire at night after adding ingredients collected during the day.

This is
Cape Town

South Africa's 'Mother City', dominated by Table Mountain and surrounded by the wild Atlantic, has unquestionably one of the most beautiful city backdrops in the world. Despite being a considerable urban hub, its surroundings are surprisingly untamed, characterized by a mountainous spine stretching between two seaboards and edged by rugged coast and dramatic beaches.

Central Cape Town with its grandiose colonial buildings and beautiful public gardens crammed up against modern skyscrapers lies in the steep-sided bowl created by Table Mountain. Atmospheric Victorian suburbs stretch around the lower slopes, while the Atlantic Seaboard with its promenade and dense crop of holiday flats and the popular V&A Waterfront development hug the coast. Further out on False Bay are the Cape Flats, their sprawling townships a lasting testimony of the Apartheid era.

Cape Town's population is the most cosmopolitan in the country, with a mix of cultures, ethnicities and religions that drive the very pulse of the city. The mishmash of people, including white descendants of Dutch and British settlers, a black African population and the distinctive 'Cape Coloured' community, results in a vibrant cultural scene.

It is this mixture of environments and communities that makes Cape Town such an instantly likeable and captivating city. Few places in the world can offer mountain hiking, lazing on a beach, tasting world-class wines and drinking beer in a township shebeen all in one day. Put simply, it is a city worth crossing the

Essential Cape Town

Finding your feet

To get the best idea of Cape Town's layout, head to the top of Table Mountain. From its summit, the city stretches below in a horseshoe formed by the mountains: Table Mountain is in the centre, with Devil's Peak to the east and Lion's Head and Signal Hill to the west. Straight ahead lies the City Bowl, the Central Business District (CBD) backed by leafy suburbs. This is also the site of Cape Town's historical heart and where all the major museums, historical buildings and sights are. Beyond, on the shores of Table Bay, is the V&A Waterfront, a slick development of shopping malls and restaurants. Following the coast around to the west, you come to the modern residential districts of Green Point and Sea Point, which are dominated by the enormous Cape Town Stadium, which was built for the 2010 FIFA World Cup™. In the opposite direction the southern suburbs stretch west and south, dipping from the mountain's slopes, and here, under a blanket of trees, are Cape Town's largest mansions as well as the beautiful Kirstenbosch National Botanical Garden.

Best places to stay

Taj Cape Town, page 53
Mount Nelson, page 54
The Backpack, page 55
Ellerman House, page 56
Cape Grace, page 57
Vineyard Hotel & Spa, page 58

Best time to visit

The weather is good all year round and at its most pleasant in summer (October-February). December/January is high season with long, warm sunny days and is the busiest time for domestic tourism. July/August are the coldest and rainiest months but see lots of European visitors. Book accommodation and car hire ahead during these periods. See also Practicalities, page 211.

Getting around

Most of Cape Town's oldest buildings, museums, galleries and the commercial centre are concentrated in a relatively small area and are easily explored on foot. However, to explore more of the city, and to visit Table Mountain, the suburbs or the beaches, there are several public transport options, and taxis are affordable. There are also a number of day tours to join and, for the greatest flexibility, it's always a good idea to rent a car.

Public transport in Cape Town is well organized and very efficient. For all public transport enquiries call the 24-hour, toll-free City of Cape Town's **Transport Information Centre** (T0800-65 64 63), which offers assistance for **MyCiTi** (including the airport bus) and **Golden Arrow** bus services, **Metrorail** services, and can help with the location of minibus and regular taxi rank locations. See Transport, page 74, for further details.

City Sightseeing Cape Town, T021-511 6000, www.citysightseeing.co.za, daily from 0830, is a red double-decker open-top hop-on hop-off bus that is ideal if you don't want to drive and stops at all the major sights, such as the Lower Cableway Station, Camps Bay, Kirstenbosch, the Castle of Good Hope, and as far south as Hout Bay on the peninsula. Audio-commentary is available in 16 languages and there's a special kids' channel. The main ticket and information kiosks are outside the Two Oceans Aquarium on Dock Road at the V&A Waterfront (bus stop 1), and at 81 Long Street in the city centre (bus stop 5). However you can buy tickets on the bus or online (for a discount) and join anywhere on the routes. A one-day ticket costs R150, children (5-15) R80, under fives free, and a two-day ticket is R250/R170. The buses are wheelchair friendly. There are two main routes; the **Red City Tour** has 11 stops and runs every 20 minutes, while the **Blue Mini Peninsula Tour** has 14 stops and runs every 35 minutes. There are also add-on options; off the red route, the **Yellow Downtown Tour** is a loop around the city centre museums, while off the blue route, the **Purple Wine Tour** is an extension into the Constantia Valley. Then two free guided walking tours can be added – The **Historic City Walk** (1100) and the **Bo-Kaap Walk** (1500) – both of which start and finish at the Long Street kiosk (bus stop 5) where the red, blue and yellow routes converge. The **Night Tour** is not a hop-on hop-off tour like the others, but it's a three-hour after-dark circular tour from the V&A Waterfront (bus stop 1) that includes a stop on Signal Hill to watch the sunset (picnics can be ordered). Check the website for all the options.

Time required

Three days to explore the V&A Waterfront and the major sights in the City Bowl. Allow half a day each to visit Table Mountain, Robben Island and the Kirstenbosch National Botanical Garden. Another day is required for a full tour around the Cape Peninsula.

Best restaurants

Africa Café, page 59
Miller's Thumb, page 60
Giovanni's, page 61
Gold Restaurant, page 61
The Test Kitchen, page 63

⬚ Cape Town orientation

Sights
Cape Town

Cape Town's icon and one of the world's most recognizable landmarks

Cape Town is defined, first and foremost, by Table Mountain. Rising a sheer 1073 m from the coastal plain, it dominates almost every view of the city, its sharp slopes and level top making it one of the world's best-known city backdrops. For centuries, it was the first sight of Cape Town afforded to seafarers, its looming presence visible for hundreds of kilometres. Certainly, its size continues to astonish visitors today, but it is the mountain's wilderness, bang in the middle of a bustling conurbation, that makes the biggest impression. Table Mountain sustains over 1400 species of flora, as well as baboons, dassies (large rodents) and countless birds. The Table Mountain National Park encompasses the entire peninsula stretching from here to Cape Point. Between September and March you have the additional pleasure of seeing the mountain covered in wild flowers. The most common vegetation is fynbos, of which there is an extraordinary variety, but you'll also see proteas plus the rare silver tree, *Leucadendron argenteum*.

The most popular ascent of the mountain directly above the City Bowl is described below; other parts of the park are covered later in the chapter (see page 86).

Table Mountain Aerial Cableway

Tafelberg Rd, information line T021-424 8181, www.tablemountain.net; the first car up is at 0800, the last car down varies from 1800 to 2130 depending on the time of year, both the information line and the website has up-to-the-minute details of times and, given Cape Town's unpredictable weather, will tell you if the cableway is open or not (always check before going up to the Lower Cableway Station). Return ticket R225, children (4-18) R110, one-way ticket R115, children (4-18) R58, under 4s free. Also check the website for special offers; 2 for the price of 1 on summer evenings to watch the sunset for example. Tickets bought online (not a bad idea to avoid lengthy queues at the ticket office at the Lower Cableway Station in summer) are valid for 14 days. The cableway is closed for annual maintenance for 2 weeks end Jul/ beginning Aug (check the website for exact dates). The cableway is wheelchair accessible, and some parts at the top are too. There are a number of options of getting to the Lower Cableway Station: you can drive and parking is along Tafelberg Rd on either side of the station (but note: parking is almost impossible on busy, sunny days, and you may end up more than 1 km away); go by taxi and once you come back down there is a taxi rank at the station or call a Rikki or Uber taxi to pick you up: by the City Sightseeing Cape Town bus, or by MyCiTi bus – the routes that run between the V&A Waterfront, Civic Centre and Camps Bay (106 and 107) stop at the top of Kloof Nek, swap there on to the MyCiTi shuttle (110) that runs up Tafelberg Rd to the Lower Cableway Station (this shuttle operates whenever the cableway is open).

The dizzying trip to the top in the Aerial Cableway is one of Cape Town's highlights. The first cableway was built in 1929, and since then has had three upgrades, the latest being in 1997. It's estimated to have carried up some 20 million people to date. There are two cars, each carrying up to 65 passengers, and as you ride up the floor rotates, allowing a full 360° view. Journey time is just under five minutes. In the base of each car is a water tank that can carry up to 4000 litres of fresh water to the top. There is the **Table Mountain Café** at the top station, which also has a deli for takeaway sandwiches, cheese and sushi platters and other light meals. To conserve water, they use compostable plates and containers. Naturally, souvenirs of your visit can be bought at **The Shop at the Top**. A network of paths has been laid out from the top station in three circular walks that lead to different lookout points with stunning views of the City Bowl, Cape Flats, Robben Island and back along the peninsula. There are also free 30-minute guided walks, which depart from the **Twelve Apostles Terrace** (below the café) daily on the hour between 0900 and 1500.

Hiking

For the more adventurous there are numerous paths climbing to the top as an alternative to getting the cableway. The most popular route starts 2 km beyond the Lower Cableway Station and follows a course up Platteklip Gorge; there's another path from Kirstenbosch National Botanical Garden. Both take about two to three hours to the top, although they are both fairly tough and should not be taken lightly – do not be misled by the 3-km distance from bottom to top. Given Table Mountain's size and location, conditions can change alarmingly quickly. The weather may seem clear and calm when you set out, but fog (the famous 'Table Cloth' which flows from the top) and rain can descend without warning.

Before venturing out, make sure you have suitable clothing, food and water. Take warm clothes, a windbreaker, a waterproof jacket, a hat, sunscreen, sunglasses, plenty of water (2 litres per person) and energy foods. Never climb alone and the group should hike at the rate of the slowest member and should never split up, and inform someone of which route you're taking and what time you should be back. Also be aware that if the weather is too unfavourable for the cableway to be open, you can't rely on it being open to take you back down, so allow enough daylight hours to make the descent on foot.

Signal Hill

Signal Hill's summit offers spectacular views of the city, the Twelve Apostles (the mountainous spine stretching south from Table Mountain) and the ocean. It is possible to drive to the 350-m summit, which means that it can get pretty busy around sunset. Nevertheless, watching the sun dip into the Atlantic from this viewpoint with a cold sundowner in hand is a highlight of a visit to Cape Town. Avoid being there after dark, as there have been reports of muggings, although the presence of security officers has now reduced this considerably. From the town centre, follow signs for the Lower Cableway Station and take a right at Kloof Nek opposite the turning for the cableway station.

Lion's Head

Halfway along the road up Signal Hill you pass Lion's Head, a popular hiking spot. The signposted climb to the 669-m peak is fairly challenging and takes about two to three hours. The path spirals around the head to reach a part with chains that help climbers over a particularly rocky section; the 360° views from the top are incredible. Many local people tackle it during full moon and are rewarded with a glittering view of Cape Town by night. In the 17th century the peak was known as Leeuwen Kop (Lion's Head) by the

Dutch, and Signal Hill was known as Leeuwen Staart (Lion's Tail), as the shape resembles a crouching lion.

City Bowl
natural amphitheatre with the city's most interesting and historic sights

From the Table Mountain Lower Cableway Station, you look out over the central residential suburbs of Tamboerskloof (Drummers' Ravine), Gardens, Oranjezicht (Orange View) and Vredehoek (Peaceful Corner), and beyond here lie the high-rise blocks of the business district. Together these form the City Bowl, a term inspired by the surrounding mountains.

Closest to the mountain is **Oranjezicht**, a quiet district that was, up until 1900 the area was a farm of the same name. On the boundary with Gardens are the **De Waal Park** and **Molteno Reservoir**, originally built as a main storage facility for the city in 1881, which now provides a peaceful wooded spot from where you can enjoy a view of the city.

There is nothing peaceful about **Vredehoek** today, as the De Waal Drive (M3) brings rush hour traffic into the top end of town from the southern suburbs and beyond. Most of the area has been given over to ugly high-rise apartments, though the residents benefit from some excellent views. This was the area in which many Jewish immigrants from Eastern Europe settled, and have to a large part remained.

Gardens is a lively neighbourhood with a choice of quality restaurants and comfortable guesthouses. Cape Town's best-known hotel, the **Mount Nelson**, is situated here in its own landscaped gardens. The grand gateway to the hotel was built in 1924 to welcome the Prince of Wales.

From here the land slopes gently towards the harbour and the V&A Waterfront, with the commercial heart of the city laid out in between. This was the area where the Dutch East India Company first created fruit and vegetable gardens to supply the ships' crews who suffered greatly from scurvy. Across Orange Street from the entrance to the Mount Nelson Hotel is the top end of **Government Avenue**, a delightful pedestrian route past Company's Garden and many of the city's main museums. Originally sheltered by lemon trees, it is now lined with oaks and myrtle hedges, and is one of Cape Town's most popular walks.

South African Museum and Planetarium
25 Queen Victoria St, at the top end of Company's Garden, T021-481 3800, www.iziko.org.za, 1000-1700, R30, children (6-18) R15, family of 4 ticket R75, under 5s free.

This, the city's most established museum, specializes in natural history, ethnography and archaeology, and is a good place to take children. There are extensive displays of the flora and fauna of southern Africa, including the popular Whale Well and interactive Shark World area, but the highlight is the 'IQe – the Power of Rock Art' exhibition. The displays of ancient San rock art have been in the museum for almost 100 years but, following a process of consultation and dialogue with Khoi-San communities, they have been re-interpreted in a far more sensitive and illuminating manner. The exhibits focus on the significance and symbolism of San rock art, with some fascinating examples including the beautifully preserved Linton panel, which depicts the trance experiences of shamans. Other themes explored include rainmaking and the significance of animal imagery; the eland, for example, appears more often than any other animal in San rock art, and it holds a central role in all major rituals, from teenage initiation to marriage and rainmaking. The

To Cape Town International Convention Centre (CTICC) & Docks

To N1 & N2

To 2

To Helen Suzman Blvd and V&A Waterfront

To Green Point, Sea Point & De Waterkant

To N2 & Woodstock

To Noon Day Gun

To Lower Cableway Station for Table Mountain

To De Waal Drive, M3 & Southern Suburbs

➡ Cape Town maps

1 Cape Town orientation, page 25
2 Cape Town Centre, page 29
3 Gardens & Tamboerskloof, page 31
4 V&A (Victoria & Alfred) Waterfront, page 43
5 De Waterkant, V&A Waterfront & Green Point, page 44

200 metres
200 yards

Where to stay 🛏
15 on Orange 3 E2
The Backpack 1 E1
Cape Diamond 18 C2
Cape Heritage 8 B1
Cape Town Lodge 6 C1
Daddy Long Legs 16 C1
Grand Daddy 12 B1
Hilton Cape Town 7 C1
Inn on the Square 9 B2
Long St Backpackers 11 D2
Protea Hotel Fire & Ice! 4 E1
Taj Cape Town 10 C2
Urban Chic 19 D1
Westin Cape Town 2 A1

Restaurants 🍴
95 Keroom 4 D2
Aubergine 13 E3
Africa Café 1 C1
Biesmiellah 9 C1
Bukhara 8 C2
Café Mozart 11 C2
Company's Garden 3
Dias Tavern 10 C3
Eastern Food Bazaar 15 C2
Mama Africa 5 D1
Marco's African Place 6 B1
Mr Pickwicks 7 D1
Royale Eatery 12 D2
Savoy Cabbage 2 B1

Bars & clubs 🍸
31 16 B2
Assembly 20 C3
Chrome 14 D1
Coco 21 B1
Mercury Live & Lounge 22 D3
Zula 19 D1

whole exhibition, although short, is beautifully arranged and accompanied by the sound of San singing, a disjointed and haunting sound.

Nearby are the ethnographic galleries, offering interesting displays on the San, Khoi and Xhosa, among others, as well as the original Lydenburg Heads. There is also a small display of pieces recovered from Great Zimbabwe that illustrate its importance as a trade centre – there are beads from Cambay, India, Chinese Celadon ware, 13th-century Persian pottery and Syrian glass from the 14th century. The Stone Bones is an exhibition about the fossilized skeletons found in the Karoo, which date back 250 million years – predating dinosaurs. There are life-sized reproductions of the reptile-like creatures, including walk-around dioramas and examples of the actual fossils. Every year in spring the museum hosts the excellent BBC Wildlife Photographer of the Year exhibition. Contact the museum for exact dates.

Next door, at the **Planetarium** ⓘ *T021-481 3900, www.iziko.org.za, 1000-1700, show times vary depending on what's on; check the website, R40, children (under 18) R20*, presentations change every few months, but usually a view of the current night sky is shown and visitors receive a star map to find the constellations and planets that are visible each month. Shows last an hour and are fascinating. Children (aged 5-10) will enjoy the Davy the Dragon show, which sends Davy off into space to learn how to be the best flying dragon ever.

Bertram House
Corner of Government Av and Orange St, T021-424 9381, www.iziko.org.za, Mon-Fri 1000-1700, R20, children (6-18) R10, under 5s free.

This early 19th-century red-brick Georgian House has a distinctly English feel to it. The building houses a collection of porcelain, jewellery, silver and English furniture, the majority of which was bequeathed by Ann Lidderdale. Winifred Ann Lidderdale was an important civic figure in Cape Town in the 1950s. After her marriage to Henry Maxwell Lidderdale, she lived in England and the USA, but in 1951 the couple returned to Cape Town for their retirement. It was her desire to establish a house museum to commemorate the British contribution to life at the Cape. Downstairs the two drawing rooms contain all the trappings of a bygone elegant age – card tables, a Hepplewhite settee, a square piano and a fine harp. Three rooms have wallpaper from London, a very expensive luxury for the period.

Jewish Museum
88 Hatfield St, T021-465 1546, www.sajewishmuseum.co.za, Sun-Thu 1000-1700, Fri 1000-1400, closed on Jewish and public holidays, R40, under 16s free.

Inside this excellent, contemporary museum is a rich and rare collection of items depicting the history of the Cape Town Hebrew Congregation and other congregations in the Cape Province. The history of the community is interesting in itself: in 1841 a congregation of 17 men assembled for the first time in Cape Town to celebrate Yom Kippur. At the meeting they set about the task of raising funds to build a synagogue, and in 1862 the foundation stone was laid for the first synagogue in southern Africa. The following year the building was completed and furnished – quite a feat for such a small community at the time. On display upstairs are bronze Sabbath oil lamps, Chanukkah lamps, Bessamin spice containers, Torah scrolls, Kiddush cups and candlesticks. There is a beautiful stained-glass window depicting the Ten Commandments in Hebrew. From here a glass corridor leads you to a newer section of the museum that is devoted to the history of Jewish immigration to the Cape, mainly from Lithuania. A lot of thought has been put into the displays, which include photographs, immigration certificates, videos and a full reconstruction of a Lithuanian *shtetl*, or village. There are special displays outlining the stories of famous Jewish South Africans, including Helen Suzman and Isie Maisels. The museum complex also houses a library, café and bookshop.

Holocaust Centre
88 Hatfield St, T021-462 5553, www.ctholocaust.co.za, Sun-Thu 1000-1700, Fri 1000-1400, entry by donation.

An intelligent and shocking examination of the Holocaust can be found next door at this modern museum. Exhibits follow a historical route, starting with a look at anti-Semitism in Europe in previous centuries, and then leading to the rise of Nazism in Germany, the creation of ghettos, death camps and the Final Solution, and liberation at the end of the war. Video footage, photography, examples of Nazi propaganda and personal accounts of the Holocaust produce a vividly haunting and shocking display. The exhibits cleverly acknowledge South Africa's emergence from Apartheid and draw parallels between both injustices, as well as looking at the link between South Africa's Greyshirts (who were later assimilated into the National Party) and the Nazis. The local context is highlighted further at the end of the exhibition, with video accounts of Jews who survived the Holocaust and moved to Cape Town.

South African National Gallery
Government Av, T021-467 4660, www.iziko.org.za, 1000-1700, R30, children (6-18) R15, family of 4 ticket R75, under 5s free.

3 Gardens & Tamboerskloof

Where to stay
15 on Orange **5**
Ashanti Lodge **2**
Cape Cadogan **4**
Cape Milner **8**
Kensington Place **12**
Leeuwenvoet
  House **13**
Mount Nelson **15**
Parker Cottage **17**
The Backpack **3**
Zebra Crossing
  Backpackers **21**

Restaurants
Arnold's **1**
Chef Pon's Asian Kitchen **8**
Emily's **5**
Manna Epicure **2**
Miller's Thumb **3**
Saigon **4**
Societi Bistro **6**
Vida e Caffè **9**
Yindee's **11**

Bars & clubs
Rafiki's **5**
Rick's Café Américain **10**

Cape Town maps
1 Cape Town orientation, page 25
2 Cape Town Centre, page 29
3 Gardens & Tamboerskloof, page 31
4 De Waterkant, V&A Waterfront & Green Point, page 44
5 V&A (Victoria & Alfred) Waterfront, page 43

200 metres
200 yards

BACKGROUND
Under the British

Cape Town's history was closely related to events in Europe, particularly the French Revolution. The ideas put forward by the Revolution of Liberty, Fraternity and Equality were not welcome in colonies such as the Cape. The Dutch East India Company was seen to be a corrupt organization and a supporter of the aristocracy. When the French invaded Holland, the British decided to seize the Cape to stop it from falling into French hands. After the Battle of Muizenberg in 1795, Britain took over the Cape from the representatives of the Dutch East India Company, which was bankrupt. In the Treaty of Amiens (1803) the Cape was restored to the Batavian Republic of the Netherlands. In 1806 the British took control again at the resumption of the Anglo-French wars.

When the British took over power it was inevitable that they inherited many of the problems associated with the colony. The principal issue was how to manage European settlement. The Dutch East India Company had only encouraged settlement as a cheap and efficient means of supplying their base in Cape Town. Thereafter they were only interested in controlling the Indian Ocean and supplying ships. By the time the British arrived, the Dutch settler farmers (the Boer) had become so successful that they were producing a surplus. The only problem was high production costs due to a shortage of labour. To alleviate the situation, a policy of importing slaves was implemented. This in turn led to decreased work opportunities for the settler families. Gradually the mood changed and the Boer looked to the interior for land and work. They were not impressed by the British administration and in 1836 the Great Trek was under way.

The National Gallery houses a permanent collection but also hosts some excellent temporary exhibitions that include the best of the country's contemporary art. The original collection was bequeathed to the nation in 1871 by Thomas Butterworth Bailey, and features a collection of 18th- and 19th-century British sporting scenes, portraits and Dutch paintings. Far more interesting are the changing exhibitions of contemporary South African art and photography. Check the website to see what's on. There's a good souvenir shop on site.

Rust en Vreugd
78 Buitenkant St, T021-467 7205, www.iziko.org.za, Mon-Fri 1000-1700, R20, children (6-18) R10, family of 4 ticket R50, under 5s free.

A few hundred metres east of the National Gallery, hidden behind a high whitewashed wall, is this 18th-century mansion. Today it houses six galleries displaying a collection of watercolours, engravings and lithographs depicting the history of the Cape. Of particular note are Schouten's watercolour of Van Riebeeck's earth fort (1658), watercolours by Thomas Baines (a British artist who travelled extensively in South Africa and Australia) of climbing Table Mountain, lithographs by Angas of Khoi and Zulus, and a collection of cartoons by Cruikshank depicting the first British settlers arriving in the Cape.

Company's Garden
T021-400 2521, daily 0700-1900, closes 1800 Jun-Aug, café 0730-1700.

Running alongside Government Avenue are the peaceful Company's Garden, situated on the site of Jan van Riebeeck's original vegetable garden, which was created in 1652 to grow produce for settlers and ships bound for the East. Cape Town's earliest records show that the garden was originally divided into rectangular fields protected by high trimmed myrtle windbreaks, and watered via a system of open irrigation furrows fed by mountain streams. The design was typical Dutch agricultural practice of the time, apart from the furrows, which had been adapted to suit the region's weather. It is now a small botanical garden, with lawns, a variety of labelled trees, ponds filled with Japanese koi and a small aviary. Situated just across from the Rose Garden, some of the original garden was laid out in a quadripartite pattern and replanted in 2014. The vegetables, herbs and medicinal plants are thriving. It's a popular spot with office workers at lunchtime. The grey squirrels living amongst the oak trees were introduced by Cecil Rhodes from America. There are also a couple of statues here: opposite the South African Public Library at the lower end of the garden, is the oldest statue in Cape Town, that of Sir George Grey, governor of the Cape from 1854 to 1862. Close by is a statue of Cecil Rhodes, pointing northwards in a rather unfortunate flat-handed gesture, with an inscription reading, "Your hinterland is there", a reminder of his ambition to paint the map pink from the Cape to Cairo. There is a lovely and stylish café in the garden, the **Company's Garden Restaurant** (see page 60), which replaced the old tea room. It's now a fashionable spot for brunch, lunch or tea beneath the trees and look out for the giant swings which are made to resemble weaver bird nests.

National Library of South Africa
5 Queen Victoria St, behind St George's Cathedral, T021-424 6320, www.nlsa.ac.za, Mon-Fri 0900-1700, free.

Adjoining the garden is the South African Public Library, which opened in 1818. It is the country's oldest national reference library and was one of the first free libraries in the world. Today it houses an important collection of books covering South Africa's history. The building also has a bookshop and Wi-Fi access.

Houses of Parliament
Entry via Plein St gate, T021-403 2911, www.parliament.gov.za, phone ahead to book free 1-hr tours that take place 0900-1200 Mon-Fri, overseas visitors must present their passports.

On the other side of the avenue are the Houses of Parliament. The building was completed in 1885, and when the Union was formed in 1910 it became the seat for the national parliament. In front of the building is a marble statue of Queen Victoria, erected by public subscription in honour of her Golden Jubilee. It was unveiled in 1890.

St George's Cathedral
5 Wale St, T021-424 7360, www.sgcathedral.co.za, Mon-Fri 0800-1600 and during services in the evenings and at weekends.

The last building on Government Avenue and on the corner of Wale Street is St George's Cathedral, best known for being Archbishop Desmond Tutu's territory from 1986 until 1996 (see box, page 34). It is from here that he led over 30,000 people to City Hall to mark the end of Apartheid, and where he coined the now universal phrase 'Rainbow Nation'.

PEOPLE
Desmond Tutu

Desmond Tutu was a stalwart opponent of Apartheid and, like Nelson Mandela, became an influential and respected figure far beyond the borders of South Africa. His powerful oration and his simple but brave defiance of the Apartheid state impressed the world, and won him the Nobel Peace Prize in 1984. He was born in Klerksdorp in 1931 and, after being educated in church schools in Johannesburg and at university in England, he rose through the ranks to become secretary general of the South African Council of Churches from the 1970s. He first caught the international headlines with his call for the international community to stop buying South African goods, which lead to economic sanctions from 1985 to pressurize the government towards reform.

Tutu's opposition to Apartheid was vigorous and unequivocal, and he was outspoken both in South Africa and abroad. As a result, the government twice revoked his passport and he was jailed briefly in 1980 after a protest march. However, it was thought by many that Tutu's increasing international reputation and his rigorous advocacy of non-violence protected him from harsher penalties. He became the first black Anglican Archbishop of Cape Town from 1986 until 1996, and it was from this position that he consistently advocated reconciliation between the parties as Apartheid began to be dismantled.

After Apartheid, Tutu chaired the hearings of the Truth and Reconciliation Commission in 1996, and argued forcibly that the policy of granting amnesty to all who admitted their crimes was an important step in healing the nation's scars. Since then, Tutu has used his voice in the fight against AIDS, poverty and racism in South Africa, and in international conflict resolution. Nelson Mandela once said of him, "sometimes strident, often tender, never afraid and seldom without humour, Desmond Tutu's voice will always be the voice of the voiceless".

The building was designed by Sir Herbert Baker in the early 20th century. Inside, some of the early memorial tablets have been preserved, while over the top of the stairs leading to the crypt is a memorial to Lady D'Urban, wife of Sir Benjamin D'Urban, the Governor of the Cape from 1834 to 1838. Under the archway between the choir and St John's Chapel is a bronze recumbent statue of Archbishop West Jones, the second Archbishop of Cape Town (1874-1908). The Great North Window is a fine piece of stained glass depicting the pioneers of the Anglican church. The cathedral's choir is superb and they regularly perform at evensong.

Slave Lodge
T021-460 8242, www.iziko.org.za, Mon-Sat 1000-1700, R30, children (6-18) R15, family of 4 ticket R75, under 5s free.

On the corner of Adderley and Wale streets is Slave Lodge, the second oldest building in Cape Town. The building has had a varied history, but its most significant role was as a slave lodge for the VOC (see page 92); between 1679 and 1811 the building housed up to 1000 slaves. Local indigenous groups were protected by the VOC from being enslaved; most slaves were consequently imported from Madagascar, India and Indonesia, creating the most culturally varied slave society in the world. Conditions at the lodge were appalling and up to 20% of the slaves died every year.

It has now been developed into a museum chartering the history of the building and slavery in South Africa. At the entrance to the exhibition is a slick cinema room, with two TVs showing a 15-minute film on the history of slavery in the Cape, highlighting the rules under which slaves lived, the conditions in which they were imported and sold, and the fundamental role slavery played in the success of Cape Town. Beyond here, the museum has a series of displays, including a model of a slave ship and images and sounds of what life was like in the lodge. The top floor houses a muddle of British and VOC weapons, household goods, furniture and money, as well as relics from Japan and ancient Rome, Greece and Egypt.

Groote Kerk
T021-422 0569, www.grootekerk.org.za, 1000-1900, free guided tours available.

Nearby is one of Cape Town's older corners, **Church Square**, site of the Groote Kerk. Up until 1834 the square was used as a venue for the auctioning of slaves from the Slave Lodge, which faced onto the square. All transactions took place under a tree – a concrete plaque marks the old tree's position.

The Groote Kerk was the first church of the Dutch Reformed faith to be built in South Africa (building started in 1678 and it was consecrated in 1704). The present church, built between 1836 and 1841, is a somewhat dull, grey building designed and constructed by Hermann Schutte after a fire had destroyed most of the original. Many of the old gravestones were built into the base of the church walls, the most elaborate of which is the tombstone of Baron van Rheede van Oudtshoorn. Inside, more early tombstones and family vaults are set into the floor, while on the walls are the coats of arms of early Cape families. Note the locked pews, which were rented out to wealthy families in the 19th century. Two of the Cape's early governors are buried here – Simon van der Stel (1679-1699) and Ryk Tulbagh (1751-1771).

District Six Museum
25A Buitenkant St, T021-466 7200, www.districtsix.co.za, Mon-Sat 0900-1600, R30, R45 guided tour, children (under 16) R5, café and bookshop.

Housed in an old Methodist Church, this is one of Cape Town's most powerful museums and gives a fascinating glimpse of the inanity of Apartheid. District Six was once the vibrant, cosmopolitan heart of Cape Town, a largely coloured inner-city suburb renowned for its jazz scene. In February 1966, PW Botha, then Minister of Community Development, formally proclaimed District Six a 'white' group area. Over the next 15 years, an estimated 60,000 people were given notice to leave their homes and were moved to the new townships on the Cape Flats. The area was razed, and to this day remains largely undeveloped. Over the years there has been much talk about relocating some of those who were originally displaced to new housing in the area, but as yet there has been no progress.

The museum contains a lively collection of photographs, articles and personal accounts depicting life before and after the removals. There are usually a couple of musicians at the back, tinkering away at their guitars and tin pipes and adding immeasurably to the atmosphere of the place. Highlights include a large map covering most of the ground floor on which ex-residents have been encouraged to mark their homes and local sights. The **Namecloth** is particularly poignant: a 1.5-m-wide length of cloth has been provided for ex-residents to write down their comments, part of which hangs by the entrance. It has grown to over 1 km, and features some moving thoughts. A display in the back room looks at the forced removals from the Kirstenbosch area.

City Hall and Grand Parade

From Adderley Street, a short walk down Darling Street will take you to the City Hall and the Grand Parade. The latter is the largest open space in central Cape Town and was originally known as Wapen Plein (Square of Arms), which was the site of Jan van Riebeck's original fort in the 1650s before the castle was built and the square was used for garrison parades. In 1994, after his release from prison, Nelson Mandela made his first speech from City Hall to over 250,000 people. The neoclassical City Hall, built to celebrate Queen Victoria's golden jubilee and built of honey-coloured Bath stone imported from England, overlooks the parade. Its clock tower is a half-size replica of Big Ben in London. In 1979 the municipal government moved to a new Civic Centre on the Foreshore, a dominant tower block which straddles Hertzog Boulevard. The hall is now a function venue and is regularly used by the Cape Town Philharmonic Orchestra (see page 66) because of its fine 3165-pipe organ. Its specifications were drawn up by Sir George Martin, organist of St Paul's Cathedral in London at the time. Adjacent to City Hall on the corner of Darling and Parade streets is the Old Drill Hall, which was originally built in 1884 as an indoor venue for garrisons during bad weather as an alternative to the Grand Parade. It has been remodelled a number of times since then and now houses the **Cape Town Central Library** ① *T021-444 0209, Mon-Thu 0900-2000, Fri 0900-1800, Sat 0900-1600.*

Castle of Good Hope

Buitenkant St, entry from the Grand Parade side, T021-481 7223, www.castleofgoodhope. co.za, www.iziko.org.za, 0900-1600, R30, children (5-16) R15, under 5s free, reduced rates on Sun. Free guided tours Mon-Sat 1100, 1200 and 1400. Expect to have any bags checked since the castle is still used as the regional offices for the National Defence Force.

Beyond the Grand Parade, on Darling Street, is the main entrance of South Africa's oldest colonial building, the Castle of Good Hope. Work was started in 1666 by Commander Zacharias Wagenaer and completed in 1679. Its original purpose was for the Dutch East India Company to defend the Cape from rival European powers, and today it is an imposing sight, albeit a rather gloomy one. Under the British, the castle served as government headquarters and since 1917 it has been the headquarters of the South African Defence Force, Western Cape.

Today the castle is home to three museums. The **William Fehr Collection** is one of South Africa's finest displays of furnishings reflecting the social and political history of the Cape. There are landscapes by John Thomas Baines and William Huggins, 17th-century Japanese porcelain and 18th-century Indonesian furniture. Upstairs is an absurdly huge dining table which seats 104, in a room still used for state dinners.

To the left of the William Fehr Collection is the **Secunde's House**. The Secunde was second in charge of the settlement at the Cape, responsible for administrative duties for the Dutch East India Company. None of the three rooms contains original furniture from the castle, but they do recreate the conditions under which an official for the Dutch East India Company would have lived in the 17th, 18th and early 19th centuries. The third museum is the **Military Museum**, a rather indifferent collection depicting the conflicts of early settlers. More absorbing are the regimental displays of uniforms and medals.

The free guided tours are informative and fun, although a little short. Tour highlights include the torture chambers, cells, views from the battlements and Dolphin Court, where

Lady Anne Barnard was supposedly seen bathing in the nude by the sentries. While waiting for a tour you can enjoy coffee and cakes at a small café, or explore van der Stel's restored wine cellars, where you can taste and buy wines. There is full ceremonial changing of the guard at noon, which coincides with the firing of the Noon Gun from Signal Hill.

Adderley Street and Heerengracht

Adderley Street is one of the city's busiest shopping areas, and is sadly marred by a number of 1960s and 1970s eyesores, but it does still boast some impressive bank buildings. On the corner of Darling Street is the **Standard Bank Building** (1880), a grand structure built shortly after the diamond wealth from Kimberley began to reach Cape Town. Diagonally across is the equally impressive **Barclays Bank Building** (1933), a fine Ceres sandstone building which was the last major work by Sir Herbert Baker in South Africa. At the corner of Adderley Street and Strand Street stands a modern shopping mall complex, the **Golden Acre**. On the lower level of the complex the remains of an aqueduct and a reservoir dating from 1663 can be viewed.

Continuing down towards the docks, Adderley Street passes Cape Town Railway Station and becomes Heerengracht. At the junction with Hans Strijdom Street is a large roundabout with a central fountain and a bronze statue of Jan van Riebeeck, given to the city by Cecil Rhodes in 1899. At the bottom end of Heerengracht on the foreshore are statues of Bartholomew Dias and Maria van Riebeeck, donated respectively by the Portuguese and Dutch governments in 1952 for Cape Town's tercentenary celebrations. The palm trees here once graced a marine promenade in this area, a further indication of how much additional land has been reclaimed from Table Bay over the years. At the end of Heerengracht, on the corner of Coen Steytler Street, is the Cape Town International Convention Centre (CTICC). This is a much-used venue with several exhibition spaces that regularly holds events for the public such as the **Design Indaba**, **Cape Town Good Food & Wine Show**, **Decorex** and the **Cape Town International Jazz Festival**. Check press for details or visit www.cticc.co.za.

Greenmarket Square

A couple of blocks south of the junction of Strand Street and St George's Mall, a pedestrianized road lined with shops and cafés, is Greenmarket Square, the old heart of Cape Town and the second oldest square in the city. It has long been a meeting place, and during the 19th century it became a vegetable market. In 1834 it took on the significant role of being the site where the declaration of the freeing of all slaves was made. Today it remains a popular meeting place, with a busy market (Monday to Saturday) selling African crafts and jewellery.

Dominating one side is the **Inn on the Square** hotel (see Where to stay, page 54), housed in what was once the headquarters of Shell Oil – note the shell motifs on its exterior. It was erected in two stages, in 1929 and 1941, and was modeled on Shell Mex House on the Thames Embankment in London. Diagonally opposite is the **Old Town House** ① *T021-481 3933, www.iziko.org.za, Mon-Sat 1000-1700, R20, children (6-18) R10, family of 4 ticket R50, under 5s free,* (1751), originally built to house the town guard. It became the first town hall in 1840 when Cape Town became a municipality. Much of the exterior remains unchanged, and with its decorative plaster mouldings and fine curved fanlights, it is one of the best preserved Cape baroque exteriors in the city. The first electric light in Cape Town was switched on in the Old House on 13 April 1895. Today the white double-storeyed building houses the Michaelis Collection of Flemish and Dutch paintings. At the entrance to the house is a circle set into the floor which marks the spot from which all distances to and from Cape Town are measured.

Koopmans-De Wet House

35 Strand St, T021-481 3935, www.iziko.org.za, Mon-Fri 1000-1700, R20, children (6-18) R10, family of 4 ticket R50, under 5s free.

Just off St George's Mall, is the delightfully peaceful Koopmans-De Wet House. The house is named in memory of Marie Koopmans-De Wet, a prominent figure in cultured Cape Society who lived here between 1834 and 1906. The inside has been restored to reflect the period of her grandparents who lived here in the late 18th century. All of the pieces are numbered and a small catalogue gives a brief description. Though not too cluttered, there is a fascinating collection of furnishings which gives the house a special tranquil feel. Look out for the early map of the Cape coastline at the head of the stairs, dating from 1730 – Saldanha Bay and Cape Agulhas are clearly visible. At the back of the house is a shaded courtyard and the original stables with the slave quarters above.

Evangelical Lutheran Church

96-100 Strand St, T021-421 5854, www.lutheranchurch.org.za, Sunday service 1000.

A few blocks west of Koopmans-De Wit House is the Evangelical Lutheran Church, and next door is the **Martin Melck House**, built and named after a wealthy merchant. Originally the house served as a clandestine Lutheran church, as in the 18th century the Dutch authorities refused to tolerate any churches other than those belonging to the Dutch Reformed Church. However, following a number of petitions from German, Danish and Scandinavian officials at the Cape, in 1779 the VOC relented and decided to give Lutherans permission to erect their own church. This was converted from a barn in 1785 and the present church with its fine clock tower and spire replaced it in 1820. A sexton's house was added on the opposite side of the church from Martin Melck House, which has been the Netherlands Consulate since the 1950s. The complex of three buildings was declared a National Monument in 1948. Today the church is open for Sunday service and Martin Melck House is at the time of writing being converted into a history museum.

Long Street

Stretching for more than 20 blocks in the CBD, Long Street is one of the trendiest and most energetic streets in Cape Town and it gets particularly lively at night. Lined with street cafés, fashionable shops, bars, clubs and backpacker hostels, it has a distinctly youthful feel about it, although a clutch of new boutique hotels, posh apartment complexes and upmarket restaurants are injecting the area with a new sophisticated edge. Long Street is also home to some fine old city buildings. One of Cape Town's late Victorian gems is at No 117, now an antiques shop. On the outside is an unusual cylindrical turret with curved windows; inside is a fine cast-iron spiral staircase leading to a balustraded gallery.

The **Slave Church Museum** ⓘ*No 40, T021-423 6755, Mon-Fri 0900-1600, by donation*, is the oldest mission church in South Africa, built between 1802 and 1804 as the mother church for missionary work carried out in rural areas by the South African Missionary Society. It was used for religious and literacy instruction of slaves in Cape Town. Inside are displays of missionary work throughout the Cape, and behind the pulpit are displays showing early cash accounts and receipts for transactions such as the transfer of slaves.

Heritage Square

Two blocks north of Long Street, the entrance is on Shortmarket Street, is this renovated block of 17th- and 18th-century townhouses, which is home to a clutch of excellent

BACKGROUND
Noon Day Gun

Above Bo-Kaap on the lower slopes of Signal Hill, at Lion Battery at the top end of Military Street (look out for signs on Buitengracht Street) is the Noon Day Gun, which is fired at noon every day except Sunday and public holidays. The two cannons arrived in Cape Town with the British in 1795, and it is thought that they were used in combat during the Battle of Muizenberg. After which they were at the castle and fired to announce the arrival of ships, and were then moved to Signal Hill in 1902 as time-keeping instruments. In fact every Capetonian came to rely on the gun for the accurate time – pocket watches in the early 1900s were unreliable and were reset each day to the gun, and a resident of Cape Town could expect to be asked if he had the correct 'gun time'. Today they are loaded every day by the South African Navy at about 1140 with 3.1 kg of gunpowder. The second gun is loaded as a standby in case the first misfires. At 1155 the Bravo flag is raised (an international maritime signal used for military explosives), and the guns are fired at noon. You can watch and listen – it's a massive boom that gives most people in Cape Town a fright even when they are expecting it. The view from here takes in the high-rises in the commercial area of the City Bowl, and the harbour and V&A Waterfront.

restaurants including the **Africa Café** (see Restaurants, page 59) and the **Cape Heritage Hotel** (see Where to stay, page 53). In the centre is a cobbled courtyard holding the Cape's oldest living grape vine, which was planted in 1781. **Signal Hill Winery** ⓘ *100 Shortmarket St, T021-424 5820, www.winery.co.za, Mon-Fri 1100-1700, Sat 1200-1600*, has alfresco tables in the courtyard for wine tasting accompanied by light snacks.

Bo-Kaap and the Bo-Kaap Museum

About 600 m west along Wale Street is Bo-Kaap, Cape Town's historical Islamic quarter and one of the city's most interesting residential areas. It was developed in the 1760s and today feels a world away from the nearby CBD. Here the streets are cobbled and tightly woven across the slopes of Signal Hill, and the closely packed houses are painted in bright hues of lime, pink and blue. The name means 'upper Cape' and it developed as a working-class district for freed slaves, who were mostly imported by the Dutch from Malaysia, Indonesia and other parts of Asia. Today's Cape Malay community in Bo-Kaap are the descendents of these. It was this community who also introduced Islam to South Africa and the Owal Mosque on Dorp Street, built in 1794, is the oldest mosque in the country and there are nine other mosques in the district. The air here rings with muezzin calls before the five daily prayers. Opposite the museum on Wale Street, **Atlas Trading** is a shop worth stopping by to see the shelves stacked with relishes and pickles and at the back the wooden boxes of spices used in Cape Malay cooking. You can do a great half-day tour of Bo-Kaap with **Andulela Experience** (see page 72), which includes a walkabout, a visit to the museum and a cookery class and lunch in a local family's home. To the west, Bo-Kaap blends into the trendy new shopping and nightlife area of De Waterkant (see below).

Bo-Kaap Museum ⓘ *71 Wale St, T021-481 3938, www.iziko.org.za, Mon-Sat 1000-1700, R20, children (6-18) R10, family of 4 ticket R50, under 5s free.* Housed in an attractive 18th-century house, the museum is dedicated to the Cape's Malay community and contains the furnishings of a wealthy 19th-century Muslim family. There are antique furnishings and Islamic heirlooms such as an old Koran and *tasbeh* beads set in front of the mihrab alcove, while the back room has displays dedicated to the input that slaves had in the economy and development of Cape Town. The photos are the most interesting articles, giving a fascinating glimpse of life in the Bo-Kaap in the early 20th century. The house itself is one of the oldest buildings in Cape Town surviving in its original form. It was built by Jan de Waal for artisans in 1763 and it was here that Abu Bakr Effendi started the first Arabic school and wrote important articles on Islamic law. He originally came to Cape Town as a guest of the British government to try and settle religious differences amongst the Cape Muslims.

De Waterkant, Green Point and Sea Point

fashionable residential suburbs on the slopes of Signal Hill

De Waterkant

De Waterkant – once a run-down area of flaking bungalows – is now Cape Town's most fashionable district, with beautifully restored Victorian and Georgian homes painted in bright hues crammed into a tight cobbled grid of streets, climbing up towards Signal Hill. This is not only the city's main gay area, but has an excellent choice of nightlife, super-trendy restaurants, bars and boutiques. Most of these are in the **Cape Quarter** ① *T021-421 1111, www.capequarter.co.za*, a shopping/dining complex with two charming outside piazzas surrounded by restaurants with central water features and trees with twinkly lights. Recently extended, this now covers several large blocks between Waterkant Street and Somerset Road, and the Victorian façades on Somerset Road have been incorporated into the complex. The origins of the district come from when the first merchant, a Michiel Christiaan Vos, developed the land for commercial use in 1817. Vos Lane still exists (and now serves as the main entrance to the Cape Quarter), as do Hudson and Dixon streets, also named after early merchants.

Green Point

About 500 m beyond the Cape Quarter, along Somerset Road, is the start of Green Point, where there is a large roundabout with a turning northeast to the V&A Waterfront. From here, Somerset Road turns into Main Road and then runs through Green Point and the length of Sea Point. Both are upmarket suburbs of high-rise apartment blocks on the side of Signal Hill with ocean views and all the conveniences along Main Road, such as shopping malls and restaurants. Flanking the roundabout is the unmissable new Cape Town Stadium, built for the 2010 FIFA Football World Cup™ at a cost of US$600 million. At 52 m high and surrounded by 60 ha of parkland, it accommodates 55,000 seated spectators (although nearer 65,000 when standing on the pitch is included, as attested to during the 2013 Justin Bieber Believe Tour™). When a sports event or concert is on, Cape Town City Council widely publishes information locally about road closures, parking and special public transport.

To the west of the stadium, the main entrance gates to the **Green Point Urban Park** (0700-1900; free) is off Helen Suzman Boulevard or opposite the lighthouse on Beach Road, although there are also several others around its perimeter. Another legacy of the development for the 2010 FIFA Football World Cup™, it's a series of perfectly manicured lawns and beds planted with indigenous flowers and trees, and it shares ponds and water features with the neighbouring Metropolitan Golf Club (see page 70). Interestingly, the

BACKGROUND
Table Bay and the Portuguese

The first evidence of human inhabitants in the Cape has been dated back to nearly 30,000 years ago. Rock art found in the area was created by nomadic San people (also known as Bushmen), a hunter-gatherer group which roamed across much of southern Africa. Some San groups survive today, mostly in Namibia and Botswana, despite continuing persecution. The original San were replaced about two thousand years ago by Khoi groups, a semi-nomadic people who settled in the Cape with herds of sheep and cattle.

António de Saldanha, a Portuguese admiral who lost his way going east, landed in Table Bay in 1503. They called the bay Aguada da Saldanha (it was renamed Table Bay in 1601 by **Joris van Spilbergen**). Saldanha and a party of the crew went ashore in search of drinking water. They followed a stream to the base of Table Mountain and then proceeded to climb to the top. From here Saldanha was able to get a clear view of the surrounding coastline and the confusion caused by the peninsula. On their return they found the crew unsuccessfully trying to barter with local indigenous Khoi for livestock. The trade quickly developed into a row which ended in bloodshed. There was another battle between the Portuguese and the Khoi in March 1510. On this occasion the Khoi had struck back after children and cattle were stolen by the sailors. Seventy-five Portuguese were killed, including **Dom Francisco de Almeida**, who had just finished five years as the first Portuguese Viceroy to India. Few Portuguese ships landed in Table Bay after this.

whole of this green area in Green Point was vested land that was granted to the Cape Town City Council in 1923 by the Union Government as 'commonage' for general public recreation and sports fields.

Running parallel to Main Road is Beach Road which winds its way from the V&A Waterfront and around Mouille Point, where there is another smart row of apartment blocks and the 20-m-tall red and white candy-striped **Green Point Lighthouse**. This is the oldest working lighthouse on the South African coast, built by Herman Schutte (a German builder) in 1824, and electrified in 1929.

Sea Point

The pleasant **Sea Point Promenade** follows the length of Beach Road from Mouille Point to Bantry Bay, a distance of about 5 km. It's intercepted by short stretches of beach and has an adjoining strip of park where there are attractions for children such as a mini-train, maze, mini-golf and playgrounds, plus outdoor gyms for adults and various public art installations and sculptures. Primarily it's a place where local people jog, rollerblade or walk their dogs and there are good views of Table Bay and some surf spots below the promenade wall. The beach is unsafe for swimming, but there are a couple of rock pools and an excellent open-air swimming pool (see page 72).

The V&A (Victoria and Alfred) Waterfront, Cape Town's original Victorian harbour and the city's most popular attraction, receives in excess of 25 million visitors a year. The whole area was completely restored in the early 1990s, and today it is a lively district packed with restaurants, bars and shops, and there is a whole host of things to see and do.

The V&A Waterfront derives its name from the two harbour basins around which it is developed. It started off with a small jetty, built by Jan van Riebeeck in 1654, as part of his task to establish a refreshment station at the foot of Africa for the VOC. Then in June 1858 serious winter storms wrecked over 30 vessels and as a consequence Lloyd's of London refused to insure ships wintering in Table Bay. Construction began in 1860, when Midshipman HRH Prince Alfred, Queen Victoria's second son, tipped the first load of stone to start the building of the breakwater for Cape Town's first harbour. Thanks to the discovery of gold and diamonds in South Africa, it wasn't long before the Alfred Basin could not handle the increased shipping volumes and subsequently a larger basin, the Victoria Basin, was built. Original buildings stand shoulder to shoulder with mock-Victorian shopping malls, museums and cinemas, all crowding along a waterside walkway with Table Mountain towering beyond. Despite being geared towards tourists it remains a working harbour, which provides much of the area's real charm. To explore the harbour and beyond, there are boat companies along Quay 5 in front of Victoria Wharf offering all manner of boat cruises, from short half-hour harbour tours to two-hour sails to Camps Bay by schooner.

The choice of shops, restaurants and entertainment is unrivalled. When the main mall **Victoria Wharf** opened, it was similar to any other South African shopping mall and featured the usual chain stores. Over the years and with growing popularity the quality of shops has shifted upmarket. The majority now sell clothes, souvenirs, jewellery and specialist items, with luxury brands such as Gucci, Jimmy Choo and Burberry. There are more than 80 restaurants. However, the location and popularity come at a price, and the cost of a meal here is considerably more than elsewhere in Cape Town.

Clock Tower

At the narrow entrance to the Alfred Basin, on the Berties Landing side, is the original Clock Tower, built in 1882 to house the port captain's office. This is in the form of an octagonal Gothic-style tower and stands just in front of the **Clock Tower Centre**, a modern mall with a collection of shops, offices and restaurants. The Clock Tower Centre houses the Nelson Mandela Gateway to Robben Island, from where you catch the main ferry to the island (see page 47). Just next to the Clock Tower Centre, is the small **Chavonnes Battery**

Museum ① *T021-416 6230, www.chavonnesmuseum.co.za, 0900-1600, R35, children (10-18) R15*, which lies underneath a modern office building and displays relics of a fortified structure built by the Marquais of Chavonnes of the Dutch East India Company in 1726. Built in an arc shape, it once held a battery of 16 cannons ready to fire out to sea over

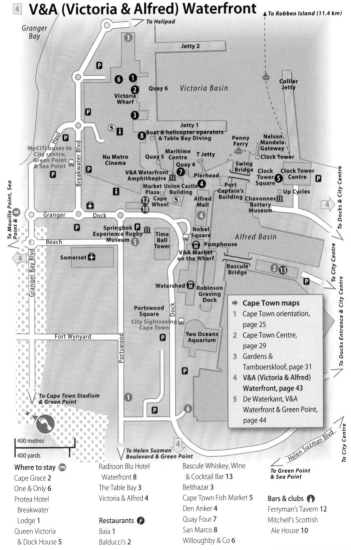

| 4 | V&A (Victoria & Alfred) Waterfront | ▲ To Robben Island (11.4 km) |

➡ **Cape Town maps**
1 Cape Town orientation, page 25
2 Cape Town Centre, page 29
3 Gardens & Tamboerskloof, page 31
4 **V&A (Victoria & Alfred) Waterfront, page 43**
5 De Waterkant, V&A Waterfront & Green Point, page 44

Where to stay 🛏
Cape Grace **2**
One & Only **6**
Protea Hotel
  Breakwater
  Lodge **1**
Queen Victoria
  & Dock House **5**

Radisson Blu Hotel
  Waterfront **8**
The Table Bay **3**
Victoria & Alfred **4**

Restaurants 🍴
Baia **1**
Balducci's **2**

Bascule Whiskey, Wine
  & Cocktail Bar **13**
Belthazar **3**
Cape Town Fish Market **5**
Den Anker **4**
Quay Four **7**
San Marco **8**
Willoughby & Co **6**

Bars & clubs 🍸
Ferryman's Tavern **12**
Mitchell's Scottish
  Ale House **10**

a 180° angle. It remained in service until 1860 when the construction of Alfred Basin began and some of the demolished walls were used to fortify the new docks. Parts of the remaining walls can be seen, there are exhibits about Cape Town's history as a military outpost, and visitors can help load an 18-pound cannon. This side of the Waterfront is connected to the bulk of the area by a swing bridge, which swings open every 10 minutes to allow boats to pass underneath.

Union Castle Building

Walking across the swing bridge (look out for the Cape fur seals on a landing to your right as you cross), you come to the stocky square building known as **Union Castle Building** (1919), designed by the firm of architects owned by Sir Herbert Baker. The Union Steamship Company and the Castle Line both ran monthly mail ships between Britain and South Africa in the late 19th century. In 1900 they amalgamated and from then on mail was delivered every week. The last Union Castle ship to sail to England

5 De Waterkant, V&A Waterfront & Green Point

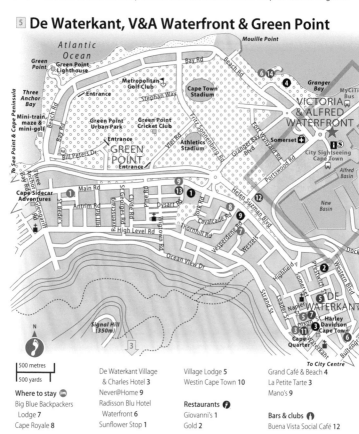

Where to stay	De Waterkant Village & Charles Hotel **3**	Village Lodge **5**	Grand Café & Beach **4**
Big Blue Backpackers Lodge **7**	Never@Home **9**	Westin Cape Town **10**	La Petite Tarte **3**
Cape Royale **8**	Radisson Blu Hotel Waterfront **6**	**Restaurants**	Mano's **9**
	Sunflower Stop **1**	Giovanni's **1**	**Bars & clubs**
		Gold **2**	Buena Vista Social Café **12**

with the mail was the *Windsor Castle* in 1977. This is now home to the **Maritime Centre** ⓘ *T021-405 2880, www.iziko.org.za, 1000-1700, R20, children (6-18) R10, family of 4 ticket R50, under 5s free*, a collection of model ships and objects associated with the era of mail ships. It also holds an archive of over 20,000 photographs of ships that visited Cape Town from the 1920s to the 1960s.

Opposite the Union Castle Building is the **Victoria & Alfred Hotel**. Now a luxury four-star hotel and shopping mall, the building was originally a coal store before being converted into Union Castle's warehouse and customs baggage store.

To the south of the hotel is **Nobel Square** ⓘ *www.nobelsquare.com*, which was opened on 16 December 2006, the Day of Reconciliation, and pays tribute to four of South Africa's Nobel Peace Prize laureates – the late Nkosi Albert Luthuli (1961), Archbishop Desmond Tutu (1984) and FW de Klerk and Nelson Mandela who jointly won it in 1993. Slightly larger than life-size statues of the four formidable men stand next to each other with a backdrop of Table Mountain and, in front of the sculpture, the Laureates' preferred quotations engraved in their chosen language. In the middle of the square, the Peace and Democracy sculpture – a narrative work of a jumble of people and faces on top of each other – represents the contribution made by women and children to the attainment of peace in South Africa. Flanking the square is the entrance to the V&A Market on the **Wharf** ⓘ *T021-276 0200, www.marketonthewharf.co.za, Apr-Oct 1000-1730, Nov-Mar 1000-1900*, a lively market in the Waterfront's historical Pumphouse with over 60 food stalls serving anything from coffee and muffins to Mexican and Thai snacks and oysters with a glass of bubbly and there's an artisanal beer bar.

Market Square

Beyond the Union Castle Building and Quay 4 is Market Square, an open plaza-like area in front of one of the main entrances to Victoria Wharf. It's a popular spot for buskers and is lined with restaurants and pubs with alfresco tables, as well as the main food court of Victoria Wharf that has numerous takeaway counters and a communal seating area. The attractions here include the **V&A Waterfront Amphitheatre** ⓘ *daily at 1700 in summer, and weekends at 1600 in winter, check the programme on the website*, an outdoor semi-circle of brick steps overlooking a stage where there are free concerts and children's entertainment, and the **Cape Wheel** ⓘ *T021-418 2502, www.*

Victoria Basin

South Arm

Port

➡ **Cape Town maps**
1 Cape Town orientation, page 25
2 Cape Town Centre, page 29
3 Gardens & Tamboerskloof, page 31
4 V&A (Victoria & Alfred) Waterfront, page 43
5 De Waterkant, V&A Waterfront & Green Point, page 44

Duncan Rd

... Rd

ⓟ Caltex

☐ SUP Cape Town

Customs Gate

Flyover

10

Cape Town International Convention Centre (CTICC) ✉

Long St

Walled

2 S Sisulu Av

To Airport & Winelands

Café Manhattan **11**
Crew Bar **5**
Fireman's Arms **6**
The Piano Bar **7**
Slug & Lettuce **13**
Tobago's **14**

BACKGROUND

The growth of the city and the port

Industrialization in Europe brought great change, especially when the first steamship, the *Enterprise*, arrived in Table Bay in October 1825. After considerable delay and continual loss of life and cargoes, work began on two basins and breakwater piers. The first truckload of construction rocks was tipped by Prince Alfred, the 16-year-old son of Queen Victoria, on 17 September 1860. The Alfred Basin was completed in 1870 and a dry dock was added in 1881.

No sooner had the first basin been completed than diamonds and gold were discovered in South Africa. Over the next 40 years Cape Town and the docks were to change beyond recognition. In 1900 work began on a new breakwater which would protect an area of 27 km. After five years' work the **Victoria Basin** was opened. This new basin was able to shelter the new generation of ships using Table Bay but was unable to cope with the increase in numbers during the **Anglo-Boer War**. A third basin was created to the east of Victoria Basin in 1932 and for a while this seemed to have solved the problem, but fate was against Cape Town. In January 1936 the largest ship to visit South Africa docked with ease at B berth in the new basin. The boat, which was being used to help promote tourism in South Africa, was filled with wealthy and famous visitors. The morning on which she was due to sail, a strong southeasterly wind blew up and pressed the liner so firmly against the quay that she couldn't sail. In one morning all of the new basin's weaknesses had been exposed.

The next phase of growth was an ambitious one, and it was only completed in 1945. The project involved the dredging of Table Bay and the reclaiming of land. The spoil from the dredging provided 140 sq km of landfill, known as Foreshore. This new land extends from the present-day railway station to **Duncan Dock**. As you walk or drive around Cape Town today, remember that just over 50 years ago the sea came up to the main railway station.

capewheel.co.za, Mon-Thu 1200-2100, Fri-Sat 1000-2200, Sun 1000-2100 R100, children (4-12) R50, family of 4 ticket R270, under 4s free, an observation wheel and a mini-replica of the London Eye. It has 30 air-conditioned cars, two of which can accommodate wheelchairs, and the ride takes about 15 minutes to an optimum height of 40 m. It offers superb views of the V&A, Table Mountain, Cape Town Stadium and Robben Island.

Dock Road

Heading south, on the other side of Dock Road on Portswood Ridge above the car park, is the **Springbok Experience Rugby Museum** ⓘ *T021-418 4741, www.sarugby.co.za, 1000-1800, R65, children (6-18) R40, under 5s free*, which will appeal to sports fans and celebrates the history of the Springboks and South African rugby from the 1860s to the present day. Historic objects on display include famous trophies, jerseys, boots and other memorabilia, many legendary matches can be analyzed on TV and interactive exhibits include the 'Springbok Trials' zone where visitors can test their kicking, passing, fitness and reaction skills. Next to it on the corner of Dock Road is the 1894 **Time Ball Tower**; its purpose was to act as an accurate reference for ships' navigators who set their clocks as the ball on the roof fell. Correct time was vital for navigators to be able to determine precise longitude. Across the road is the newly developed **Watershed** (formerly the Waterfront Craft Market), which is home to more than 150 stalls selling quality craft and design products (see page 68). Walking through here is a good option to get to the aquarium.

Two Oceans Aquarium
Dock Rd, T021-418 3823, www.aquarium.co.za, 0930-1800, R131, children (4-13) R63 (14-17) R102, under 4s free, online tickets are 10% less.

Focusing on the unique Cape marine environment created by the merging of the Atlantic and Indian Ocean, this aquarium is the top attraction on the Waterfront. The display begins with a walk through the Indian Ocean, where you'll follow a route past tanks filled with a multitude of colourful fish, turtles, seahorses and octopuses. Highlights include giant spider crabs and phosphorescent jellyfish floating in a mesmerizing circular current. Then you walk past touch pools, where children can pick up spiky starfish and slimy sea slugs. Free puppet shows and face painting keep children busy at the **Alpha Activity Centre** in the basement. The main wall here looks out into the water of the actual harbour, and you can watch Cape fur seals dart and dive before the glass. Upstairs is a vast tank holding the Kelp Forest, an extraordinary tangle of giant kelp that sways drunkenly in the artificial tides. The highlight is the Predators exhibit, a circular tank complete with glass tunnel, holding ragged-tooth sharks, eagle rays, turtles and some impressively large hunting fish. There are daily feeds at 1500 and, with an Open Water diving certificate, you can arrange to dive with the sharks for R740. The **Shoreline Café** overlooks the yacht marina and has a children's play area with childminders.

★Robben Island
former prison synonymous with Nelson Mandela; now a museum reached by ferry

Lying 12 km off Green Point's shores, Robben Island is best known as the notorious prison that held many of the ANC's most prominent members, including Nelson Mandela and Walter Sisulu. It was originally named by the Dutch, after the term for seals, 'rob' – actually a misnomer as none are found here.

Tours to the island are run by the **Robben Island Museum** ① *T021-413 4220, www.robben-island.org.za.* The Nelson Mandela Gateway at the Clock Tower Centre is the embarkation and disembarkation point for tours. The Gateway also houses a shop, the ticket office and a small **museum** ① *open 0730-2100*, with photographic and interactive displays on Apartheid and the rise of African nationalism. An air-conditioned catamaran completes the half-hour journey to the island. Tickets cost R270, children (under 18) R150. Tours begin with a 45-minute drive around the key sites, including Sobukwe's house, the lime quarry where Mandela was forced to work, the leper cemetery and the houses of former warders. Whenever possible, tours around the Maximum Security Prison are conducted by ex-political prisoners, who paint a vivid picture of prison life here. Departures are daily at 0900, 1100, 1300 and 1500 (no 1500 ferry in winter), and the whole excursion lasts 3½ hours. You must remain with your guide throughout the tour. Be sure to book a day ahead (or several days in peak season) as tickets sell out quickly, and always phone ahead to see if the ferry is running in bad weather. Do not drink any tap water on the island.

The island's history of occupation started in 1806, when John Murray was granted permission by the British to conduct whaling from the island. During this period the

BACKGROUND
Impact of the Apartheid years

The descendants of the large and diverse slave population have given Cape Town a particularly cosmopolitan atmosphere. Unfortunately, Apartheid urban planning meant that many of the more vibrant areas of the city in the earlier part of this century were destroyed. The most notorious case is that of District Six, a racially mixed, low income housing area on the edge of the City Bowl. The Apartheid government could not tolerate such an area, especially so close to the centre of the city, and the residents, most of whom were classified as 'coloured', were moved out to the soulless townships of the Cape Flats, such as Mitchell's Plain. The area was bulldozed but few new developments have taken place on the site: this accounts for the large areas of open ground in the area between the City Bowl and the suburb of Woodstock. Happily, the government recently handed over the first pocket of re-developed land to a small group of ex-residents of District Six and their descendants. What the area will become remains to be seen – the issue remains controversial as many ex-residents feel the open, barren land should remain as a poignant testimony to the forced removals.

Other reminders of the cosmopolitan history of Cape Town can be experienced in the area to the west of Buitengracht Street. This district, known as **Bo-Kaap**, is still home to a small Islamic (Cape Malay) community that somehow managed to survive the onslaught of Apartheid urban planning. The coloured population of Cape Town has historically outweighed both the white and African populations, hence the widespread use of Afrikaans in the city. This balance was maintained by Apartheid policies that prevented Africans from migrating into the Western Cape from the Eastern Cape and elsewhere. This policy was not, however, able to withstand the pressure of the poor rural Africans' desire to find opportunities in the urban economy. Over the past couple of decades there has been an enormous growth in the African population of Cape Town. Many of these new migrants have been forced to settle in squatter areas, such as the notorious Crossroads Camp next to the N2 highway. During the Apartheid era these squatter camps were frequently bulldozed and the residents evicted but as soon as they were cleared they sprang up again. Crossroads was a hotbed of resistance to the Apartheid state and much of the Cape Flats area existed in a state of near civil war throughout much of the 1980s.

Today, Cape Town remains the most cosmopolitan city in South Africa. The official colour barriers have long since disappeared and residential boundaries are shifting. The economic balance, too, is beginning to change: and the black and coloured middle class has strengthened considerably. There are still pockets of low-income housing, notably the sprawling townships on the Cape Flats, but large areas in the northern suburbs have expanded into middle-income districts, and the Atlantic Seaboard and southern suburbs continue to boast some of the most exclusive and expensive real estate on the African continent.

authorities started to use the island as a dumping ground for common convicts; these were brought back to the mainland in 1843, and their accommodation was deemed suitable only for lepers and the mentally ill. These were in turn moved to the mainland between 1913 and 1931, and the island entered a new era as a military base during the Second World War. In 1960 the military passed control of the island over to the Department of Prisons, and it remained a prison until 1996. On 1 December 1999 the island was declared a World Heritage Site by UNESCO.

Robben Island's effectiveness as a prison did not rest simply with the fact that escape was virtually impossible. The authorities anticipated that the idea of 'out of sight, out of mind' would be particularly applicable here, and to a certain extent they were correct. Certainly, its isolation did much to break the spirit of political prisoners, not least Robert Sobukwe's. Sobukwe, the leader of the Pan African Congress, was kept in solitary confinement for nine years. Other political prisoners were spared that at least, although in 1971 they were separated from common law prisoners, as they were deemed a 'bad' influence. Conditions were harsh, with forced hard labour and routine beatings. Much of the daily running of the maximum security prison was designed to reinforce racial divisions: all the wardens, and none of the prisoners, were white; black prisoners, unlike those deemed coloured, had to wear short trousers and were given smaller food rations. Contact with the outside world was virtually non-existent – visitors had to apply for permission six months in advance and were allowed to stay for just half an hour. Newspapers were banned and letters were limited to one every six months.

Yet despite these measures, the B-Section, which housed Mandela and other major political prisoners, became the international focus of the fight against Apartheid. The last political prisoners left the island in 1991.

Southern suburbs
forests, gardens and vineyards on Table Mountain's eastern slopes

Primarily encompassing the more affluent residential areas of Cape Town, the suburbs, stretching southeast from the centre, are an interesting diversion to the usual tourist spots. Although a car is the best way to visit them, it's possible to reach all by train – the Metrorail service between the city centre and Simon's Town runs through the suburbs and there is the option of buying a hop-on hop-off ticket on this line as part of the Southern Line initiative (see page 89), but to get to the sights away from the railway line you'll need a car or the City Sightseeing Cape Town bus (page 25) stops at some.

Woodstock
The first suburb, less than 3 km from the city centre, is **Woodstock**, a mixed commercial and residential area, and historically a working-class coloured district. Today it is somewhat run down, although the back streets are an attractive mesh of Victorian bungalows, some of which have been taken over by fashionable bars and restaurants, and both Main and Albert roads are dotted with junk and decor shops. Woodstock's most popular attraction is the **Old Biscuit Mill** ① *373-375 Albert Rd, T021-447 8194, www.theoldbiscuitmill.co.za, Mon-Sat 1000-1700,* a converted mill and now home to a variety of 'lifestyle' shops – furniture, interior design and art galleries – and restaurants. The overwhelming reason to come to Woodstock is the **Neighbourgoods Market** ① *373 Albert Rd, T021-448 1438, www.*

neighbourgoodsmarket.co.za, Sat 0900-1400, held at the Old Biscuit Mill on a Saturday morning. The stalls sell organic vegetables, home-made bread, pastries, cupcakes, chutneys, jams, goat's cheese, chocolate and many more delicious goodies. You can also get food such as Indian curries, Mexican wraps, Greek kebabs, sushi and pizza, accompanied by a glass of fizz or a bloody Mary, and sit on sociable trestle tables or hay bales to eat.

Observatory

After Woodstock, Observatory is an appealing area of tightly packed houses, narrow streets and, being close to the university, student hangouts. The observatory after which the suburb is named is where Station Road intersects Liesbeeck Parkway. Aside from making astronomical observations the observatory is responsible for accurate standard time in South Africa, and has a seismograph which records earthquakes around the world. Observatory is also where you'll find the **Groot Schuur Hospital**, the site of the world's first heart transplant performed by Professor Christiaan Barnard. The **Heart of Cape Town Museum** ⓘ *Groot Schuur Hospital, Main Rd, Observatory, T021-404 1967, www. heartofcapetown.co.za, 2-hr guided tours run daily at 0900, 1100, 1300 and 1500 and must be pre-booked, R200, children (10-16) R100, under 10s free,* explains the story and has a number of rooms including the two adjoining theatres that were used for the transplant, which took place in 1967. The informative tours go a long way to recreate the tension of the night of 2 December, and the eerie waxwork figures of Barnard and his team are brought to life with a soundtrack of clinking scalpels.

Mowbray, Rosebank and Rondebosch

The next suburbs of Mowbray, Rosebank and Rondebosch lie just below the **University of Cape Town (UTC)**. Again, they are popular with students and have a good selection of restaurants and shops. **Mowbray** was originally known as Driekoppen, or three heads, after the murder by three slaves of a European foreman and his wife in 1724. On their capture they were beheaded and their heads impaled on stakes at the farm entrance to act as a deterrent. **Rondebosch,** is well known for being associated with education, and aside from the university, several important schools were founded in the district. The area was also important from a practical point of view: in 1656 Van Riebeeck realized that Company's Garden was exposed to a damaging southeast wind. His first choice of a more sheltered spot was Rondebosch. This proved a success and a grain storage barn was built. Early accounts describe the area as wild country, with the farmers frequently losing livestock to hyenas, lions and leopards – an image that is hard to imagine as you sit in the evening rush hour on Rhodes Drive. Also in Rondebosch is the **Groot Schuur Estate**, the president's official residence and the original residence of the Cape Governor over 200 years ago.

Irma Stern Museum

Cecil Rd, Rosebank, T021-685 5686, www.irmasternmuseum.org.za, Tue-Fri 1000-1700, Sat 1000-1400, R20, children (under 16) R10.

Irma Stern was one of South Africa's pioneering artists and her lovely house displays a mixture of her own works, a collection of artefacts from across Africa and some fine pieces of antique furniture from overseas, including 17th-century Spanish chairs, 19th-century German oak furniture and Swiss *mardi gras* masks. Her portraits are particularly poignant and those of her close friends are superb, while her religious art is rather more disturbing. Stern's studio, complete with paint brushes and palettes, has been left as it was when she died.

Rhodes Memorial

Cearly signposted off Rhodes Dr (M3), by the Rondesbosch turning, T021-689 9151, www.rhodesmemorial.co.za, Nov-Apr 0700-1900, May-Oct 0800-1800.

The imposing granite memorial to Cecil John Rhodes (Cape Prime Minister from 1890 to 1896) was designed by Francis Masey and Sir Herbert Baker. Four bronze lions flank a wide flight of steps which lead up to a Greek Temple. The temple houses an immense bronze head of Rhodes, wrought by JM Swan. Above the head are the words "slave to the spirit and life work of Cecil John Rhodes who loved and served South Africa". At the base of the steps (one for each year of his short 49-year life) is an immense bronze mounted figure of *Physical Energy* given to South Africa by GF Watts, a well-regarded sculptor of the time; the original stands in Hyde Park, London. Other than the memorial, the great attraction here is the magnificent view of the Cape Flats and the southern suburbs. Behind the memorial are a number of popular trails leading up the slopes of Devil's Peak. Also tucked away here is an excellent little tea house (0900-1700) set in a garden of blue hydrangeas that serves breakfasts, light meals and excellent cheesecake and cream teas. Bookings (T021-689 9151) are advised for brunch on summer weekends.

South of Rondesbosch

By this point the southern suburbs have reached right around Devil's Peak and the shadowy mountains now dominating the views represent an unfamiliar view of Table Mountain. The suburb of **Newlands** backs right up to the slopes of the mountain and is probably best known for being the home to Western Province Rugby Union and the beautiful Newlands cricket Test Ground, now known as Sahara Park. There are several good hotels and guesthouses in the area.

Newlands ⓘ *Boundary Rd, a few mins' walk from Newlands Station, T021-659 6700, www.newlandstours.co.za, a scheduled tour runs every Tue at 1000 or pre-book a tour for Mon-Fri 0900-1500, from R48, children (under 16) R35.* The first official rugby match at Newlands was played in 1890 and the stadium was a venue for 1995 World Cup matches. The first recorded cricket match in Africa took place between officers in the British army in Cape Town in 1808, and the Newlands cricket oval opened in 1888. In 2003 it hosted the Cricket World Cup opening match. There are a number of fun options here run by Newlands Tours. You can visit the rugby stadium and enter through the players' entrance, see the changing rooms and run through the players' tunnel. At the cricket ground you can walk across the pitch and visit the scorer's and third umpire's booths.

Opposite Newlands and also on Boundary Road, **Josephine Mill** ⓘ *T021-686 4939, www.josephinemill.co.za, Mon-Fri 1000-1600, Sat 1000-1400, R10, milling demonstrations Mon-Fri 1100 and 1500, R20,* the only surviving watermill in Cape Town, has been restored as a working flour mill; note the massive iron waterwheel. The building is in the style of a Cornish red-brick mill, built by a Swede, Jacob Letterstedt in 1840, and named in honour of his Crown Princess, Josephine. The mill is tucked away near the rugby stadium and has a shop selling organic stone-milled flour and bread and a peaceful tea garden and deli.

★Kirstenbosch National Botanical Garden

Off Rhodes Dr (M3) and clearly signposted, T021-799 8783, www.sanbi.org, Sep-Mar 0800-1900, Apr-Aug 0800-1800, R50, children (6-17) R10, under 6s free. By far the easiest way of getting here is by car. Otherwise there are trains to the nearest station at Mowbray, 10 mins from the city centre. From here there is an erratic Golden Arrow bus service or a very long walk.

Alternatively, take a taxi, most of the organized city tours also include the garden on their itinerary and the City Sightseeing Cape Town bus stops here.

Kirstenbosch, 13 km south of the city centre is South Africa's oldest, largest and most exquisite botanical garden. The gardens stretch up the eastern slopes of Table Mountain, merging seamlessly with the fynbos of the steep slopes above. Cecil Rhodes bought Kirstenbosch farm in 1895 and promptly presented the site to the people of South Africa with the intention that it become a botanical garden. It was not until 1913 that it was proclaimed a National Botanical Garden – the Anglo-Boer War had caused the delay. The first director of the gardens was Professor Harold Pearson, who died just three years after the garden's creation. A granite Celtic Cross marks his grave in the Cycad garden. There is a fitting epitaph: "If ye seek his monument, look around you." The real development was under Professor RH Compton, who cared for the gardens for 34 years. The herbarium, named after him, houses over 250,000 specimens, including many rare plants.

A great deal of time and effort has been put into making the gardens accessible to the general public, ensuring they provide pleasure for both serious botanists and families enjoying a day out on the slopes of Table Mountain. In the **Fragrance Garden** herbs and flowers are set out so as to make appreciating their scents effortless. On a warm day, when the volatile oils are released by the plants, there are some rather overpowering aromas. The plaques are also in Braille. The **Dell** follows a beautifully shaded path snaking beneath ferns and along a stream. Indigenous South African herbs can be inspected in the **Medicinal Plants Garden**, each one identified and used by the Khoi and San peoples in the treatment of a variety of ailments. The plants' uses are identified on plaques, and it seems that most ailments are covered – kidney trouble, rheumatics, coughs, cancer, piles and bronchitis. For a sense of the past, it is worth visiting what is known as **Van Riebeeck's Hedge**. Back in 1660 a hedge of wild almond trees (*Brabejum stellatifolium*) was planted by Van Riebeeck as part of a physical boundary to try and prevent cattle rustling. Segments still remain today within the garden. Built to commemorate Kirstenbosch's 100th anniversary in 2013, the curvy **Tree Canopy Walkway** has also been dubbed the 'Boomslang' which means 'tree snake' in both Afrikaans and Dutch. Made of steel and timber, the 130-m-long walkway starts at ground level and winds and dips to some 12m above the trees of the Arboretum; there are marvelous views from top. At the back of the Fragrance Garden is the start of the **Skeleton Gorge path**, which can be followed all the way to the summit of Table Mountain. It starts off as a stepped path, but becomes fairly steep near the top with ladders in places; take special care in the wet season.

Perhaps the most enjoyable way of experiencing the gardens is at one of the Sunday sunset concerts held throughout summer (see Music, page 66). Also available for a small fee are eco-adventure tours, and tours by motorized golf cart. Just beyond the entrance is a shop and café on the courtyard terrace. The shop has the usual collection of curios, along with a good choice of books on South Africa and a selection of indigenous plants. With far nicer views is the **Kirstenbosch Tea Room** (see page 63) inside the gardens, which serves good meals (until 1700). And, for a reasonable price, you can have a ready-made picnic with wine and join the Capetonians on the lush lawns.

Tourist information

Cape Town Tourism
The Pinnacle, corner of Burg and Castle streets, T021-487 6800, www.capetown. travel, Oct-Mar Mon-Fri 0800-1900, Sat 0830-1400, Sun 0900-1300, closes 1 hr earlier in winter (Apr-Sep).
The official city tourist office is an excellent source of information and a good first stop in the city. In addition to providing practical information about Cape Town, it can help with accommodation bookings and has plenty of information on nightlife and events. It is also home to **Western Cape Tourism** (same contact details) and there is a desk for **South Africa National Parks** (SANParks), www.sanparks.co.za, where you can make reservations for the parks. There's also a café, gift shop and free Wi-Fi. There are 12 other branches/desks around Cape Town including at the Table Mountain Lower Cableway Station and Kirstenbosch National Botanical Garden.

Where to stay

Cape Town has an excellent selection of accommodation from large flashy 5-star hotels to good-value small guesthouses and backpacker hostels. Book well ahead for Christmas and the New Year when Cape Town is especially popular with domestic tourists. All accommodation options can organize airport transfers. Several agencies specialize in medium- and long-term holiday lets of private homes or self-catering flats. These are good value for families or groups. Try www.sa-venues.com or www.capeletting.com.

City Bowl
City centre

$$$$ Taj Cape Town
Wale St, T021-819 2000, www.tajhotels.com.
Impressive offering from the Taj luxury hotel group opposite St George's Cathedral; the façades of the old South African Reserve Bank have been kept. 177 palatial rooms. **Bombay Brasserie** is a superb Indian restaurant, there's a champagne and oyster bar, gym and spa.

$$$$ Westin Cape Town
Convention Sq, Lower Long St, T021-412 9999, www.westincapetown.com.
This huge grey-glass structure overlooks the convention centre and has 483 rooms, in modern and minimalist style. Facilities include popular rooftop spa, gym and pool, 5 restaurants and bars, and service is impressively swift and efficient.

$$$$-$$$ Hilton Cape Town
112 Buitengracht St, T021-481 3700, www3.hilton.com.
Modern Hilton with top-class facilities and 137 rooms, outdoor heated pool, 3 restaurants: **Signal Hill Terrace**, Arabic food and shisha pipes, **Mezbaan**, Indian food, and **Bistro 126** for Mediterranean and seafood. Walking distance to museums and Bo-Kaap district.

$$$ Cape Heritage Hotel
Heritage Sq, 90 Bree St, T021-424 4646, www.capeheritage.co.za.
Charming hotel set in a rambling renovated town house dating from the late 17th century. The 17 huge rooms are individually styled, with muted coloured walls and contemporary decor, but retain the high teak ceilings and yellowwood floors.

$$$ Grand Daddy
38 Long St, T021-424 7247, www.granddaddy.co.za.
Long St's most eccentric boutique hotel, with 45 rooms and, like its sister hotel, **Daddy Long Legs** (see below), it is decorated throughout by local artists and the design element is simply stunning. Talk

of the town are the 7 vintage Airstream trailers (**$$**) on the roof that are again individually decorated; it's a unique way to sleep in Cape Town. **Daddy Cool** is a sexy and stylish cocktail bar and the **Showroom Cafe** offers good food with an organic and low-calorie slant.

$$$ Urban Chic
Corner of Long and Pepper streets, T021-426 6119, www.urbanchic.co.za.
Italian-owned hotel with 20 rooms (prices rise the higher you go, as the mountain views improve). Beautiful, airy decor, with pale colours and modern art on the walls, on the 1st floor is the stylish **Blue Horizon Sushi & Grill** with a covered glass-fronted balcony overlooking bustling Long St.

$$$-$$ Cape Town Lodge
101 Buitengracht St, T021-422 0030, www.capetownlodge.co.za.
A striking tower block with 119 rooms with CBD views. Rooftop swimming pool, gym, 2 bars, excellent steak restaurant – **The Famous Butcher's Grill** on the ground floor decorated with photos of District Six.

$$$-$$ Protea Hotel Fire & Ice!
Corner of New Church and Victoria streets, T021-488 2555, www.proteahotels.co.za.
Fashionable place with spacious modern lobby with cocktail bar, restaurant specializing in gourmet burgers, a cheeky smoking room where seats are fashioned as coffins, and themed elevators (Table Mountain cableway or a shark cage-dive). The 189 rooms are small but neat with all mod cons.

$$ Cape Diamond Boutique Hotel
Corner of Longmarket and Parliament streets, T021-461 2519, www.africanskyhotels.com.
Round the corner from Government Av and a short walk from Long St and set in a restored art deco diamond dealership with 60 small but comfortable and good-value rooms, contemporary decor, bar and restaurant. The rooftop terrace has excellent views of Table Mountain and the City Bowl.

$$ Daddy Long Legs
134 Long St, T021-422 3074, www.daddylonglegs.co.za.
Described as an art hotel, with 13 rooms spread across a town house, offering funky, artistic rooms – each is individually themed and designed by a local artist. Rooms are small, but the stylish, original decor makes up for it. Good value and refreshingly different.

$$ Inn on the Square
10 Greenmarket Sq, T021-423 2050, www.threecities.co.za.
Set in the historical Shell building right on Greenmarket Sq, 165 rooms with pleasant neutral decor. Small pool deck on the 8th floor with view of Table Mountain, restaurant and cigar bar, the **Dish**, on the ground floor with tables overlooking the market.

$ Long St Backpackers
209 Long St, T021-423 0615, www.longstreetbackpackers.co.za.
Sociable hostel with 80 beds in cramped dorms and doubles spread around leafy courtyard, fully equipped kitchen, TV/DVD lounge, pool room, internet, travel centre, balcony overlooking Long St; can be noisy but handy for nightlife.

Gardens and Tamboerskloof

$$$$ Cape Cadogan
5 Upper Union St, Tamboerskloof, T021-480 8080, www.capecadogan.com.
Ultra-elegant 2-storey 19th-century mansion with 12 spacious rooms, private terraces, 4-poster beds and stone walk-in showers for 2. Shady courtyard with small pool, and a startlingly all-white dining room.

$$$$ Mount Nelson
76 Orange St, Gardens, T021-483 1000, www.mountnelsonhotel.co.za.
Cape Town's famous colonial hotel which opened in 1899 and has always welcomed celebrity guests, with 209 luxurious rooms in 6 wings overlooking Table Mountain, the

parkland-type gardens, or 1 of the 2 vast heated swimming pools. Rates vary widely from R3700-13,400 depending on room and season. The celebrated **Planet Restaurant** serves Cape specialities and contemporary fare to live jazz, while the **Oasis Restaurant** is well worth visiting for the daily cream teas on the veranda.

$$$ 15 On Orange
15 Orange St, Gardens, T021-469 8000, www.africanpridehotels.com.
Great location near sights and restaurants, sleek glass-and-steel hotel with 112 large rooms. Vast 7-storey central atrium with white marble floors and retro furnishings, bar, restaurant and luxury spa.

$$$ Cape Milner
2a Milner Rd, Tamboerskloof, T021-426 1101, www.cape milner.com.
Fashionable hotel with 57 rooms with neutral pale grey decor and slick dark-wood furniture. Small infinity pool and cocktail bar. It's a popular local meeting place and has a decent restaurant serving good Capetonian cuisine.

$$$ Kensington Place
38 Kensington Gardens, Higgovale, T021-424 4744, www.kensingtonplace.co.za.
Cape Town's original luxury boutique hotel in a quiet, leafy area with excellent and friendly service and great views over the city. The 8 beautiful and good-sized rooms are individually styled with Afro-chic furnishings. Bar, small pool in tropical gardens, breakfast is served until a decadent 1300.

$$$-$$ Parker Cottage
3 Carstens St, Tamboerskloof, T021-424 6445, www.parkercottage.co.za.
Award-winning B&B set in 2 restored Victorian bungalows, 10 rooms, with clawfoot baths, fireplaces, polished wood floors, lots of antiques and flamboyant colours. Gay-friendly and an easy stroll to restaurants on Kloof St.

$$ Leeuwenvoet House
93 New Church St, Tamboerskloof, T021-424 1133, www.leeuwenvoet.co.za.
Historical guesthouse in cottage built in 1892, with original Oregon pine floors and doors, antique decor, 12 a/c rooms, some with Victorian baths. Heated swimming pool, easy walking distance to shops and restaurants but retains a peaceful atmosphere.

$$-$ Ashanti Lodge
11 Hof St, Gardens, T021-423 8721, www.ashanti.co.za.
One of Cape Town's best-known and most popular hostels, not least for its party atmosphere. Dorms and doubles in huge old house with polished wooden floors and communal balconies. There's a courtyard and small pool and a couple of spaces for camping. Lively bar serving good snacks, with pool table and DSTV, plus good booking centre. Also has a guesthouse ($$) nearby with smart en suite double rooms and spotless kitchen, and a 2nd hostel at 23 Antrium Rd in Green Point.

$$-$ The Backpack
74 New Church St, Tamboerskloof, T021-423 4530, www.backpackers.co.za.
Cape Town's 1st hostel.and today one of the best run in town. Set across several houses with spotless dorms, doubles and singles. Polished wood floors, upmarket decor, tiled courtyard and pool, lovely bar with TV, meals and snacks served throughout the day, one of the best backpacker travel centres around.

$$-$ Zebra Crossing Backpackers
82 New Church St, T021-422 1265, www.zebra-crossing.co.za.
Quiet, friendly backpacker hostel straddling 2 Victorian bungalows, spotless dorms plus small double rooms, Wi-Fi and travel centre, shady courtyard café, bar and good views of Table Mountain.

De Waterkant and Green Point

$$$$-$$$ Cape Royale
47 Main Rd, Green Point, T021-430 0500, www.caperoyale.co.za.
Impressive new block but with a Victorian façade, 95 1- to 2-bedroom suites with contemporary furniture and luxurious fabrics, kitchenettes, balconies with V&A Waterfront views. Excellent **Bistro 1800°** restaurant, rooftop bar and pool with Table Mountain views, gym and spa.

$$$ Village Lodge
49 Napier St, De Waterkant, T021-421 1106, www.thevillagelodge.com.
Spread across 2 converted houses with 15 smallish a/c rooms, decor is trendy greys and white, with shimmery black-stone bathrooms and magnificent Table Mountain views. **Soho** restaurant serves breakfasts and Thai food. Also has a choice of cottages and apartments in the area.

$$$-$$ De Waterkant Village
Reception, The Charles, 137 Waterkant St, De Waterkant, central reservations, T021-490 2500, www.dewaterkant.com.
Village and Life manage over 40 historical Bo-Kaap style houses and apartments in trendy De Waterkant, each stylishly and individually decorated in either cutting-edge modern decor or with traditional antiques, sleeping 1-6, many have delightful roof terraces. They also have **De Waterkant House** (**$$**), www.dewaterkanthouse.com, a guesthouse with 9 chic rooms, a splash pool, beautiful lounge and terrace, and **The Charles** (**$$**), www.thecharles.co.za, a gay-friendly guesthouse with 9 lovely bright rooms, some with Victorian bath, and good views from the spacious wooden decks, which also serves as the central reception.

$$-$ Big Blue Backpackers Lodge
7 Vesperdene Rd, Green Point, T021-439 0807, www.bigblue.za.net.
An airy backpacker hostel set in a gorgeous mansion dating from 1885, with 86 beds in spacious dorms, single or doubles (some en suite). Pleasant breakfast room, bar, small pool, Wi-Fi, travel centre, TV room, kitchen.

$ Never @ Home
107 Main Rd, Green Point, T021-434 9282, www.neverathomeworld.com.
Well located on Main Rd, a few mins' walk to the V&A and directly opposite the stadium, this backpackers has dorms, twins and doubles, small pool deck at back, Wi-Fi, restaurant; is also above the popular **Slug & Lettuce** pub facing onto the street.

$ Sunflower Stop
179 Main Rd, Green Point, T021-434 6535, www.sunflowerstop.co.za.
Dorms with a bit more room than most, smallish doubles, kitchen, garden with swimming pool and outdoor bar with braai, tours and travel advice. Good location close to restaurants and bars on Main Rd.

Sea Point

$$$$ Ellerman House
180 Kloof Rd, T021-430 3200, www.ellerman.co.za.
Award-winning luxury boutique hotel with sweeping ocean views, 9 elegant suites with quality furnishings and fabrics, valuable South African art on the walls, balconies. Beautiful well-tended gardens, pool, spa and gym, gourmet dining and wine cellar with a staggering 7500 labels.

$$$$-$$$ The Clarendon
67 Kloof Rd, T021-434 6854, www.clarendon.co.za.
Luxurious guesthouse with 10 grandly furnished rooms, some with views of Lion's Head. Large pool, breakfast and afternoon tea served on terrace, and beautiful lounge. Also has a similar upmarket guesthouse nearby in Bantry Bay at 158 Kloof Rd.

$$$ Winchester Mansions
221 Beach Rd, T021-434 2351, www.winchester.co.za.
A well-run hotel in Cape Dutch style with 76 mountain- or ocean-view rooms, some

with 2 bedrooms for families. Pleasant pool deck and **Ginkgo Spa**. Also has **Harvey's** restaurant, offering fusion cuisine and jazz brunches on Sun.

$$$-$$ The Glen
3 The Glen, T021-439 0086,
www.glenhotel.co.za.
Gay-friendly boutique hotel in an Italian-style villa with views of Signal Hill, 24 rooms with classy decor. Tropical garden with palm trees and pool, steam room, and can organize temporary gym membership.

$$$-$$ Radisson Blu Le Vendome Hotel
14 London Rd, T021-826 5100,
www.radissonblu.com.
Close to Sea Point Promenade with tasteful French-themed decor and good ametites in 143 rooms and suites, views towards Signal Hill or ocean, pool, restaurants including **La Mer Restaurant and Grill**.

$$ Cascades on the Promenade
11 Arthurs Rd, T021-434 5979,
www.cascadescollection.com.
Stylish boutique hotel in a Cape Dutch heritage building near the Sea Point promenade and swimming pool. Each of the 8 rooms has an Apple Mac with Wi-Fi, Nespresso coffee machine, and there's a terrace restaurant.

V&A Waterfront
Generally hotels at the V&A Waterfront are aimed at the high-spending foreign visitor, and all are expensive. For cheaper accommodation with easy access to the V&A, consider Green Point, above.

$$$$ Cape Grace
West Quay Rd, T021-410 7100,
www.capegrace.com.
One of the most luxurious hotels in Cape Town, and an iconic feature of the V&A. 122 enormous rooms with plush decor, balconies have mountain or harbour views. 2 bars and the celebrated **Signal** restaurant, attractive swimming pool and deck, and there's a lovely rooftop spa.

$$$$ One&Only
Dock Rd, T021-431 5888,
www.oneandonlyresorts.com.
Sol Kerzner's (of Sun City fame) super-luxury 131-room hotel and as you can imagine it's stunning. Rooms have balconies or terraces overlooking Table Mountain or the ocean, 2 islands in the marina have a clutch of villas – if you are in this league you can park your yacht outside – plus a vast heated swimming pool (the largest in Cape Town) and a tranquil spa. The giant lobby has a cocktail bar, which is also used for high tea, a branch of famed Japanese restaurant **Nobu**, and the gourmet **Reuben's** restaurant, which has a wall of 5000 bottles of wine (also see Restaurants in Franschhoek, page 123).

$$$$ Radisson BLU Hotel Waterfront
Beach Rd, Granger Bay, T021-441 3000,
www.radissonblu.com/hotel-capetown.
Quality large hotel in an unbeatable location right on the ocean's edge and a short walk from the V&A. All 177 rooms are spacious with sunny decor. Infinity pool, state-of-the-art spa and **Tobago's** restaurant and bar is very popular for sundowners.

$$$$ The Table Bay
Quay 6, T021-780 7878,
www.suninternational.co.za.
Enormous luxury offering from the Sun International Group, with 329 top-notch rooms; what they lack in character they make up for in facilities and comfort. Large pool and sun deck, spa, bar and good restaurant. Efficient service but feels ostentatious (note the sculpture by the main entrance commemorating the stays of celebrities and politicians).

$$$ Victoria & Alfred
Pierhead, T021-419 6677,
www.newmarkhotels.com.
Stylishly converted warehouse (1904) with 96 rooms, spacious with contemporary and comfortable furnishings, some rooms have jacuzzis on the balconies. Excellent restaurant serving seafood and steaks, pool,

gym and spa. Also has a similar properties: the 35-room **Queen Victoria Hotel ($$$$)**, and the 34-room **Dock House Boutique Hotel ($$$)**, in the precinct of heritage buildings on Portswood Ridge, accessed from Portswood Rd.

$$ Protea Hotel Breakwater Lodge
Portswood Rd, T021-406 1911, www.protea hotels.com.
Housed in what was once the Breakwater Prison (1859), this is the least expensive option at the V&A. The 191 rooms are fairly small but comfortable in appealing muted grey colours, some have 2 bedrooms for families, 2 restaurants, bar, gym, and Wi-Fi in the 2 lounges.

Woodstock and Observatory

$$ DoubleTree by Hilton Cape Town – Upper Eastside
31 Brickfield Rd, Woodstock, T021-404 0570, www.uppereastsidehotel.co.za.
The Hilton brand aimed at business travellers with 183 small rooms, an impressive lobby built of steel girders and white pillars, colourful upholstery and modern pictures, and excellent value. Bar and restaurant. Free shuttle to the V&A 4 times a day.

$ Green Elephant Backpackers
57 Milton Rd, Observatory, T021-448 6359, www.green elephant.co.za.
Long-established and relaxed backpacker joint set across 3 old Observatory houses. Dorms and doubles, kitchen, garden with pool and jacuzzi, small bar and Wi-Fi. Short stroll to cafés and bars on Lower Main Rd in Observatory.

South of Rondesbosch

$$$$-$$$ Vineyard Hotel & Spa
Colinton Rd, off Protea Rd, Newlands, T021-657 4500, www.vineyard.co.za.
Set around a country house originally built for Lady Anne Barnard in 1799, with 208 a/c rooms set in 2.5 ha of lovely landscaped parkland full of birds. Top-class facilities

include spa, gym, indoor and outdoor heated pools, **The Square** and **Myoga** restaurants (see page 63).

$$$ Andros Boutique Hotel
Corner of Phyllis and Newlands roads, Upper Claremont, T021-797 9777, www.andros.co.za.
Grand old Cape Dutch house built in 1908 by Herbert Baker with 8 elegant rooms, white and cream decor, relaxing terrace, pool, sauna and spa. The smart restaurant has candlelit tables and marble floors and a French-influenced menu.

$$ Harfield Guest Villa
26 1st Av, Claremont, T021-683 7376, www.harfield.co.za.
Award-winning, elegant B&B with 9 individually designed rooms, with views of Table Mountain. Lounge/bar, sun deck and pool, breakfast room and dinner on request. Walking distance to Cavendish Sq shopping mall.

Restaurants

The best source of restaurant listings are the annual *Eat Out* magazine (www.eatout. co.za), available at Exclusive Books and other bookshops, and the website www. dining-out.co.za. Hotels often offer an excellent choice for dining.

City Bowl

City centre

$$$ 95 Keerom
95 Keerom St, T021-422 0765, www.95keerom.com. Thu-Fri 1200-1430, Mon-Sat 1830-2230.
Beautifully presented and expensive Italian Milanese cuisine and favourites include the meat and fish wafer-thin carpaccio, soft polenta with parmesan, and *osso buco* (braised veal shanks). The restored façade is part of the original stables and slave quarters of the Company's Garden that date to 1682.

$$$ Africa Café
Heritage Sq, 108 Shortmarket St, T021-422 0221, www.africacafe.co.za. Open 1800-2300.
African-themed restaurant geared at tour groups, offering an excellent introduction to the continent's cuisines. The menu is a set 'feast' and includes 13 dishes from around Africa, such as Egyptian-smoked fish, Kenyan maize patties, Cape Malay mango chicken curry and springbok stew. A great experience, but it's pricey and very touristy.

$$$ Aubergine
39 Barnet St, T021-465 4909, www.aubergine. co.za. Tue-Fri 1200-1400, Mon-Sat 1900-2230.
Sophisticated and award-winning menu, with a modern slant on classical European dishes such as foie gras and quail, the 3- to 5-course degustation menu is an elaborate affair when wine is paired to food.

$$$ Bukhara
33 Church St, T021-424 0000, www.bukhara. com. Mon-Sat 1200-1500, daily 1830-2300.
Cape Town's best Indian, which also has branches at Victoria Wharf in the V&A Waterfront and Grand West Casino. Delicious melt-in-your-mouth aromatic north Indian dishes, plush decor, superb service and award-winning wine list. You can watch the chefs in the open kitchen.

$$$ Savoy Cabbage
Heritage Sq, 101 Hout St, T021-4242626, www.savoycabbage.co.za. Mon-Fri 1200-1430, Mon-Sat 1900-2230.
One of the best restaurants in Cape Town, serving beautifully prepared contemporary South African cuisine. The menu changes daily, and includes dishes such as gemsbok carpaccio, free-range duck breast and a gorgeous soft-centred chocolate pudding. Bookings essential.

$$ Mama Africa
178 Long St, T021-424 8634. Tue-Fri 1200-1600, Mon-Sat 1900-late.
Popular restaurant and bar serving 'traditional' African dishes with a great atmosphere and often with live music. The food is tasty, despite the notoriously slow service. Centrepiece is a bright green carved mamba-shaped bar.

$$ Marco's African Place
15 Rose St, T021-423 5412, www. marcosafricanplace.co.za. Tue-Sun 1500-late.
Good-value 'African' menu covering everything from slow-roasted Karoo lamb to samp and beans, plus popular Pan-African platter with assortment of grilled game. Live music in the evening when a cover charge is added to the bill.

$$-$ Dias Tavern
15 Caledon St, off Buitenkant St, T021-465 7547, www.diastavern.co.za. Mon-Sat 1130-1500, 1800-2200.
Old-fashioned pub near the Fugard Theatre so ideal for a quick pre-show meal. Serves authentic Portuguese fare like peri-peri chicken, chorizo sausage, sardines, *trinchado* (beef in red wine) and *espetada* (a towering steak skewer).

$ Biesmiellah
2 Upper Wale St, T021-423 0850, www.biesmiellah.co.za. Open 0930-2300.
Lacking in trimmings, but a prime position in colourful Bo-Kaap, this is one of the better-known and well-established Cape Malay restaurants. Try the sweet lamb and chicken curries and sticky malva pudding. No alcohol, but wash a meal down with a *falooda* – milk, rosewater and almonds.

$ Eastern Food Bazaar
Entrances on both Darling and Longmarket streets, T021-461 2458, www. easternfoodbazaar.co.za. Open 1000-2100.
On the ground floor of the Wellington Fruit Growers building designed by Herbert Baker's office in 1902, this food emporium has a long line of self-service counters for delicious and very cheap Indian, Turkish and Cape Malay spicy food. No alcohol and strictly halal.

$ Royale Eatery

273 Long St, T021-422 4536,
www.royaleeatery.com. Mon-Sat 1200-2300.
Ultra-trendy eatery specializing in over 50
gourmet burgers – try the 'Miss Piggy' with
bacon and guacamole, served with sweet
potato fries. **The Waiting Room**, upstairs,
is a popular bar with balcony and great
views of Long St.

Cafés

Café Mozart

37 Church St, T021-424-3774, www.themozart.
co.za. Mon-Fri 0700-1600, Sat 0900-1530.
With tables spilling out among the stalls of
Church St Antiques Market, this 30-year-
old café serves excellent breakfasts, filled
baguettes and croissants, and mains of
seafood and inventive salads.

Company's Garden Restaurant

Access from Queen Victoria St or from
within the garden, T021-423 2919, www.
thecompanysgarden.com. Open 0700-1800.
This used to be the old tea room and has
been revamped into a stunning and stylish
family-friendly garden café – expect to
queue on a sunny day. The menu features
gourmet sandwiches and burgers, giant
salads, fisherman's and ploughman's platters
and the table of cakes must not be missed.

Lola's

228 Long St, T021-423 0885, www.lolas.co.za.
Open 0730-1700.
A streetside favorite and a good stop on a
walk along Long St, best known for their
warm croissants, mussel chowder and fresh
juices. Uses organic produce and fair-trade
principles, portions are generous, and
friendly, quick service.

Mr Pickwicks

158 Long St, T021-423 3710. Open 0800-0200.
Trendy spot, a favourite with pierced and
tattooed Long St locals, and sells tickets to
Cape Town's major club nights and gigs.
Excellent baguettes, toasties, healthy salads,
large pasta portions and milkshakes.

Gardens and Tamboerskloof

$$$ Miller's Thumb

10b Kloof Nek Rd, T021-424 3838,
www.millersthumb.co.za. Tue-Fri 1230-1430,
Mon-Sat 1830-2230.
Beloved by locals, bookings essential, this
place serves delicious seafood, plus steaks
and some veggie choices, lots of spices and a
Creole or Mozambique twist on some dishes.

$$ Emily's

55 Kloof St, T021-424 0882, www.emily-s.com.
Mon-Sat 1000-2200.
Café by day and bistro from 1900, tables are
centred around the open kitchen or on the
garden terrace. The weekly changing menu
has a South African slant; expect the likes of
bobotie with pumpkin fritters or quail with
ostrich stuffing.

$$ Saigon

Corner of Camp and Kloof streets, T021-424
7670. Sun-Fri 1200-1430, daily 1800-2230.
Superb Vietnamese and Japanese cuisine,
very popular place set on a corner
overlooking busy Kloof St and roof terrace
with views of Table Mountain. Good choice
for vegetarians and sushi bar.

$$ Societi Bistro

50 Orange St, Gardens, T021-424 4100,
www.societi.co.za. Mon-Sat 1200-2300.
A neighbourhood favourite with a bistro-
style menu and cosy rooms with bare brick
walls and fireplaces, snug bar with leather
couches, and garden with tables under
palms. On some weekday nights does a meal
deal with movie tickets at the nearby Labia
Cinema (see page 66).

$$ Yindee's

22 Camp St, Tamboerskloof, T021-422 1012,
www.yindees.com. Mon-Fri 1230-1430,
Mon-Sat 1830-2300.
An excellent Thai restaurant serving
authentic spicy curries, stir-fries, soups and
unusual deep-fried coconut ice cream for
dessert. Served in a sprawling Victorian
house with traditional low tables.

$$-$ Arnold's
60 Kloof St, Gardens, T021-424 4344,
www.arnolds.co.za. Open 0745-2300.
Bustling good-value spot on busy Kloof
St, good salads, pastas, burgers and more
substantial meals like ostrich steak. Fast,
friendly service, happy hour 1630-1830, may
have to queue for a table at weekends for the
legendary cooked breakfasts.

$$-$ Chef Pon's Asian Kitchen
12 Mill St, Gardens, T021-465 5846,
www.chefpons.co.za. Mon-Sat 1800-2230.
Long menu of favourite dishes from across
Asia, and everything arrives freshly cooked
and sizzling hot but it's the Thai food that
wins hands down. Decor is simple and dark,
but cosy on a winter's night, and lingering
after your meal is discouraged if they need
the table (which they frequently do).

Cafés

Manna Epicure
151 Kloof St, Tamboerskloof, T021-426 2413,
www.mannaepicure.com. Tue-Sat 0800-
1700, Sun 0800-1600.
A white and bright café in an old house
on trendy Kloof St. Great for elaborate
breakfasts, open sandwiches made from the
famous Manna's artisanal breads, and gooey
cakes and pastries. Also a takeaway bakery.

Vida e Caffè
www.vidaecaffe.co.za. Mon-Fri 0700-1800,
Sat-Sun 0700-1700.
The original of what has become South
Africa's most successful coffee chain, with
its trademark quirky atmosphere, excellent
coffees and a choice of muffins and melting
hot paninis. The minimalist red and white
interior is packed throughout the day.

De Waterkant and Green Point

$$$ Gold Restaurant
15 Bennett St, Green Point, T021-421 4653,
www.goldrestaurant.co.za. Open 1830-2300.
Popular with tour groups and deservedly
so, this full-on African extravaganza offers

interactive drumming, Malian puppets,
acapella singing, and a hand-washing
ceremony. The menu of 14 dishes from Cape
Malay lamb bobotie to West African peanut
chicken is served as a set menu to share.

$$$ Grand Café & Beach
Granger Bay Rd, Granger Bay, T021-425 0551,
www.grandafrica.com. Tue-Sat 1200-late,
Sun 1200-1600.
Set in a restored warehouse adjacent to the
V&A with its own beach created between
the rocks of Granger Bay and lovely interior
design. Interesting fusion menu but
overpriced, better for sundowner cocktails
on sofas in the sand.

$$ Mano's
39 Main Rd, Green Point, T021-434 1090,
www.mano.co.za. Mon-Sat 1200-2200.
The affable Mano oversees this small
Mediterranean restaurant with simple decor
and a short but pleasing menu. The steak
and pommes frites and lamb cutlets are
always popular and there's a good choice
of wine.

Cafés

Giovanni's
103 Main Rd, Green Point, T021-434 6593.
Open 0730-0900.
Cape Town's best and busiest deli, and a
favourite with regulars who come to chat
at the coffee bar and buy the imported
cheese, cold meats and olives, fresh bread
and pastries and hard to come buy groceries
from Italy and the UK. The delicious ready
meals can be eaten here or taken away.

La Petite Tarte
*Shop A11, Cape Quarter, Dixon
St, De Waterkant, T021-425 9077.*
Mon-Fri 0830-1630, Sat 0830-1500.
Charming French-style sidewalk café
decorated with antique furniture, floral
cushions and shelves of dainty china,
serves breakfasts, light lunches and cakes,
best known for the croque monsieur and
chocolate gateau.

Sea Point

$$$ La Mouette
78 Regent Rd, Sea Point, T021-433 0856, www.lamouette-restaurant.co.za. Open Tue-Sun 1800-2230, Sun lunch 1200-1500.
Set in a historic Tudor-style house with terrace, fine old fireplaces, and multiple elegant dining rooms, this has both à la carte and 6-course tasting menus of classically French food with a few global twists.

$$ La Perla
Corner Church and Beach roads, T021-434 2471, www.laperla.co.za. Open 0900-2300.
Long-term Sea Point favourite opened in 1959, with an extensive and traditional Italian menu with over 200 dishes of seafood, excellent anitpasto, plenty of vegetarian options, and wonderful desserts.

$$ Posticino
323 Main Rd, T021-439 4014, www.posticino.co.za. Open 1200-2300.
Popular with local residents and always has a buzzy atmosphere, this good-value Italian is well known for its thin-based pizzas and you can make up your own pasta sauce.

V&A Waterfront
With over 80 restaurants and cafés, the Waterfront is one of the most popular districts in Cape Town for eating out and gets very busy. There is a wide range of places to eat but they generally charge unashamedly high tourist prices. Nevertheless, to experience superb cuisine and impeccable service with unparalleled harbour and mountain views, a V&A restaurant is usually on most visitors' agendas.

$$$ Baia
Victoria Wharf, T021-421 0935, www.baiarestaurant.co.za. Open 1200-1500, 1900-2300.
Fine seafood restaurant spread over 4 terraces with views of Table Mountain. Expensive but delicious seafood dishes follow a Mozambique theme – try the spicy coconut prawns – and some rare wine vintages.

$$$ Balducci's
Victoria Wharf, T021-421 6002, www.balduccis.co.za. Open 0900-2230.
Contemporary restaurant with seats overlooking the harbour, good choice of pasta dishes and mains ranging from ostrich steak and luxury lamb burgers, to confit de canard and blackened kingklip.

$$$ Belthazar
Victoria Wharf, T021-421 3753, www.belthazar.co.za. Open 1200-2300.
Top-of-the-range steakhouse with tables overlooking the harbour. Excellent Karan dry- and wet-cured steaks, plus range of seafood and a staggering 600 South African wines.

$$$ Cape Town Fish Market
Clock Tower, T021-413 5977, www.ctfm.co.za. Open 1100-2300.
Now a quality chain found in the other main cities and there's a branch in London; this is the original. Seafood restaurant with a fisherman's theme, but the best reason to come here is to watch the Japanese chefs at the revolving sushi bar and to get an outside table overlooking the swing bridge.

$$$ Den Anker
Pierhead, T021-419 0249, www.denanker.co.za. Open 0900-2300.
Popular Belgian restaurant with a bar with Belgian beer on tap, views across Alfred Basin. Best known for tin pots of mussels with crispy bread and steak tartare with pommes frites.

$$ Quay Four
Quay 4, T021-419 2008, www.quay4.co.za. Open 1100-2400.
Hugely popular tavern and bistro with great views over the water from the broad wooden deck. Seafood is the focus and the calamari and fish and chips served in giant frying pans are excellent value. There's often live music in the evening.

$$ Willoughby & Co
Lower level, Victoria Wharf, T021-418 6115, www.willoughbyandco.co.za. Open 1130-2230.
Surrounded by shops in Victoria Wharf with tables 'outside' in the mall, this is so popular expect to queue. Best known for its delectable sushi, but the extensive menu also has as a few pastas and beef and seafood mains and all wines are available by good-value carafes.

Cafés

San Marco
Victoria Wharf, T021-418 5434, www.eatalian.co.za. Open 0830-2300.
Alfresco tables with views of the mountain and the V&A's street performers serving a full menu of coffees and alcoholic drinks, enormous salads, stuffed paninis and gelato ice cream.

Woodstock and Observatory

$$$ The Test Kitchen
The Old Biscuit Mill, 375 Albert Rd, Woodstock, T021-447 2337, www.thetestkitchen.co.za. Tue-Sat, lunch seating 1230-1330, dinner 1900-2030.
Run by British-born gourmet chef Luke Dale-Roberts and a Cape Town foodies' favourite and listed in the World's 50 Best Restaurants awards; book well ahead for a table. Every dish is technically precise, deliciously original and beautiful to look at. The open-plan kitchen lets diners be part of the creative experience.

Cafés

Obz Café
115 Lower Main Rd, Observatory, T021-448 5555, www.obzcafe.co.za. Kitchen 0900-2230, bar until 0200.
Popular student haunt open all day for light meals, coffee or cocktails, great salads and sandwiches, also has main meals in the

evenings and occasional live music and stand-up comedy.

South of Rondesbosch

$$$ Myoga
Vineyard Hotel, see Where to stay, page 58, T021-657 4545, www.vineyard.co.za. Tue-Sat 1130-1500, 1830-2230.
A very smart award-winning hotel restaurant with a great global fusion menu. Lunch is buffet style with a weigh-by-plate charging system and dinner is à la carte. The desserts are very creative – think violet ice cream with dissolving candy floss.

$$ Barristers Grill
Corner of Kildare and Main streets, Newlands, T021-671 7907, www.barristersgrill. co.za. Mon-Fri 1100-late, Sat 0900-late, Sun 1100-2200.
A popular mock-Tudor steakhouse that has expanded into a bistro/café during the day with plenty of alfresco tables. Given that it's in Newlands, it's a popular spot on a Sat afternoon to watch rugby on the giant TVs.

Cafés

The Kirstenbosch Tea Room
Kirstenbosch National Botanical Garden, T021-797 4883, www.ktr.co.za. Open 0830-1700.
Lovely terrace with views of the gardens and mountain looming behind. Offers breakfasts, sandwiches and salads and lunchtime mains like sweet and spicy bobotie and ostrich burgers. The cakes, scones and artisan breads are baked on the premises. Also offers a picnic hamper service.

Bars and clubs

City Bowl
There's plenty of edgy youthful nightlife around Long St and this is the place to come for local live music and the latest dance sounds. The best source of advice on gigs and club nights is in the cafés on Long St where you can pick up fliers. The more

sophisticated bars and clubs are in Green Point, the V&A Waterfront and Camps Bay. Nightclubs charge an entry fee and bars a cover charge for live music.

31
31st Floor, Absa Centre, 2 Riebeeck St, T021-421 0581, www.thirtyone.co.za. Open Fri-Sat 2000-0400.
Stylish and sophisticated club with an oval bar and cocktail lounge and spectacular nighttime views of the city and ocean from the top floor of this bank building. No guys under 23 and girls under 21.

Assembly
61 Harrington St, T021-465 7286, www.theassembly.co.za. Wed, Fri-Sat 2100-0400.
Cavernous place in a converted loft with a very long bar, a mixed bag of music from DJs and live bands.

Chrome
6 Pepper St, between Long and Loop streets, T021-422 3368, www.chromect.com. Wed-Sun, 2200-0500.
Aimed firmly at the serious dance crowd, mostly hip hop and R&B, large dance floor, sophisticated lighting and sound system.

Coco
70 Loop St, T072-673 6869, www.cococpt.co.za. Fri-Sat 2100-0300.
Upmarket spot with leather couches and banquettes, upstairs VIP seating and downstairs dance floors, house and lounge music, strictly glamorous dress code.

Mercury Live & Lounge
43 de Villiers St, T021-465 2106. Mon, Wed-Sat 2100-0200.
With a stage and a bar in a darkened room, this is Cape Town's leading live indie music venue for rock, punk and hip hop acts, with a lively, young crowd.

Zula
196 Long St, T021-424 2242, www.zulabar.co.za. Tue-Sat 1200-late.
Fashionable bar and cocktail lounge with several small rooms, great balcony overlooking Long St, and occasional live music. Sells snacks like pizzas, burgers and nachos and non-alcoholic smoothies.

Gardens and Tamboerskloof

Rafiki's
13 Kloof Nek Rd, Tamboerskloof, T021-426 4731, www.rafikis.co.za. Open 1200-0200.
Popular bar overlooking Kloof Nek with a huge wrap-around balcony perfect for a sundowner. DJs and occasional live music in the evenings, simple food like pizzas and burgers.

Rick's Café Américain
2 Park St, Gardens, T021-424 1100, www.rickscafe.co.za. Mon-Sat 1100-0200.
Just off fashionable Kloof St, in a rambling old Victorian house decorated with cushion-laden couches, mirrors and elaborate candlesticks. Cocktails, beer on tap, and good inexpensive food including tapas.

De Waterkant and Green Point

Buena Vista Social Café
14 Alfred House, Portswood Rd, Green Point, T021-421 0348, www.buenavista.co.za. Open 1200-1200.
Cuban-themed bar and restaurant where a fashionable crowd tuck into a mix of tapas and Tex-Mex-style dishes washed down with mojitos. Splashes of vibrant colour and fireplaces create a warm atmosphere.

Café Manhattan
74 Waterkant St, De Waterkant, T021-421 6666, www.manhattan.co.za. Open 1000-late.
Cape Town's most established gay venue (though not exclusively) in a lovely Victorian building with a wrap-around balcony, mischievous Wild West decor, a long bar, good varied food, especially the burgers.

Crew Bar
30 Napier St, De Waterkant, T021-418 0118. Mon-Sun 1900-0400.
Popular gay club in a historic De Waterkant

house with 2 dance floors, balconies with Table Mountain views. Mostly men but women are welcome and may also appreciate the bare-chested gogo-dancers.

Fireman's Arms
corner Buitengracht Mechau Sts, T021-419 0207, www.firemansarms.co.za. Mon-Sat 1200-2300.
Historic pub set in what was Cape Town's first fire station built in 1864, still complete with fire pole and fireman's hats. Best known as a place to watch sports and its get packed out on rugby match days. Good homely menu of pub grub such as liver and onions or bangers and mash.

The Piano Bar
47 Napier St, De Waterkant, T021-418 1096, www.thepianobar.co.za. Mon-Fri 1500-2400, Sat-Sun 1630-2400.
New York-inspired revue bar and eatery in the middle of De Waterkant village with broad terrace and live music most nights including African-infused jazz.

V&A Waterfront

Bascule Whiskey Wine & Cocktail Bar
Cape Grace (see Where to stay, page 57), www.capegrace.com. Open 1000-2400.
Overlooking the gleaming yachts in the V&A Waterfront's marina, social butterflies meet for sundowners at this glamorous bar. Has over 400 whiskies, numerous Cape wines, and the light menu features savoury and sweet tapas.

Ferryman's Tavern
East Pier Rd, T021-419 7748, www.ferrymans.co.za. Open 1100-2300.
A popular haunt with restaurant upstairs, huge outside seating area, TV continually showing sports action, a lively mixed crowd.

Mitchell's Scottish Ale House
East Pier Rd, T021-419 5074, www.mitchells-ale-house.com. Open 1100-2300.
Next door to **Ferryman's** this is an English-style wood-panelled pub and it brews its own beer including bitter and stout, which are not common in South Africa. Sports are shown on TV and there's simple pub fare.

Tobago's Radisson BLU Hotel Waterfront
See Where to stay, page 57, T021-441 3000, www.radissonblu.com. Open 0900-2300.
Super-stylish hotel bar set around an infinity pool, with great ocean views, a long list of cocktails. A perfect spot for sundowners and attracts a mixed crowd of tourists and after-work drinkers.

South of Rondesbosch

Forester's Arms
57 Newlands Av, T021-689 5949, www.forries.co.za. Open 1100-late.
Old-fashioned English-style pub, popular with sports fans who come to watch important matches. A fun-loving, boozy scene with a leafy beer garden and fire inside in winter.

Tiger Tiger
103 Main Rd, Claremont, T021-683 2220, www.tigertiger.co.za. Tue, Thu-Sat 2030-late.
This is the southern suburbs' most commercial and modern nightclub with several bars, plenty of seating areas, a large sunken dance floor and mainstream pop music. Attracts the odd local rugby or cricket star given its proximity to Newlands.

Entertainment

Casino
GrandWest Casino & Entertainment World, *1 Vanguard Dr, Goodwood, T021-505 7777, www.suninternational.com. Most facilities 1000-2400, casino 24-hr.* Around 12 km to the east of the city centre in Goodwood, this multifaceted Vegas-style entertainment complex has a casino, a 6-screen Nu Metro cinema, ice-rink, 10-pin bowling alley, several restaurants and bars, and the 5000-seat Grand Arena that regularly hosts pop and rock concerts and comedy from international artists.

Cinema

The 2 major cinema groups are **Nu Metro** (*www.numetro.co.za*), and **Ster-Kinekor** (*www.sterkinekor.com*). There are multi-screen cinemas in all the large shopping malls including Canal Walk, the V&A Waterfront and Cavendish Sq. The latter 2 also have a separate **Cinema Nouveau**, which screens international and art-house films (information and bookings also at Ster-Kinekor). For Encounters Documentary Film Festival, see Festivals, below.

Labia Cinema, *68 Orange St, Gardens, T021-424 5927, www.labia.co.za*. Cape Town's most enjoyable cinema, showing independent international films in a historic building that used to be the Italian Embassy's ballroom and was named after an Italian princess. It has a café serving good pre-movie snacks that is licensed, so you can take your glass of wine into the movie.

Music

All tickets for live performances can be purchased online from **Computicket** *(T011-340 8000, www.computicket.com)*, or there are kiosks at the V&A Waterfront and Cavendish Sq and the other larger malls, as well as in **Checkers** and **Shoprite** supermarkets.

See also Bars and clubs, page 63, for live music venues.

Cape Town Opera, *see Artscape (below), T021-410 9807, www.capetownopera.co.za*. The acclaimed Cape Town Opera's season is usually from May-Nov, and includes at least one well known crowd pleaser, such as *Madame Butterfly*.

Cape Town Philharmonic Orchestra, *T021-410 9809, www.cpo.org.za*. Based at Artscape (see below) where they accompany the Cape Town Opera and Cape Town City Ballet; the orchestra also plays symphonies in the City Hall.

Kirstenbosch Summer Concerts, *at Kirstenbosch National Botanical Garden (see page 51), T021-799 8782, www.sanbi.org. Nov-Mar every Sun at 1700*. Summer concerts from folk and jazz to classical and opera, and the occasional international pop star, in an idyllic setting where you can picnic on the lawns. The programme is published at the beginning of Oct and ticket prices vary but include garden entry.

Theatre

Tickets from **Computicket**, see above.
Artscape, *DF Malan St, Foreshore, T021-410 9800, www.artscape.co.za*. Cape Town's major complex offering opera, ballet, theatre and music, with several stages and a main theatre seating 1500.

Baxter Theatre, *Main Rd, Rondebosch, T021-685 7880, www.baxter.co.za*. Hosts community theatre and children's performances, as well as international productions and musicals.

Fugard Theatre, *Caledon St, off Buitenkant St, City Centre, T021-461 4554, www.thefugard.com*. Cape Town's newest theatre named after renowned South African playwright Athol Fugard is located in the restored historical Sacks Futeran Building, which used to house tailors and seamstresses in the District Six days. Shows musicals, plays and comedy.

Festivals

There are a number of events throughout the year; many of which fall over public holiday weekends. See www.capetown.travel for full listings. Islamic holidays are celebrated across Cape Town as the majority of Cape Coloureds are Muslim, while the Christian holidays are celebrated by other communities.

2 Jan Karnaval (also known as **Kaapse Klopse**). This carnival, staged by the Cape Coloured community, begins in Bo-Kaap, ends up near the Green Point Stadium, and includes a procession of competing minstrel bands, with painted faces, straw boaters and bright satin suits.

Jan J&B Metropolitan Handicap, last Sat in Jan, www.jbmet.co.za. South Africa's major horse racing meet at Kenilworth Race Course, where everyone is expected to dress up and there's plenty of TV coverage for the fashion and social events.

Jan/Feb Shakespeare-in-the-Park, Maynardville Open Air Theatre in Maynardville Park, Wynburg, www.artscape.co.za/maynardville-open-air-theatre. **Artscape** (see page 66) presents a season of Shakspeare and performances by the Cape Town City Ballet on this lovely stage surrounded by trees.

Feb/Mar Cape Town Pride, www.capetownpride.org. The biggest gay event in town, with floats and a parade around Green Point culminating in a street party in De Waterkant.

Mar Cape Town Carnival, www.capetowncarnival.com. A fabulous and extravagant 1-km procession of floats, dancers and musicians along Somerset Rd in Green Point between De Waterkant and the Cape Town Stadium followed by a street party with local DJs. Cafés and street vendors serve snacks and beverages along the route. In just a few years since its conception, this has become one of Cape Town's most popular annual events.

Mar Cape Town Festival, www.capetownfestival.co.za. Music festival held over the weekend of the Human Rights' Day public holiday on 21 Mar at various venues, with a main stage in Company's Garden. It features many of Cape Town's home-grown musicians.

Mar Cape Argus Pick 'n' Pay Cycle Tour, www.cycletour.co.za. The world's largest timed cycling event taking an impressive 109-km route around Table Mountain and along the shores of the peninsula. It's open to international cyclists and attracts some 40,000 participants each year.

Apr Two Oceans Marathon, www.twooceansmarathon.org.za. Dubbed as one of the most beautiful marathons in the world, it runs on a 56-km route around the Cape Peninsula, and attracts over 26,000 runners; there's also a half marathon and a number of fun runs, and again they are open to international competitors.

Apr Cape Town International Jazz Festival, www.capetownjazzfest.com. Held at the Cape Town International Convention Centre (CTICC), where 5 stages host a huge array of local and international jazz artists and on 1 night there's a free concert in Greenmarket Sq. This celebrated event now attracts in excess of 30,000 people.

Apr Taste of Cape Town, www.tasteofcapetown.com. Held at the Cape Town Cricket Club in Green Point next to the Cape Town Stadium with stalls and marquees, some of the city's top gourmet restaurants showcase their food; buy a book of coupons and a wine glass for tastings.

May Cape Times V&A Waterfront Wine Affair, www.waterfront.co.za. You can taste over 350 wines from 95 estates, and food is from participating V&A Waterfront restaurants.

May Good Food & Wine Show (2nd weekend). At the Cape Town International Convention Centre (CTICC), www.goodfoodandwineshow.co.za. This celebrates gourmet food and good wine, with tastings and Cape Town's best restaurants serving up tempting mini-plates, plus hands-on cooking experiences and demonstrations from celebrity chefs.

May-Jun Cape Town Funny Festival, Baxter Theatre, www.baxter.co.za. A month-long program of performances showcasing local and international comedy talent.

Jun Encounters Documentary Film Festival, www.encounters.co.za. Films screened at the Labia Cinema and Cinema Nouveau at the V&A Waterfront.

Aug Mercedes-Benz Cape Town Fashion Week, www.mbfashionweeksa.co.za. Runway shows at the Cape Town International Convention Centre (CTICC) showcase young and established designers from across Africa, which concludes with a dazzling display of evening wear.

Sep   Chelsea Festival at Kirstenbosch, www.sanbi.org. The best time to see the flowers in full bloom, special events include gardening talks, flower arranging contests and fine art exhibitions, but the real reason to come is to see Kirstenbosch's entry to the Chelsea Flower Show in London, for which they have won countless gold medals.

Sep   Hermanus Whale Festival, www. whalefestival.co.za. Marks beginning of calving season of southern right whales, when there is excellent land-based whale watching over Walker Bay from the cliff-tops in Hermanus. This is an easy day trip from Cape Town and features live music, a craft market, and a marquee displaying exhibits on whales. A whale-crier blows his horn when a whale is spotted.

Dec   Mother City Queer Project, www. mcqp.co.za. The city's biggest annual gay-themed party and a colourful and fun event which attracts thousands. Different venue and different dress-up code each year; there's a no costume, no entry policy.

Dec   Kirstenbosch Summer Concerts (every Sun until Mar). This is a perfect way to enjoy the gardens with a picnic on the lawns; the concerts vary from rock, folk and jazz to classical and opera. A popular venue for international stars (www.sanbi.org).

Shopping

Arts, crafts and curios

African Image, *52 Burg St, T021-423 8385, www.african-image.co.za. Mon-Sat 0900-1700.* Excellent alternative to the tired souvenir shops, this sells contemporary African art, such as bags made from traditional weavings and beautiful baskets, plus quirky souvenirs like coke-bottle-top bags and old township signs.

Church St Antiques Market, *on Church St, between Long and Burg streets. Mon-Sat 0900-1400.* Offbeat antiques, nautical equipment, crockery and jewellery.

Greenmarket Square, *Mon-Sat 0900-1600.* A lively arts and crafts market selling goods from across Africa on the picturesque square flanked by several terrace cafés.

Monkeybiz, *43 Rose St, Bo-Kaap, T021-426 0636, www.monkeybiz.co.za. Mon-Fri 0900-1700, Sat 0900-1300.* Something of a local sensation, **Monekybiz** creates employment for women (many of them HIV positive) in the townships of Mandela Park and Khayelitsha. The women create beautiful and quirky one-off bead works, including figures, animals and accessories.

Out of This World, *Victoria Wharf, V&A Waterfront, T021-419 3246. Open 0900-2100.* One of the more tasteful selections of the many African arts and crafts shops at the V&A, and there's also carefully chosen ethnic interior decor items collected from around the world.

The Pan African Market, *76 Long St, T021-426 4478, www.thepanafricanmarket.com. Mon-Fri 0900-1700, Sat 0900-1500.* 2-storey centre set in a converted Victorian house, selling crafts from across the continent, good local crafts made from recycled material, beadwork, ceramics. Café specializing in African food, plus a book shop and holistic healing area.

Streetwires, *77 Shortmarket St, T021-426 2475, www.streetwires.co.za. Mon-Fri 0900-1700, Sat 0900-1300.* Another wire-sculpture cooperative supporting local communities, useful place to browse these interesting South African crafts without feeling under pressure from the usual street vendors. You can also meet the artists.

Watershed, *Dock Rd (next to the Two Oceans Aquarium), V&A Waterfront, www.waterfront. co.za. Open 1000-1900.* Huge warehouse that is home to more than 150 stalls selling quality African-made items from ceramics and furniture to textiles, fashion and jewellery. On the mezzanine level is Wellness at the Watershed that offers body and soul products and walk-in therapies such as reflexology or scalp massages.

Books and maps

Clarke's Bookshop, *211 Long St, T021-423 5739, www.clarkesbooks.co.za.* Mon-Fri 0900-1700, Sat 0900-1300. A mass of antiquarian, second-hand and new books in a muddled old shop, a must for any book lover, and also specializes in books on Southern Africa art.

Exclusive Books, *www.exclusivebooks. co.za.* National bookshop chain, the best branches are at Victoria Wharf at the V&A Waterfront and Cavendish Sq Mall, which also have cafés. Particularly good for maps, guidebooks and coffee-table books on Cape Town and Africa and carry a full range of international magazines and newspapers.

Select Books, *232 Long St, T021-424 6955. www.selectbooks.co.za. Mon-Fri 0900-1700, Sat 0900-1300.* This small friendly bookshop specializes in classics, antiquarian and Africana books, with a strong emphasis on Cape Town's and South African history, plus sports like cricket and rugby.

Music

The African Music Store, *134 Long St, T021-426 0857. Mon-Fri 0900-1800, Sat 0900-1400.* Stocks an excellent choice of music by major African artists as well as compilations and reggae. The staff are incredibly helpful and are happy to let you listen to any number of CDs before purchasing. Can ship worldwide.

Mabu Vinyl, *2 Rheede St, Gardens, T021-423 7635, www.mabuvinyl.co.za. Mon-Sat 0900-1800, Sun 1100-1500. Just off Kloof St*, this is a relative Aladdin's Cave of vinyl LPs and 12"s, cassettes, turntables, comics and new CDs of independent South African artists. The shop has reached pop-culture icon (and a minor tourist attraction) status after the 2013 Oscar-winning documentary *Searching for Sugarman*, which tracks one of the co-owner's quest to find the much-loved South African guitarist and singer Sixto Rodriguez.

Musica, *Victoria Wharf, V&A Waterfront, T021-418 4722, www.musica.co.za. Open 0900-2100.* The national music and movie store with branches in the larger shopping malls, selling CDs and DVDs. Has an extensive range of South African contemporary and African traditional music.

Shopping malls

Canal Walk, *Century Blvd, Century City, Milnerton, T021-555 4444, www.canalwalk. co.za. Open 0900-2100.* On the N1 about 10 km north of the city, this is one of South Africa's largest malls with over 400 retail outlets, local chain stores as well as international brands, cinema, entertainment atrium, food court and restaurant piazza.

Cavendish Square, *Dreyer St, Claremont, T021-657 5600, www.cavendish.co.za. Mon-Sat 0900-1900, Sun 1000-1700.* A stylish mall with 230 stores, 20 restaurants, cinema, food court, the Cavendish Connect section features individual boutiques.

Gardens Centre, *Mill St, Gardens, T021-465 1842, www.gardensshoppingcentre.co.za, Mon-Fri 0900-1900, Sat 0900-1700, Sun 0900-1400.* Large branches of supermarkets, plus 85 specialist shops for homeware, fashion, decor and gifts.

Victoria Wharf, *V&A Waterfront, T021-408 7600, www.waterfront.co.za. Open 0900-2100.* With over 400 upmarket shops, this is Cape Town's premier shopping mall with many specialist shops for curios, jewellery and international brand designer fashion, plus over 80 restaurants and 2 cinemas.

What to do

Abseiling and kloofing

Abseil Africa, *T021-424 4760, www. abseilafrica.co.za.* Operates one of the world's highest and longest commercial abseils – 112 m down Table Mountain – R750 excluding cableway fee. Also runs day trips to other abseil points around the Cape and kloofing (canyoning) trips, which involve hiking, boulder-hopping and swimming along mountain rivers.

Cricket

Sahara Park Test Ground, *161 Camp Ground Rd, Newlands, for fixtures and tickets Computicket, T011-340 8000, www. computicket.com.* A beautiful cricket oval where a few of the famous old oak trees remain and it is still possible to watch a game from a grassy bank with Table Mountain as a backdrop. You can take a tour of Newlands, see page 51.

Boat tours

See also page 47 for Robben Island Tours and page 100 for boat trips from the peninsula.

There are more than 20 boats of varying types and sizes operating from Quay 5, the Pierhead or the Clock Tower at the V&A Waterfront. Just take a stroll around and the touts at the various kiosks will tell you what's on offer and when the next departure is. You can choose from a sail on a schooner to Camps Bay, a quick ferry trip across one of the docks, a guided tour of the working harbour, a sunset cruise with champagne, or a fast inflatable jet boat ride. All companies are listed at www.waterfront.co.za.

Jolly Roger Pirate Boat, *Quay 5, T021-421 0909, www.pirateboat.co.za.* A swashbuckling adventure for children, this themed boat goes out on daily 1-hr trips with an interactive pirate show, R120, children (under 12) R60, family of 4 ticket R300.

Tigresse, *Quay 5, T021-421 0909, www. tigresse.co.za.* Daily departures on luxury catamarans for a 1½-hr sail out to Table Bay; R240 with champagne, discounts for children (4-12), and on *Tommy the Tugboat*, a half-hour harbour cruise to see the seals, R50, children (under 12) R25.

Waterfront Charters, *Quay 5, T021-418 5806, www.waterfrontcharters.co.za.* Boats to choose from include a large catamaran and stylish schooner called the *Esperance*, and a range of boat tours including around (not to) Robben Island, whale watching, sunset and dinner cruises. Example prices: ½-hr seal cruise, R80; 1½-hr sunset cruise, R250; 1-hr jet boat, R700.

Golf

For further details visit the website of the **Western Province Golf Union**, *www.wpgu. co.za.* Expect to pay green fees of around R300-550 for 18 holes and clubs, carts and caddies can be hired.

Metropolitan Golf Club, *Fritz Sonnenberg Rd, Green Point, T021-430 6011, www. metropolitangolfclub.co.za.* The 1st golf club was founded here in 1885, and after the land was turned into a military camp by the British during the Anglo-Boer War, reopened again as the Metropolitan Golf Club in 1902. In 2010, the course layout was changed to accommodate the new Cape Town Stadium, and now the 18-hole course has a magnificent location immediately beneath the outer rim of the impressive stadium as well as sweeping ocean views.

Rondebosch Golf Club, *Klipfontein, Rondebosch, T021-689 4177, www. rondeboschgolfclub.com.* A tidy course with the Black River flowing through it and good views of Table Mountain.

Royal Cape Golf Club, *174 Ottery Rd, Wynberg, T021-761 6551, www.royalcapegolf. co.za.* An old club with a history dating back to 1885, which has been the venue for major professional tournaments.

Helicopter flights

Without doubt, seeing Cape Town from a low-flying helicopter is an incredible experience. You can pre-book, or if it's a clear wind-free day, just turn up at Quay 5 at the V&A Waterfront where there are several offices. All companies are listed at www. waterfront.co.za. Passengers are transferred from there by golf cart to the helipad beyond the Table Bay Hotel. Flights start from R800 per person for 15-20 mins.

Sport Helicopters, *Quay 5, V&A Waterfront, T021-419 5907, www.sporthelicopters.co.za.* As well as scenic flights, offers exciting rides over Table Bay and the West Coast in an ex-Vietnam Huey helicopter.

The Hopper, *Quay 5, V&A Waterfront, T079-513 2254, www.thehopper.co.za.* The 15-min flight goes along the coast to Camps Bay, then turns back through Kloof Nek to see the top of Table Mountain and the City Bowl. Longer 20-, 30- and 60-min flights take in other parts of the peninsula.

Hiking
Downhill Adventures, *Shop 10 Overbeek Building, corner of Kloof, Long and Orange streets, Gardens, T021-422 0388, www. downhilladventures.com.* Guided half-day hikes on Table Mountain for R750: full-day R850. Also organizes a number of other adventure activities; see below.

Kiteboarding
Cabrinha, *Eden On The Bay Shopping Centre, corner of Sir Baird & Otto Du Plessis drives, Bloubergstrand, T021-554 1729, www.cabrinha. co.za.* Rents out equipment to experienced kiteboarders and offers 4-hr beginner's lessons for R1390 on Langebaan Lagoon, a 1-hr drive north of Cape Town.
Downhill Adventures, *www.downhill adventures.com, see above.* Beginners' tuition at Dolphin Beach at Table View, north of the city centre from R950 per 2-hr lesson and recommends 3 sessions before going alone.

Mountain biking
Downhill Adventures, *www.downhill adventures.com, see above.* Organizes the popular Table Mountain double descent, which is a 90% downhill trail around Devil's Peak for R850, as well as rides around Cape Point and the Winelands Meander. Also offers bike and helmet rentals for R400 per day.
Homeland, *305 Long St, T021-689 5431, www. homeland.co.za.* Mountain-bike rentals cost R140 for 24 hrs; cheaper rates the longer you hire. Also rents out surf boards, paddle skis, wet suits and camping equipment.

Paragliding
Para-Pax, *T082-881 4724, www.parapax.com.* Tandem paragliding from Lion's Head is very popular, with gliders landing on Sea Point

Promenade. Flights cost R1150 and for R200 you get photos and DVD.

Rugby
The rugby season is from mid-May to mid-Jul. International games are played at the **Western Province Rugby Union** ground *(Boundary Rd, Newlands, T021-659 4600, www.wprugby.co.za).* Tickets through **Computicket**, *T011-340 8000, www. computicket.com.* You can take a tour of Newlands, see page 51.

Sandboarding
Downhill Adventures, *www.downhill adventures.com, see above.* Not as fast as snowboarding, but can be a fun day out and trips are to dunes about 1 hr north of Cape Town. Half-day R750; full-day R950.

Scuba diving
The Cape waters are cold but good for wreck and kelp diving. The best season for diving is during the winter months when the weather ensures the sea is flat as the prevailing winds blow offshore. Water temperatures are 12-18°C; visibility is usually 5-10 m.
    For dive operators on the Cape Peninsula, see page 101. A number of dive companies also specialize in great white shark-cage diving offshore from Gansbaai, 165 km southeast of Cape Town. Full-day excursions are available from Cape Town, see page 146. Experienced divers can also dive with sharks in the predator tank in the Two Oceans Aquarium, see page 47.
Table Bay Diving, *Quay 5, V&A Waterfront, T021-419 8822, www.tablebaydiving.com.* Dive charters and full range of PADI courses.

Skydiving
Skydive Cape Town, *T082-800 6290, www. skydivecapetown.za.net.* Offers tandem jumps on the West Coast for R2000; extra R600 for DVD and photos. There are fantastic views back across to Cape Town and Robben Island.

Standup paddleboarding (SUP)

Cape Town provides a variety of good environments for 'Sup-ing' from flat canals to ocean surf.

Cabrinha, *Eden On The Bay Shopping Centre, corner of Sir Baird & Otto Du Plessis drives, Bloubergstrand, T021-554 1729, www.cabrinha. co.za*. From their base in Big Bay, offers 1-hr lessons for R490 with boards, which can be combined with kiteboarding (see above).

SUP Cape Town, *the clubhouse is accessed off Walter Sisulu Avenue, cross the bridge opposite the Caltex petrol station, V&A Waterfront, T082-789 0411, www.supcapetown.co.za*. Rent boards from R200 per hour and they can arrange introductory lessons on the Waterfront Canal, while during summer (Dec-Feb) they are also stationed in a bedouin tent on Clifton Fourth Beach (page 79).

Surfing

Surfing is a serious business in Cape Town, and there are excellent breaks catering for learners right through to experienced surf rats. Some of the best breaks are on **Long Beach, Kommetjie, Noordhoek, Llandudno, Kalk Bay, Muizenberg** and **Bloubergstrand**. To check out the local scene visit www. wavescape.co.za.

Downhill Adventures, *www.downhill adventures.com, see above*. Promises to get absolute beginners standing up on a wave by the end of a day. Half-day R750; full-day R950 including equipment. Also rents out surfboards, R350 per day, and wet suits (essential), R250 per day, to experienced surfers. As does **Homeland**, see Mountain biking, above.

Swimming

Sea Point Swimming Pool, *Beach Rd, Sea Point, T021-434 3341. Oct-Apr 0700-1900, May-Sep 0830-1700, R20, children (under 16) R10.* Some (probably Cape Town people) regard this as being the most stunning location for a public swimming pool in the world. Indeed, it is a sparkling bright blue outdoor Olympic-sized pool built right on the rocks next to the ocean with superb mountain and sea views. It has 2 splash pools for kids, a springboard diving pool, and terraces for sunbathing.

Tour operators

There is a diverse range of day tours in and around Cape Town available through the operators below. Expect to pay in the region of R450 for a ½-day tour and R900 for a full day. The 3 most popular are tours of the Cape Peninsula, the Winelands and the townships. Peninsula tours generally go down the west side to Hout Bay and offer an optional boat trip to see the seals on Duiker Island, then go over Chapman's Peak Drive (if its open) and into the Table Mountain National Park to Cape Point. They return to the city on the eastern side with a stop to see the penguins at Boulders Beach. Winelands tours take in about half a dozen vineyards in the Stellenbosch and Paarl regions. Township tours usually begin at the District Six Museum and continue to Langa and Khayelitsha, and companies work with the communities they visit, putting back some of the proceeds. If you want to combine a ½-day township tour with the excursion to Robben Island, all operators will drop off at the ferry. Below is a small selection of the numerous tour operators offering day tours. Any hotel can make recommendations and for a full list of tour operators, visit www.capetown.travel.

Day tours

African Eagle, *T021-464 4266, www.daytours. co.za*. Offers a full choice of local tours to the Peninsula, townships, Winelands, Whale Coast and 4-day, 3-night tours of the Garden Route. Has regular scheduled departures that single travellers can join.

Andulela Experience, *T021-790 2590, www. andulela.com*. Very different township tours that focus on music and poetry, jazz and soccer and a day trip in Bo-Kaap that includes a walking tour, Cape Malay cookery lessons and meals.

Cape Capers, *T021-448 3117, www.tour capers.co.za.* Range of trips, including ½-day tours looking at Cape Town's slave history, District Six and Bo-Kaap tours and the Cape Care Route that goes to social and environmental projects on the Cape Flats.

Cape Discovery Tours, *T021-461 9652, www.discoverytours.co.za.* Can organize private tailor-made tours for 2-5 people for day trips around Cape Town, plus the West Coast, Garden Route and as far as the private game reserves and Addo Elephant National Park in the Eastern Cape.

Cape Rainbow Tours, *T021-551 5465, www.caperainbow.com.* Tours in many European languages to the townships, Winelands, Peninsula and, in season, to the West Coast to see the flowers and Hermanus for whales.

Day Trippers, *T021-511 4766, www.day trippers.co.za.* Peninsula tours which include 1 or 2 hrs of cycling at Cape Point, Winelands, township, Table Mountain hike and the Whale Coast. Good value and fun, popular with backpackers.

Flamingo Tours, *T021-557 4496, www.flamingotours.co.za.* Tour operator specializing in disabled travel, tailor-made tours are led by a registered guide and nurse (if necessary) and can organize day tours of Cape Town with sign language.

Footsteps to Freedom, *T083-452 1112, www.footstepstofreedom.co.za.* From R250 per person depending on group size. A historical 3-hr walking tour of central Cape Town which goes to the Castle, District Six Museum and Company's Garden and can be combined with a township minibus tour later in the afternoon. A good way to learn about the city centre's historical past.

Friends of Dorothy, *T021-465 1871, www.friendsofdorothytours.co.za.* Gay-friendly tours, including a Four Passes tour, Peninsula, Winelands and whale-watching trips. Gay drivers and guides, max 7.

Hylton Ross, *T021-511 1784, www.hylton ross. com.* Full range of day tours, Cape Point with optional boat ride to see the seals from Hout Bay, Winelands, township, and longer trips to the Garden Route.

Transport

Air

Cape Town International Airport *(airport enquiries T021-937 1200, flight information T0867-277888, www.acsa.co.za)*, is 22 km east of the city centre on the N2, or, out of rush hour, a 20-min drive. Domestic and international arrivals/departures are linked by one long terminal and a retail mall. The airport has a full range of facilities including Wi-Fi, money exchange counters and ATMs. Within international arrivals, **Cape Town Tourism** *(T021-934 1949, www. capetown.travel, Mon-Fri 0600-2100, Sat-Sun 0800-2000)* can arrange accommodation and provide maps and leaflets. You can hire mobile phones and buy local SIM cards at **Vodacom's Vodashop** *(www.vodacom.com)*, or from **MTN's Fone 4 Hire** *(www.mtnsp. co.za)*, which both have desks at international and domestic arrivals, open 0500-2400.

Car hire outlets are across the road from the Transport Plaza (the concourse outside the terminal building). Several shuttle services run from kiosks in the international and domestic arrivals halls and drop off at accommodation in central Cape Town; tickets cost around R240 per person plus R30 for each additional person from the same group. Alternatively you can pre-book one through your hotel, guesthouse or backpacker hostel, or directly through **Citi Hopper** *(T021-936 3469, www.citihopper. co.za)*, **Cape Town Shuttles** *(T021-556 5606, www.capetownshuttles.co.za)*, **Sport Shuttle** *(T021-934 3477, www.sportshuttle.co.za)*, or **The Backpacker Bus** *(T021-439 7600, www. backpackerbus.co.za)*. Taxis running between the airport and city centre should have a special airport licence and they must use their meter by law. **Touch Down Taxis** *(T021-919 4659)* is the authorized airport taxi company and again kiosks are in the arrivals halls; expect to pay around R280-350 to the city centre, depending on traffic.

The **MyCiTi Bus** (see below) runs between the airport bus station (immediately outside arrivals), and the Civic Centre on Hertzog Blvd in central Cape Town, from where services continue to other destinations. Airport buses depart every 20-30 mins 0530-2130 from the airport, and 0500-2100 from the Civic Centre. The journey takes around 30 mins (45-55 mins during peak hours); some airport buses continue on to the V&A Waterfront, which means you don't have to swap at the Civic Centre. You will need a myconnect card loaded with money (see below) which are available at the airport station for arrivals, and the fare from the airport to the city is R68.70 during peak hours (0600-0830, 1600-1800), R65.60 at all other times.

Airlines

There are frequent connections from Cape Town to all the other South African cities with the domestic airlines. You can either book directly, or through **Computicket** *(T011-915 8000, www.computicket.com)*. Domestic carriers include: **British Airways/ Comair** *(www.britishairways.com)*; **FlySafair** *(www.flysafair.co.za)*; **Kulula** *(www.kulula. com)*; **Mango**, *www.flymango.com*; and **South African Airways** (**SAA**) *(www.flysaa. com)*. For details of international flights, see page 205.

Bus
Local

MyCiTi buses *(T0800-656463, www.myciti. org.za)* are part of the city's new **Integrated Rapid Transport** (**IRT**) system. The main bus station is at the Civic Centre on Hertzog Blvd in the city centre, near the railway station. Buses operate every 10-20 mins, 0630-2200. All stations and buses are wheelchair friendly and bicycles can be accommodated. Services from the Civic Centre include a non-stop bus to/from the **airport** (see above); to the **Gardens Centre** via Long St and Orange

St, which returns via Loop St; to the **V&A Waterfront** via **Green Point**; to Queens Beach in **Sea Point**; to **Camps Bay** and **Hout Bay** via Sea Point; to Camps Bay via **Tamboerskloof** and **Kloof Nek** (for **Table Mountain**); to Salt River via Woodstock; and the West Coast suburbs to the bus station at **Table View**, from where there are feeder services as far as **Blouberg**. Timetables can be found on the website. Fares start from R6.80 for a short journey, but rise during peak hours (Mon-Fri 0630-0830 and 1600-1800); children under 4 travel free. Passengers need a **myconnect** card loaded with money. Cards are 'tapped' in and out on the bus so the fare is calculated and they can be bought (R35) and loaded at the Civic Centre (and other main stations) or from some local convenience shops such as 7-Eleven or Spar (look for the 'Top Up Here' signs).

Golden Arrow buses *(T0800-656463, www.gabs.co.za)* follow all the major routes across Cape Town's metropolitan area at regular intervals and bus stops are clearly marked. Timetables and fares are published on the website (though few services run after 2100). A short journey costs around R7.20 (children 5-11 half price; under 5s free) and payment is made on board. The central bus station is on Strand St across the road from the railway station and next to the Grand Parade.

Long distance

Intercape *(www.intercape.co.za)*, **Greyhound** *(www.greyhound.co.za)*, and **Translux** *(www. translux.co.za)*, long-distance buses all depart from/ arrive at Cape Town railway station on Adderley St. Booking offices are here or book through **Computicket** *(T011-915 8000, www. computicket.com)*, or their kiosks at the V&A Waterfront and Cavendish Sq, as well as in Checkers and Shoprite supermarkets.

The budget **Baz Bus** *(www.bazbus.com)* has a daily service from Cape Town to **Port Elizabeth**. The service continues from Port Elizabeth to **Durban**, the following day, and then the day after continues to

Johannesburg and Tshwane (Pretoria). See page 207 for details.

Bike hire

Cape Town is easy to navigate by bike and there are a few bike lanes in the city centre. The Sea Point Promenade (see page 41) is well-recommended for cycling for the whole family (especially at sunset). For mountain biking, see page 71.

Up Cycles

Cape Town's first drop-and-go bike rental company. There are 3 stations: on the **Sea Point Promenade** *(next to the Sea Point Swimming Pool)*; at **Clock Tower Square** *(at the V&A Waterfront)*; and at **Mandela Rhodes Place** *(corner of Wale and Burg streets in the city centre, T076-135 2223, www.upcycles.co.za. Open 0830-sunset)*. Bikes are comfortable uprights suitable for novice cyclists, and there are children's bikes and child seats for toddlers. Helmets and locks are included. From 1-hr: R50, to a full-day: R200.

Car hire

It's always a good idea to shop around for rates and pre-book a car in peak seasons. See page 208 for further advice on car hire and driving.
Around About Cars, *T021-422 4022, www.aroundaboutcars.com.*
Atlantic Car Hire, *T021-385 0178, www.atlanticcarhire.co.za.*
Avis, *T021-934 0330, www.avis.co.za.*
Budget, *T021-380 3180, www.budget.co.za.*
Britz Africa, *T021-385 0403, www.britz.co.za.* Contact for camper vans and motorhomes for travel in and beyond South Africa. Good all-inclusive deals.
Cape Car Hire, *T021-914 0723, www.capecarhire.co.za.*
Europcar, *T021-412 9053, www.europcar.co.za.*
First Car Rental, *T021-934 7499, www.firstcarrental.co.za.*
Hertz, *T021-935 4800, www.hertz.co.za.*
Tempest, *T021-481 9860, www.tempestcarhire.co.za.*

Minibus taxis

The usefulness of minibus taxis has generally been superseded by the much more efficient and comfortable MyCiTi buses. However there are a number which still serve areas of the city on fixed routes, and leave from the minibus terminal accessed from the top floor of the railway station on Adderley St. The exception is the minibuses from Cape Town along the Atlantic Seaboard as far as Camps Bay; these usually leave every few mins from the corner of Strand St and Plein St. They can also be flagged down from the street. Most trips cost around R7, and stop running at around 1900. Minibus taxis are generally safe to use, although you'd be advised to avoid looking like a tourist and leave all valuables at home.

Motorbike hire

There are a number of places to hire bikes around the city and they are a great way to get around in summer (and easy to park) but remember you'll need a licence. A 150cc scooter can cost as little as R180 a day (less if you rent for a week).
Big Boy Scooters, *9 Buitengracht St, corner of Castle St, T021-424 0467, www.bigboyscooters.co.za.*
Cape Bike Rentals, *186 Bree St, T021-426 5851, www.capebikerentals.com.*
Cape Sidecar Adventures, *2 Glengariff Rd, Sea Point, T021-434 9855, www.sidecars.co.za.* Rents vintage ex-Chinese Red Army motorbikes with sidecars.
Harley Davidson Cape Town, *9 Somerset Rd, Green Point, T021-401 4260, www.harley-davidson-capetown.com, rents out Harleys and provides route maps for day tours.*

Taxi

There are several ranks dotted around town – the most useful ones are outside the railway station on Adderley St, in Greenmarket Sq and on Long St. If you are outside the city centre, you will have to call one in advance or ask your hotel or restaurant to call one for you.

Rikki Taxis, *T0861-745 547/021-447 3559 (from an international phone), www.rikkis.co.za.* The fleet of London black cabs can be seen buzzing around all over Cape Town, and are a cheaper alternative to regular taxis for getting around the city. You need to call one, but they pick up several people along the route, which brings down costs. They operate 24 hrs, and costs vary from R15-35 depending on the distance. They operate in the City Bowl and Atlantic Seaboard as far as Camps Bay, but a few people can charter one to get to somewhere like Kirstenbosch, for example.

Uber, *www.uber.com/cities/cape-town.* This private-driver service operates in Cape Town, and anyone who has installed the iOS or Android app can use both the uberBlack and uberX (slightly cheaper) options. Fares are charged to Uber accounts.

Train

Cape Town railway station is on Adderley St in the city centre. For details of train travel, including luxury services between Cape Town and Tshwane (Pretoria), see page 207.

Metrorail *(T0800-656364, www. capemetrorail.co.za)* operates suburban trains across the Cape Town Metropolitan region as far as **Bellville** in the northern suburbs, **Paarl** in the Winelands, **Strand** on False Bay, and **Simon's Town** on the Cape Peninsula. Tickets cost from R7.50 (children 5-11 half price; under 5s free) for a short journey; see the website for fares and timetables. Trains generally run 0530-2000 and are fine to use in rush hour (0700-0800 and 1600-1800), but are best avoided at quieter times due to safety issues; also avoid the routes to the east, which pass through the Cape Flats. Of these routes, the Cape Town–Simon's Town route is recommended for visitors as the scenic line goes through the towns on the False Bay coast; the **Southern Line initiative** is a hop-on hop-off rail ticket designed for tourists (see page 89). Metrorail also put on special trains for certain events – rugby matches at Newlands, for example.

Cape Peninsula

The most popular day trip from central Cape Town is a leisurely loop around the Cape Peninsula. The stunning coast road winds its way through the city's swanky suburbs on the Atlantic Seaboard on the western side, down to Cape Point and the Cape of Good Hope at the southern tip of the peninsula, and then up again through the quaint fishing settlements on the False Bay coast on the eastern side. This can be done under your own steam and a day's hire car is an ideal way to explore at your own pace; alternatively, all the tour operators offer the excursion – some take mountain bikes too, for a spot of cycling in the Table Mountain National Park. As well as fine ocean and mountain views, there are a number of attractions to stop for including the boat trip from Hout Bay to see the seals on Duiker Island, the spectacularly scenic Chapman's Peak Drive, climbing to the lighthouse at Cape Point, and the penguins at Boulders Beach. There are also ample places to stop for lunch, be it simple fish and chips or a gourmet meal, and there are many tourist shops, art galleries and roadside stalls to grab your attention along the way.

Cape Peninsula

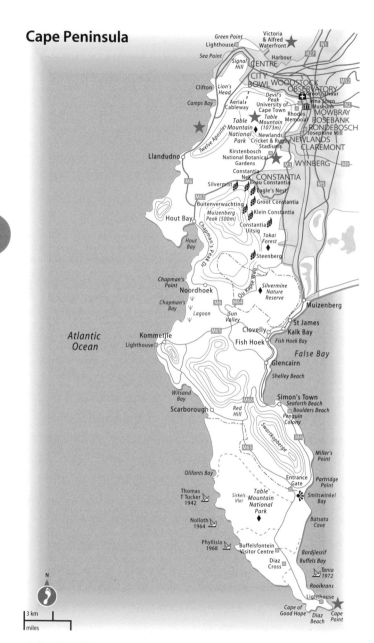

Green Point Lighthouse
Victoria & Alfred Waterfront
Sea Point
Signal Hill
Harbour
CENTRE
CITY
BOWL
WOODSTOCK
OBSERVATORY
Groot Schuur
Irma Stern Museum
Clifton
Lion's Head
Devil's Peak
University of Cape Town
MOWBRAY
ROSEBANK
Rhodes Memorial
Camps Bay
Aerial Cableway
Table Mountain (1073m)
RONDEBOSCH
Josephine Mill
Twelve Apostles
Table Mountain National Park
Newlands Cricket & Rugby Stadiums
NEWLANDS
CLAREMONT
Llandudno
Kirstenbosch National Botanical Gardens
WYNBERG
Constantia Nek
CONSTANTIA
Silvermist
Beau Constantia
Eagle's Nest
Buitenverwachting
Groot Constantia
Klein Constantia
Hout Bay
Muizenberg Peak (500m)
Constantia Uitsig
Tokai Forest
Hout Bay
Steenberg
Chapman's Peak Dr
Chapman's Point
Ou Kaapse Weg
Silvermine Nature Reserve
Noordhoek
Muizenberg
Chapman's Bay
Lagoon
Sun Valley
St James
Kalk Bay
Kommetjie
Clovelly
Fish Hoek Bay
Lighthouse
Fish Hoek
False Bay
Atlantic Ocean
Glencairn
Shelley Beach
Witsand Bay
Simon's Town
Seaforth Beach
Boulders Beach
Penguin Colony
Scarborough
Red Hill
Swartkopberge
Miller's Point
Olifants Bay
Entrance Gate
Partridge Point
Thomas T Tucker 1942
Sirkels Vlei
Table Mountain National Park
Smitswinkel Bay
Nolloth 1964
Batsata Cove
Phyllisia 1968
Buffelsfontein Visitor Centre
Diaz Cross
Bordjiesrif
Buffels Bay
Tania 1972
Rooikrans
Lighthouse
Cape of Good Hope
Diaz Beach
Cape Point

N

3 km

miles

★Atlantic Seaboard

beaches, scenic drives, sunsets and restaurants along palm-fringed promenades

The Atlantic Seaboard refers to Cape Town's wealthy suburbs on the west side of the peninsula. Exclusive Clifton, Camps Bay and Llandudno have some of Cape Town's most sought-after properties and whitewashed modern mansions and luxury apartments with their brilliantly blue swimming pools climb up the hillsides, while the pristine beaches are popular with the beautiful people. Further south the road winds its way above the rocky shoreline and below the magnificent Twelve Apostles, the spine of mountains from the back of Table Mountain. It then drops into Hout Bay and the back end of the Constantia Valley, before continuing south towards Cape Point.

Clifton Beach

Cape Town's best-known beaches stretch along Clifton, and are renowned as the playground of the young and wealthy – this is the place to see and be seen. Other than being hotpots of high society, Clifton's four sheltered beaches are stunning, perfect arches of powder-soft white sand sloping gently into turquoise water. The beaches, reached be a series of winding footpaths, are divided by rocky outcrops and are unimaginatively named First, Second, Third and Fourth. Each has a distinct character – if you're bronzed and beautiful and confident about playing volleyball in a bikini, head to First Beach. More demure visitors may feel more comfortable on Fourth, which is popular with families and has been an award-winning Blue Flag beach for many years now. It also has facilities including public toilets, changing rooms and places to buy cold drinks and snacks. The sunbathing and swimming are good on all the beaches and lifeguards are on duty, but note that the water is very cold – usually around 12°C. Umbrellas and deck chairs are available for rent. The impressive luxury houses that back the beach can be glimpsed from the winding steps leading down, and it's easy to see why fashionable Clifton is dubbed Millionaire's Row. Be warned that there is limited parking in high season, so get here early or alternatively take the MyCiTi bus.

Essential Atlantic seaboard

Getting around

On Cape Peninsula day tours, the tour operators normally first follow the Atlantic Seaboard route to Hout Bay (to stop and see the seals on Duiker Island) and then follow the road south via Chapman's Peak Drive to the Table Mountain National Park (for Cape Point). They return to the city via the penguin colony at Boulders Beach and the False Bay villages. The **City Sightseeing Cape Town** bus (see page 25) goes as far as Hout Bay on its Blue Mini Peninsula Tour either via the Atlantic Seaboard or Constantia. **MyCiTi** buses ply routes from the city centre to Camps Bay and some continue on to Hout Bay. A car is a logical option if you want to go at a more leisurely pace and stop and explore the less visited attractions and the beaches.

Camps Bay

Following the coast south, you soon skirt around a hill and come out over Camps Bay, a long arch of sand backed by the Twelve Apostles. This is one of the most beautiful (and most photographed) beaches in the world and it also has Blue Flag status, but the calm cobalt water belies its chilliness. The sand is also less sheltered than at Clifton, and sunbathing here on a windy day can be painful. But there are other distractions; the main drag along the beachfront (Victoria Road) is lined with excellent seafood restaurants, and a sundowner followed by a superb meal is quite the perfect ending to a day in Cape Town.

The drive between Camps Bay and Hout Bay runs along the slopes of the Twelve Apostles and is beautiful. Apart from the turning to Llandudno, there is no easy access to the coast until you reach Hout Bay. **Llandudno** itself is a small, exclusive settlement with only one road in and out and no shops, and a fine beach and excellent surf but again parking can be difficult on a sunny day.

Hout Bay

Hout Bay, a historical fishing harbour with an attractive beach, attracts swarms of South African families during peak season. Most come for the seafood restaurants and boat trips, but the best reason for heading here is for spectacular Chapman's Peak Drive (see below), which begins just outside town. As the sun sets in the summer months every lay-by along the road is filled with spectators, drink in hand.

Hout Bay itself is fairly attractive, with a busy fishing harbour at the western end of the bay; at the other end is a collection of shops and popular restaurants. By the harbour is a commercial complex known as **Mariners Wharf**, a popular attraction, although looking a little wind-worn these days. It is based upon Fisherman's Wharf in San Francisco, with a whole string of fish and chips restaurants, souvenir shops and stalls, and **Snoekies Fresh Fish Market**, close to the harbour gates. Even if you're not intending to buy anything it is worth a quick look to see the huge variety of fish that are caught off this coast. Boats also run from here to see the seals on **Duiker Island** (see Boat tours, page 100).

About 600 m to the east of Snoekies at the very end of Harbour Road, and located in a former fish factory, is the **Bay Harbour Market** ⓘ *T082-570 5997, www.bayharbour. co.za, Fri 1700-2100, Sat-Sun 0930-1600.* This draws a big crowd at weekends for the craft, fashion and decor stalls, but mainly for the fantastic food offered by local producers, organic farmers and artisans. There are more than 100 choices from designer cupcakes or oysters and a glass of fizz, to spit roast Karoo lamb or sushi and paella made from Hout Bay seafood. Drinks include several local ales on tap, organic wine and fruit juice, and cocktails and mocktails. Seating is at communal benches set around roaring fireplaces and a market requirement is that stallholders use biodegradable compostable cutlery and containers, and all market waste is recycled. On Friday evenings there is often live music or comedy on the small stage, and the market is so popular that successful South African bands sometimes play here 'unplugged' (when there's a cover charge).

Back in the town, next to the **tourist office** ⓘ *T021-791 8380, www.capetown.travel, Mon-Fri 0830-1730, Sat-Sun 0900-1300,* is the **Hout Bay Museum** ⓘ *4 Andrews Rd, T021-790 3474, Tue-Sat 1000-1230, 1400-1630, R5,* with displays on the history of the area, aimed at visiting school groups. More popular with families is **The World of Birds** ⓘ *Valley Rd, T021-790 2730, www.worldofbirds.org.za, daily 0900-1700, R85, children (3-16) R40, under 3s free,* with over 400 species of bird housed in impressive walk-through aviaries. There's also the **Monkey Jungle**, populated with squirrel monkeys.

Chapman's Peak Drive

T021-791 8220, www.chapmanspeakdrive.co.za, R38 per car, though from the Hout Bay side you can get a day pass for free and drive the 1st 3 km to stop at the viewpoints, but you must go back the same way.

Chapman's Peak Drive is a breathtaking 9-km route with 114 curves, carved into the cliffs 600 m above the sea. Not surprisingly, it's a favourite spot for filming car commercials. It was the brainchild of Sir Francis de Waal, a former administrator of the Cape Province (De Waal Drive in central Cape Town is named after him), and work began in 1915 and it was opened in 1922. Unfortunately, rock fall caused it to close in 2000, but, following extensive engineering works including the rigging of giant nets to catch falling rocks and an impressive cutaway section of the road right into the mountainside, it was reopened in 2003, and is now a toll road. The best time to drive along here is close to sunset in the summer, but the views of the craggy coastline and thrashing ocean, and the crescent of white sand at Hout Bay on one side, and the vast stretch of Noordhoek Beach on the other, are recommended at any time. The Drive sometimes closes in bad weather; check its up-to-the-minute status on the website.

Noordhoek

The greatest attraction here is the 8-km-long deserted beach, backed by a couple of tidal lagoons which offer excellent birdwatching. The beach also offers the Cape's finest setting for horse riding along the shore (see What to do, page 85). There's very little to the village itself, but the **Noordhoek Farm Village** ⓘ *Village Lane, at the bottom end of Chapman Peak's Drive, T021-789 2812, www.noordhoekvillage.co.za, 0900-1700,* is a collection of replica Cape Dutch whitewashed buildings around a little green and a pleasant spot for a coffee or light lunch, with four family restaurants and a deli to pick up picnic items, the **De Noordhoek Lifestyle Hotel** (see page 83), and a number of shops selling arts and crafts.

Kommetjie

The small settlement of Kommetjie means 'little basin', a reference to the natural inlet in the rocks which has been developed into a tidal pool. Long Beach is a major surfing spot and always busy with surfers, even in winter. There is an interesting walk (although go in a group as it's quite isolated) along Long Beach to the wreck of the *Kakapo*, offering a rare opportunity to examine a wreck at close quarters without having to don full scuba equipment. The *Kakapo* is a steamship which was beached here in May 1900 on her maiden voyage when the captain apparently mistook Chapman's Peak for Cape Point during a storm. The boiler and shell are still intact about 100 m above the high tide mark. Birdwatchers may be lucky to see oystercatchers roosting on the wreck. The **Slangkoppunt Lighthouse** ⓘ *Mon-Fri 1000-1500, R16, children (under 12) R8,* lies at the southern end of Long Beach and the name, also spelt Slangkop, means 'snake head'. Slender and startlingly white, it was built in 1919 and, at 41 m, is the tallest cast-iron structure in South Africa. You can climb the steep internal staircase for the views from the tiny balcony.

Off the road into the village, **Imhoff Farm** ⓘ *T4545 783-021, www.imhofffarm.co.za. 1700-0900,* is a worthy stop for families. Here are a number of attractions including a small snake and reptile park, the **Higgeldy Piggeldy Farmyard** ⓘ *Tue-Sun 1600-1200,* with petting animals, and there are a couple of camels to ride. The farm was built in 1743 by Cape commissioner, Baron Gustav Wilhelm van Imhoff, as a refreshment station for passing ships. The stables, silo, smithy, slave quarters and milking sheds are now occupied by local artists selling crafts and furniture, an excellent farm shop selling organic and free-range produce, and the **Blue Water Café**. The **Imhoff Equestrian Centre** is also here (see page 86).

Scarborough

Scarborough consists of a scattering of weekend and holiday homes on the hillside overlooking the Atlantic. The beach is broad and long but swimming is not a good idea as the water is cold and there are strong currents. Just outside Scarborough, close to the entrance to the Table Mountain National Park, is the **Cape Point Ostrich Farm** ⓘ *T021-780 9294, www.capepointostrichfarm.com, 0930-1730, R55, children (6-16) R25, under 5s free,* which is worth visiting for its in-depth tours, describing the lifecycle of the ostrich; during breeding season you can watch eggs hatching. There's a pleasant tea garden on site.

Listings Atlantic Seaboard *map p78*

Where to stay

Camps Bay

$$$$ The Bay
69 Victoria Rd, T021-438, www.thebay.co.za.
Set just across the road from the beach, with 78 modern deluxe a/c rooms all with views across the bay, pleasant contemporary feel, large pool with deck and cocktail bar, spa and beach-facing restaurant.

$$$$ Twelve Apostles
Victoria Rd, T021-437 9000, www.12apostleshotel.com.
In a gloriously scenic spot just to the south of Camps Bay beneath the Twelve Apostles, this 70-room 5-star hotel, has a commanding position overlooking the ocean and features an award-winning spa, pool, excellent restaurant, bar that also offers afternoon tea, and a small cinema.

$$$-$$ Camps Bay Resort
32 Camps Bay Drive, T021-437 9708, www.campsbayresort.com.
One of the most affordable options in Camps Bay, the resort manages 47 units spread around the blocks behind Victoria Road, no more than 150 m from the beach, from simple budget rooms and sea-facing doubles, to self-catering studios and apartments sleeping up to 6. There's access to 2 swimming pools. Breakfast vouchers are arranged at one of the restaurants.

Hout Bay

$$$$ Hout Bay Manor
Baviaanskloof, off Main Rd, T021-790 0116, www.houtbaymanor.com.
A beautifully restored manor house built in 1871, with 20 luxury a/c rooms. The decor throughout is stunning and best described as Afro-chic with bright splashes of colour. There's a pool, spa, gorgeous bar and lounge and celebrated **Pure**, restaurant (see Restaurants, page 84).

$$$$ Tintswalo Atlantic
2 km south of Hout Bay, reservations T011-300 8888, www.tintswalo.com.
Luxury option right by the waves beneath Chapman's Peak Drive, with 10 suites. Long wooden deck with pool, jacuzzi and jaw-dropping views, and there's a restaurant and bar with open kitchen where guests can interact with the chefs.

$$$-$$ Chapman's Peak Beach Hotel
Chapman's Peak Drive, T021-790 1036, www.chapmanspeakhotel.co.za.
This has 10 double rooms in the original historical building and 21 stylish more expensive rooms in a new block, some with sea views. Excellent restaurant (see page 84), and great location just across from the beach and at the start of Chapman's Peak Drive.

$$ Cube Guest House
20 Luisa Way, T071-441 8161, www.cube-guesthouse.com.
Set high up in the valley above Hout Bay with sweeping views of the mountains and

named after its modern gleaming white block architecture, 6 comfortable rooms, designer decor, pool in tropical gardens, gourmet breakfasts.

Noordhoek

$$$-$$ Monkey Valley Resort
Mountain Rd, T021-789 1391, www.monkeyvalleyresort.com.
Family resort set in woodland overlooking Noordhoek Beach, with attractive self-catering thatched log cottages sleeping 2-8 with superb views. The restaurant specializes in pizzas and seafood and serves breakfast all day.

$$ De Noordhoek Lifestyle Hotel
At the Noordhoek Farm Village (see page 81), Village Lane, T021-789 2760, www.denoordhoek.co.za.
Newly built but in traditional Cape Dutch style, this has 20 sleekly modern a/c rooms, a comfortable lounge with bar and fireplace. Restaurants are in the farm village. Strong on environmental policies – solar energy, everything is recycled, the gardens have been designed in a water-wise way.

Kommetjie

$$$$ The Last Word Long Beach
1 Kirsten Av, T021-799 6561, www.thelongbeach.com.
6 modern luxury suites with views over Long Beach, spacious airy decor in pale blues and pinks, stunning swimming pool right on the sand dunes, bar, rates include all drinks, lunch and dinner on request or a chauffeur service is available to take guests to restaurants on the peninsula.

Restaurants

Clifton Beach

$$$ Koi
34 Victoria Rd, Bantry Bay, T021-439 7258, www.koirest.co.za. Open 1200-2230.

Sophisticated restaurant with magnificent ocean views, especially at sunset. Offers Japanese and Chinese favourites with a Western twist like butternut and spinach dim sum or Norwegian salmon with wasabi purée. Free valet parking.

Camps Bay

$$$ Blues
Victoria Rd, T021-438 2040, www.blues.co.za. Open 1200-2300.
Popular restaurant and lounge/bar with superb views and a super luxurious all-white interior. Californian-style seafood menu served to a beautiful crowd, and the long cocktail menu features the signature Blues Bellini.

$$$ The Codfather
37 The Drive, T021-438 0782, www.codfather.co.za. Open 1200-2300.
Stylish laid-back place offering a range of superbly fresh seafood. No menu – the waiter takes you to a counter and you pick and choose whatever you like the look of. Also has an excellent sushi bar.

$$$ The Roundhouse
Kloof Rd, T021-438 4347, www.theroundhouserestaurant.com. Tue-Sat 1200-1600, 1830-2300.
High above Camps Bay and also accessed from the city from Kloof Nek Rd, this building has its origins as a guard house built in 1786 and was later a hunting lodge for Lord Charles Somerset. Now well known for its modern French cuisine on the curved balcony with sweeping ocean views.

$$ Tuscany Beach
41 Victoria Rd, T021-438 1213, www.tuscanybeachrestaurant.com.
0700-2300. Overlooking the beach, open all day from breakfast. Delicious seafood specials – don't miss the kingklip espetadas or the paella. Also serves wood-fired pizzas, salads, burgers and steaks. Trendy place, gets very busy for sundowners.

Hout Bay

$$$ Pure
Hout Bay Manor (see Where to stay, page 82). Tue-Sat 1900-2130, Sun 1200-1500.
A beautifully decorated restaurant almost entirely in sliver with glittering chandeliers, with 3-, 5- and 7-course tasting menus, each paired with wine, or an à la carte menu of gourmet dishes including veal, scallops, lobster, tuna and game meat.

$$ Chapman's Restaurant
Chapman's Peak Beach Hotel, see Where to stay, page 82, T021-790 1036. Open 1100-2200.
A lively restaurant and bar with wood-panelled interior, serving good seafood dishes in frying pans, also grills and pub fare. The outside terrace gets packed in summer.

$$ Dunes
Hout Bay Beach, T021-790 1876, www.dunesrestaurant.co.za. Mon-Fri 1200-2300, Sat 0900-2300, Sun 0900-1800.
Sprawling restaurant overlooking the dunes with breezy outdoor tables in the sand. Excellent seafood including Namibian oysters and West Coast mussels and popular breakfast venue at the weekend.

Cafés

Fish on the Rocks
1 Harbour Rd (about 600 m beyond Snoekies Market), T021-790 1153, www.fishontherocks. co.za. Open 1000-1900.
Delicious fresh fish and chips, deep-fried calamari and prawns, eaten from cardboard boxes at wooden tables overlooking the fishing boats in the harbour.

Noordhoek

$$$-$$ The Foodbarn
Noordhoek Farm Village (see page 81), Village Lane, T021-789 1390, www.thefoodbarn. co.za. Open 1200-1430, Wed-Sat 1900-2130.
A French restaurant with lovely white linen-clad tables in an old barn and outside on the farm stoep. The short menu features well-

thought-out dishes such as bouillabaisse or crusted rack of lamb in truffle jus. There's also a deli ($, open 0800-1700) on the other side of the village green.

$ Red Herring
Beach Rd, signposted off Chapman's Peak Drive, T021-789 1783, www.theredherring. co.za. Mon 1600-2200, Tue-Sun 1200-2200.
Cosy country-style restaurant in an old farmstead with adjoining craft shops, the outdoor deck is ideal for sundowners overlooking Noordhoek Beach. Good wood-fired pizzas and fish and chips, and daily specials on the chalk-board.

Kommetjie

$$-$ Fisherman's
Corner Main Rd and Somerset Way, T021-783 1496, www.fishermans-restaurant.co.za. Mon-Fri 1100-2400, Sat-Sun 1000-2400.
Restaurant and pub with wooden bench tables under milkwood trees where a live band plays on Sun afternoon. As the name suggests, a good choice of seafood including combos and platters, plus beers on tap.

Bars and clubs

Camps Bay
Easily the hottest place to be seen in Cape Town, Victoria Rd in Camps Bay is one long line of neon-lit restaurants and bars and the city's favourite place to watch the sun sink over the Atlantic.

Grand Café
35 Victoria Rd, T021-438 4253, www.grandafrica.com. Open 0900-late.
Sister venue to the **Grand Café & Beach** in Granger Bay (page 61), with sophisticated soft pink decor, silver candlesticks, ornate fireplaces, and balconies on 2 floors to watch the sunset. Creative cocktails and champagnes include Dom Pérignon and Cristal.

Café Caprice
Victoria Rd, T021-438 8315, www.cafecaprice.co.za. Open 0900-late.

Popular café and bar with outdoor seats, great fresh fruit cocktails. Gets packed and very noisy around sunset, loud house music played until late by a DJ every night in season and at the weekends in winter.

Dizzy Jazz Café
41 The Drive, T021-438 2686, www.dizzys. co.za. Open 1200-late.
Busy bar and music venue, popular at the weekend, mostly jazz but has everything from funk to rock and is a platform for local bands, comfortable couches, low tables, food includes sushi and pizza.

Hout Bay

Pakalolo
10 Main Rd, T021-790 0700, www.pakalolo. co.za. Open 0900-late.
An always vibey bar/restaurant with outside terraces, chill-out lounge, bar with TV for sports, regular live music and comedy. Food includes Mexican specialities like fjitas and chilli con carne, plus burgers, BBQ ribs and surf 'n turf.

Noordhoek

The Toad in the Village
Noordhoek Farm Village (see page 81), Village Lane, T021-789 2973, www.thetoad.co.za. Open 1100-2400.
Cosy pub and sports bar, gets busy and excitable at the weekend when there's an important match on, pub grub like steaks, spare ribs and *eisbein*, plus wood-fired pizzas. One of the owners is former Springbok rugby player Bobby Skinstad.

Entertainment

Theatre
Theatre on the Bay, *Link St, Camp's Bay, T021-483 3301, www.theatreonthebay.co.za.* Tickets from **Computicket**, see page 66. One of the nicest theatres in Cape Town offering an entertaining mix of plays, comedies and musicals. The restaurant here is good and

there's the option of a pre-show dinner and then dessert in the interval. It's just a few meters away from a MyCiTi bus stop so you can get here from other areas of the city.

What to do

For tour operators running day tours around the Cape Peninsula, see Cape Town, page 72.

Boat tours
Pleasure cruises depart from Hout Bay Harbour, and the most popular on a day trip around the peninsula is to see the Cape fur seal colony on Duiker Island just offshore. Some boats have underwater cameras or glass bottoms. Boats generally depart 0830-1100 (there are additional later departures in summer), which means that this determines in which direction you go around the peninsula if you want to include a morning seal excursion. The trip takes 30-40 mins and costs around R75, children (under 12) R35; no need to book just turn up at the harbour.
Drumbeat Charters, *Hout Bay Harbour, T021-791 4441, www.drumbeatcharters.co.za.*
Nauticat, *Hout Bay Harbour, T021-790 7278, www.nauticatcharters.co.za.*

Fishing
Hooked on Africa, *T021-790 5332, www. hookedonafrica.co.za.* Charter deep-sea fishing trips from Hout Bay Harbour, all gear is supplied. The most common catches are mako shark, long-fin tuna and yellowtail.
Nauticat Charters, *T021-790 7278, www. nauticatcharters.co.za.* Game fishing and boat charters, also operates from Hout Bay Harbour.

Horse riding
Trotting through the surf on the 8-km beach at Noordhoek is very popular and there are great views looking up to Chapman's Peak. Both these charge around R470 for a 2-hr ride and have horses suitable for novice riders. Departure times depend on season.

Imhoff Equestrian Centre, *Imhoff Farm, Kommetjie, T082-774 1191, www.horseriding. co.za.*
Sleepy Hollow Horse Riding, *Sleepy Hollow Lane, Noordhoek, T021-789 2341, www.sleepyhollowhorseriding.co.za.*

Snorkelling
Downhill Adventures, *Shop 10 Overbeek Building, corner Kloof, Long and Orange streets, Gardens, T021-422 0388, www. downhilladventures.com.* Downhill offers a unique chance to snorkel with the Cape fur seals at Duiker Island. The 3-hr trip costs R1250 and includes the boat ride from Hout Bay Harbour and about an hour in the water. The snorkelling site is only 2-5 m deep and has a clear view to the seabed.

★Table Mountain National Park
dramatic cliffs, stormy seas, historic lighthouse and some worthwhile hiking trails

Formerly the Cape of Good Hope Nature Reserve, Cape Point and the Cape of Good Hope are now part of the southern section of Table Mountain National Park. The reserve was originally established to protect the unique flora and fauna of this stretch of coast. In 1928 the area came under threat from developers who were looking to build seaside resorts. Those in favour of a reserve persuaded local families to sell their land, and in 1939 the reserve came into existence. Some game animals were introduced and the land has since been left to its own devices. Today, it is a dramatically wild area of towering cliffs, stupendous ocean views, some excellent hiking and, to top it all off, beautiful, deserted beaches.

Essential Table Mountain National Park

Getting around

This southernmost section of the park is visited as part of day trips from the city or you can self-drive. Given its location at the southern tip of the peninsula, you can approach from two directions: along the False Bay shoreline via Muizenberg and Simon's Town; or by the quieter M65 via Kommetjie and Scarborough. It is about 60 km from Cape Town centre to the reserve gates. There is no public transport.

A scenic drive from the gate goes to the parking area at Cape Point, which takes about 10-15 minutes and the speed limit is 60 kph. About halfway, stop at the **Buffelsfontein Visitor Centre**, T021-780 9204, 0930-1730, which showcases all the plants and animals to look out for and has details of the hiking trails.

Once at Cape Point, the **Flying Dutchman funicular railway**, every 3 minutes, 0900-1700, R55 return, R45 single, R23/18 children (6-16), under 6s free, takes visitors up from the main car park to the original lighthouse. The walk is about 500 m, is fairly steep and takes about 20 minutes.

Park information

See also page 26. T021-701 8692, www. sanparks.org, www.capepoint.co.za, October-March 0600-1800, April-September 0700-1700, R110, children (2-11) R55.

Best place to eat

Two Oceans Restaurant, next to the car park, T021-780 9200, www.two-oceans. co.za, 0900-1700, specializes in seafood. There is also a takeaway cafeteria.

Around the reserve

The Cape of Good Hope is an integral part of the Cape Floristic Kingdom, the smallest but richest of the world's six floral kingdoms. A frequently quoted statistic is that within the 7750 ha of the reserve there are as many different plant species as there are in the whole of the British Isles. In addition to all this there are several different species of antelope: eland, bontebok, springbok, cape grysbok, red hartebeest and grey rhebok, as well as the elusive cape mountain zebra, snakes, tortoises and pesky baboons.

Although the strong winds and the low-lying vegetation are not ideal for birds, over 250 species have been recorded here. There are plenty of vantage points where you can watch seabirds such as the Cape gannet, shy albatross, Sabine's gull and Cory's shearwater.

★Cape Point

Cape Point Lighthouse is nothing special in itself, but the climb is well worth it for spectacular views of the peninsula. On a clear day the ocean views stretching all around are incredible – as is the wind, so be sure to hold on to hats and sunglasses. You can take the funicular to the top, but the 20-minute walk allows better views of the coast. There are plenty of viewpoints, linked by a jumble of footpaths.

The first lighthouse came into service in May 1860, but it quickly became apparent that the most prominent point on a clear day was far from ideal in poor weather. It was quite often shrouded in cloud while at sea level all was clear. In 1872 the Lighthouse Commission decided on a lower site, but it was only after the Portuguese ship, the *Lusitania*, struck Bellows Rock in April 1911, that work started on a new lighthouse. This was built just 87 m above sea level, close to Diaz Rock and remains the Cape's most important lighthouse today. The current beam can be seen up to 63 km out to sea, and 18 km out there is a red lamp that warns ships that they are in the danger zone.

From the top point of the funicular there are still approximately 120 steps to the old lighthouse where you get some of the finest views. If you are reasonably fit and have a good head for heights, there is a spectacular walk to the modern lighthouse at Diaz Point. From the renovated old lighthouse you can see the path running along the left side of the narrow cliff that makes up the point. The round trip takes about 30 minutes, but do not attempt it if it is windy – the winds around the Cape can reach up to 55 knots.

Cape of Good Hope

Looking west across from Cape Point is the Cape of Good Hope, another rocky promontory jutting into the ocean. So named by Portugal's King John II, it has captured the imagination of European sailors since Dias who first named it the Cape of Storms in 1488 and later in 1580 Sir Francis Drake who called it the 'The Fairest Cape in all the World'. These names were derived from the fact that when following the western side of the African coastline from the equator, the Cape of Good Hope marks the point where a ship begins to travel more eastward than southward. There is a misconception that the Cape of Good Hope is the southern tip of Africa, because it was once believed to be the dividing point between the Atlantic and Indian Oceans. In fact, the southernmost point is Cape Agulhas, about 150 km to the southeast. The Cape of Good Hope is accessed by road or you can walk across from Cape Point—much of the path is on boardwalks and is fairly easy and the round trip takes about two hours. On the way, you can take a detour and walk down to beautiful Diaz Beach via Maclear's Peak and a 253-step staircase. It takes about 20 minutes, but the climb up can take twice as long as it's steep in parts. Worth it though to stand on the smooth sand and gaze up at the 200-m-high cliffs between Cape Point and the Cape of Good Hope.

Hiking Apart from visiting Cape Point and the Cape of Good Hope there are several other excellent walks around the reserve, probably the best way of appreciating the splendour of the coastline. They are marked and information is available from the Buffelsfontein Visitor Centre. They include the **Shipwreck Trails**, which start and end from the Olifantsbos parking area where yellow markers guide you through the fynbos down to the beach where you can see the wrecks of the *Thomas Tucker* (1942) and *Nolloth* (1964). The circular 3.5-km **Antoniesgat Trail** starts near Buffels Bay Beach and offers beautiful views, a moderate level of difficulty, and the opportunity to cool off in the tidal pools or enjoy a braai at one of the designated areas back at Buffels Bay at the end of the walk. More serious hikers can consider the 5.5-km **Gifkommetjie Trail**, the 5.5-km **Kanonkop Trail**, and the 7-km **Phyllisia Circuit**.

False Bay

seaside villages in a dramatic bay; penguins and whales are a highlight

On the eastern side of the peninsula lies False Bay, a popular stretch of coast thanks to the warmer waters – temperatures can be as much as 8°C higher. The area is also more sheltered and well developed for tourism, although some of the landscape seems almost dull after the Atlantic seaboard. Nevertheless, the area has some excellent beaches and gets busy with domestic tourists in summer. In spring, False Bay is the favoured haunt of calving whales, offering excellent opportunities to see southern right, humpback and Bryde whales. There are also some interesting fishing villages. False Bay is also known for its population of great white sharks. A shark watch service operates from Muizenberg, signalling alerts when sharks come in proximity of bathers and surfers.

Constantia

South of Kirstenbosch National Botanical Garden in the city's southern suburbs, lies the verdant area of Constantia and its winelands. This historical district was the first site of winemaking in South Africa and today it is an attractive introduction to the country's wines, as well as offering some fine examples of Cape Dutch architecture. There are seven estates on the Constantia Wine Route open to the public, of which Groot Constantia (see below) is the oldest and best known and definitely worth a visit. **Buitenverwachting** ⓘ *Klein Constantia Rd, T021-794 5190, www.buitenverwachting.com*, originally formed part of Groot Constantia and was sold as a sub-division in 1773. It has a wine-tasting centre and an excellent restaurant that also offers picnic baskets during the summer (November-April) from 1200-1600. **Beau Constantia** ⓘ *Constantia Rd, T021-794 8632, www.beauconstantia. com*, is a boutique modern wine farm situated at the top of Constantia Nek overlooking False Bay with a wine bar and tasting centre. **Eagles' Nest** ⓘ *Constantia Main Rd, T021-794 4095, www.eaglesnestwines.com*, traces its origins back to 1836 when it was used as a refreshment station between Wynberg and Hout Bay harbour. It offers tastings and sales and picnics are available in summer (November-March). **Klein Constantia** ⓘ *Klein Constantia Rd, T021-794 5188, www.kleinconstantia.com*, dates to 1685 and is a beautiful hilly estate with a great tasting centre, and is famed for its dessert wine, Vin de Constance, allegedly Napoleon's favourite wine. **Silvermist** ⓘ *Constantia Nek, T021-794 7601, www. silvermistvineyards.co.za*, is located at the top of the Constantia Valley and falls within the Table Mountain National Park. Established in 1984, vines are organically grown without pesticides or chemical fertilisers. It has a café and wine-tasting bar and is also the location of the **La Colombe** restaurant (see page 98). **Steenberg** ⓘ *Steenberg Rd, Tokai, T021-713 2211, www.steenbergfarm.com*, was the Cape's first agricultural farm established in 1682 by Catharina Ustings Ras, the first female landowner in southern Africa. It not only offers superb wines but has a luxurious hotel and spa, a good restaurant and a golf course (see pages 97, 98 and 100).

Essential False Bay

Getting around

False Bay can be easily accessed from the city centre by the M3, which runs around the eastern side of Table Mountain and down the middle of the peninsula. At the end of it, routes go either via Muizenberg to join the False Bay coast road (M4) or over the top of the mountains in the interior on the M64, also called Ou Kaapse Weg (Afrikaans for 'Old Cape Road'), a pass that connects the southern suburbs with the Fish Hoek Valley. There are also two routes across the mountainous spine linking the coast roads: you can cross from Noordhoek to Fish Hoek via the M65 and Sun Valley or, further south, take the Red Hill road from Scarborough to Simon's Town. Each route is convenient if your time is short, but the most scenic, and the usual route for tour operators on day tours is to follow the M65 from the Atlantic seaboard around the bottom of the peninsula and return to the city via False Bay. It is impossible to get lost as there is only one road along the shoreline.

On the False Bay side, there are a few **Golden Arrow** buses from the Strand Street bus station in the city centre to Simon's Town via Muizenberg and Fish Hoek, or there is also the option of taking the **City Sightseeing Cape Town bus**. However the **Blue Mini Peninsula Tour** only goes as far south as Constantia (where the Purple Wine Route connects to it for a tour of the Constantia Valley: stops are Groot Constantia, Beau Constantia and Eagles' Nest), before it loops across the peninsula to Hout Bay and returns to the city via the Atlantic Seaboard (or the other way around)

Alternatively, **Metrorail** ⓘ *T0800-656463, www.capemetrorail.co.za; see also page 76*, has a line running from central Cape Town through the southern suburbs to Simon's Town – the stretch following False Bay is spectacular, which in parts couldn't be closer to the sea, and this may be the only place in the world where you can spot whales from a train carriage window. From Cape Town trains leave every 30 minutes, and take one hour and 15 minutes without stops, with the last trains leaving Simon's Town at around 1930. The **Southern Line initiative** is a hop-on hop-off rail ticket designed for tourists. Tickets, R30 for a one-day pass and R50 for a two-day pass, allow unlimited travel on the line and can be purchased from any of the stations and are valid 0830-1600 (outside of commuter hours). There are seven stations on the route: Cape Town, Observatory, Newlands, Muizenberg, Kalk Bay, Fish Hoek and Simon's Town. Most tourist attractions can be reached within a 2 km radius of each station.

Groot Constantia

T021-795 5140, www.grootconstantia.co.za, www.iziko.org.za, Mon-Fri 0900-1800, Sat-Sun 1000-1800, free entrance to the main estate and orientation centre, museum 1000-1700, R30, children (6-18) R15, under 5s free, 2 restaurants: Jonkershuis has traditional Cape food; Simon's serves burgers, salads and seafood. Wine tastings at the sales centre, R40 for 5 wines; R75 chocolate and wine pairing; R50 cellar tours on the hour 1000-1600.

This old wine estate has some of the finest Cape Dutch architecture in South Africa, and with its rolling, vineyard setting and wine-tasting centre is a delightful place to spend an hour or two – although it does get swamped with tour buses in high season.

The main Manor House was originally home to Cape Governor Simon van der Stel between 1699 and 1712. He named the estate after Constantia, the daughter of the company official who had granted the land to him. Before his death, van der Stel planted most of the vines, but it was not until 1778 that the estate became famous for its wines. During this period the estate was unable to meet the demand from Europe, especially France. The house is now a museum full of period furniture and a booklet is available giving a brief description of the objects on show. The magnificent wine cellar behind the main house was designed by the renowned French architect, Louis Thibault, and today has displays on brandy and winemaking. There are two impressive giant oak vats each with a capacity of over 4000 litres. The **Orientation Centre** near the car park has some interesting storyboards on the history of the estate.

Tokai Forest

Take the Tokai Rd exit off the M3 and turn right and follow signs, T021-712 7471, www. sanparks.org, Apr-Sep 0800-1700, Oct-Mar 0700-1800, R20, children (under 16) R10, R15 car.

Tokai was set up as a forest nursery in 1883 to start a programme of reforestation. Due to this, large parts of the Constantiaberg Mountains are covered in pine trees and as they are non-indigenous there is some debate as to whether they should remain. Today, the forest is part of Table Mountain National Park. The arboretum contains 40 tree species – there are two walking trails, and horse riding and mountain biking are possible in the low-lying section (permits from the main gate).

Muizenberg

Travelling out from the city centre on the M3, Muizenberg is the first settlement you reach on False Bay and as such has long been a popular local bathing spot. The Battle of Muizenberg was a small but significant military affair that began in June 1795 and ended three months later with the (first) British occupation of the Cape. Cecil Rhodes bought a holiday cottage here in 1899 and many other wealthy people followed, building some fine Victorian and Edwardian cottages along the back streets and attracting the likes of Agatha Christie and Rudyard Kipling to its shores. Although the resort had decayed significantly over the last decade, various recent regeneration projects have meant that the area is starting to look like its old cheerful self again. The beach certainly remains beautiful: a vast stretch of powdery white sand sloping gently to the water. It is safe for swimming as there is no backwash, and it is very popular with surfers who head out to the bigger breakers. At low tide you can walk into the shallow sea for more than 300 m without having to swim.

The walk along Main Street towards St James is known locally as the **Historic Mile** and will take you past a number of interesting old buildings. Some of these are national monuments, but most are closed to the public. The first of note is the **Station building**, a fine example of art-deco architecture built in 1912. Further along on the right is the thatched and stone squat **Het Post Huijs** (**The Post House**), thought to be the oldest building in False Bay, dating back to 1742 and built by the Dutch East India Company as a toll-house to levy taxes on farmers passing by to sell their produce to ships moored in Simon's Bay. One of the early post holders was Sergeant Muys, from whom Muizenberg is thought to have got its name.

The next building of note is **Rhodes Cottage** ⓘ *246 Main St, T021-788 9140, 1000-1600, entry by donation*, which is surprisingly small and austere for someone as wealthy as Cecil Rhodes. It has been restored and now contains many of his personal items, including his diamond-weighing scale and the chest in which he carried his personal belongings, and there are displays on his life and achievements. It's a pleasant place to wander around, with a lovely garden around the side. This is where he died on 26 March 1902, and his body was transported by train with great ceremony to the Matobo Hills outside Bulawayo in Zimbabwe, where he was buried in a giant rock outcrop. The volunteers that keep the place open make charismatic and enthusiastic guides.

St James

Just beyond Muizenberg lies the more upmarket resort of St James, an appealing village with characteristic brightly coloured bathing huts lining the tidal pool. The village is named after a Roman Catholic church which was built here in 1854 to save Catholics having to travel as far as Simon's Town to attend services – interestingly, some of the early settlers were Catholic Filipino fishermen. There is a small sheltered beach and reasonable surf off **Danger Beach** and the tidal pool is a safe place for a swim.

Kalk Bay

Kalk Bay is one of the most attractive settlements on False Bay, with a bustling fishing harbour and a bohemian vibe. The town is named after the lime kilns that produced kalk from shells in the 17th century (the name Kalk is derived from the Dutch for lime). Until the arrival of the railway in 1883, the local fishermen hunted whales, seals and small fish. Today it remains a fishing harbour, worked mainly by a coloured community which somehow escaped the Group Areas Act under Apartheid. Between June and July the harbour is busy with the snoek season – look out for returning deep-sea fishing boats around the middle of the day. In the harbour itself you can see seals, who cheekily hop up to try and get to the fish at the counters. Also at the harbour, **Kalky's** (see Cafés, page 99), in a colourful wooden shed, serves up great fish and chips. **Main Road** is an appealing spot, lined with bric-a-brac and antiques shops and a handful of arty cafés. On the other side of the road is Kalk Bay's most popular attraction, the **Brass Bell**, a pub wedged between the railway tracks and the water (see Restaurants, page 99).

High up behind the town is **Boyes Drive**, an alternative route connecting Kalk Bay with Muizenburg, offering sweeping views of False Bay and it takes just 10 minutes to complete – look out for the signs from Main Road as you head out of Kalk Bay towards Simon's Town.

Silvermine Nature Reserve

At the top of Ou Kaapse Weg (M64) between Westlake (at the end of the M3 from Cape Town) and Noordhoek, T021-780 9002, www.sanparks.org, 0700-1900, R30, children (under 11) R15.

This is a popular local reserve split into two sections by the Ou Kaapseweg Road as it crosses the Kalk Bay Mountains. By car you can approach either from the Cape Town side or from Noordhoek and Fish Hoek. Note that this road is windy and has one of Cape Town's highest

BACKGROUND
The Dutch and the VOC

By the end of the 16th century British and Dutch mariners had caught up with the Portuguese and they quickly came to appreciate the importance of the Cape as a base for restocking ships with drinking water and fresh supplies as they made their long journeys to the East. Indeed, seafarers found that they were able to exchange scraps of metal for provisions to supply a whole fleet.

The first moves to settle in the Cape were made by the Dutch, and on 6 April 1652 **Jan Van Riebeeck** landed in Table Bay. His ships carried wood for building and some small cannons, the first building to be erected being a small fort at the mouth of the Fresh River. The site of the original fort is where Grand Parade in the centre of Cape Town is today. Van Riebeeck was in charge of the supply station that belonged to the Dutch East India Company (Vereenigde Oost-Indische Compagnie or VOC). After the fort was built, gardens for fruit and vegetables were laid out and pastures for cattle acquired. As the settlement slowly grew, the Khoi people were driven back into the interior. Surprisingly, the early settlers were forbidden from enslaving the Khoi; instead, slaves were imported by the VOC from Indonesia and West Africa. Although many died, these slaves were the origin of the Cape Malay community.

In 1662 Jan van Riebeeck was transferred to India. Because of rivalries in Europe, the VOC was worried about enemy ships visiting the Cape, so work started on a new stone fort in 1666. Over the next 13 years several governors came and went. During this time the French and British went to war with Holland, but the British and the Dutch East India companies joined in a treaty of

accident rates, so take care when driving. Silvermine is now part of the Table Mountain National Park, but not often visited by overseas visitors. Table Mountain and Cape Point tend to dominate the open-air attractions, and rightly so, but this reserve is well worth a visit if you enjoy hiking, plus there are great views across False Bay and the Atlantic Ocean.

Like much of the Cape, the reserve encompasses one of the oldest floral kingdoms in the world. Over 900 rare and endangered species have been recorded in the mountains, including many types of proteas, ericas and reeds. In addition to the plants there are a couple of patches of indigenous forest in the Spes Bona and Echo valleys. Ornithologists should look out for black eagles, ground woodpeckers, orange-breasted sunbirds and rock kestrels. If you're extremely lucky, you may also come across small shy mammals such as lynx, porcupine and various species of mongoose.

A tarred road leads from the western sector gates to the Silvermine Reservoir built in 1898 to supply Kalk Bay and Muizenberg with water until 1912. There is a boardwalk at the edge of the dam suitable for wheelchairs and prams and a shady picnic site under some pine trees. One of the more popular walks from here is to **Noordhoek Peak** (754 m), a circuit of about 7 km from the dam. The path is marked by stone cairns. At the summit there are spectacular views of the Sentinel and Hout Bay. Another interesting walk is from the car park to **Elephant's Eye Cave** covered with ferns and hanging plants. En route you pass the **Prinz Kasteel waterfall**. Allow about three hours for the round trip.

friendship in March 1674, and then in July of the same year a ship arrived with the news that the British and Dutch had made peace. In October 1679 one of the most energetic governors arrived in the Cape, **Simon van der Stel**. For the next 20 years van der Stel devoted his energies to creating a new Holland in southern Africa. During his period as Governor, van der Stel paid particular attention to the growth and development of Cape Town and the surrounding farmlands. The company garden was replanted, nursery plots were created and new experimental plants were collected from around the world. North of the gardens he built a large hospital and a lodge to house VOC slaves. New streets were laid out which were straight and wide with plenty of shade. New buildings in the town were covered in white limewash, producing a smart and prosperous appearance. In 1685, in appreciation for his work, he was granted an estate by the VOC, which he named **Constantia**. During his life he used the estate as an experimental agricultural farm and to grow oak trees which were then planted throughout the Cape.

One of his more significant contributions was the founding of the settlement at Stellenbosch. He directed the design and construction of many of the town's public buildings, and then introduced a number of the crops to be grown on the new farms. For many years he experimented with vines in an effort to produce wines as good as those in Europe. He was particularly pleased when in 1688 French Protestant Huguenot refugees arrived in the Cape. He saw to it that they were all settled on excellent farmlands in what became to be known as **Franschhoek** (French glen), the upper valley of the Berg River. In 1693 he had the foresight to appoint the town's first engineer to tackle problems of a clean water supply and the removal of rubbish. Van der Stel died in June 1712 at Constantia.

Fish Hoek

The centre of Fish Hoek with its cheap shops and fish and chip takeaways is fairly unremarkable, but the village is best known for its fine beach – perhaps the best for swimming after Muizenberg – which stretches almost 2 km across the Fish Hoek valley. Swimming is safe at the southern end of the bay, and boogie-boarding and kayaking are also popular. From mid-August to October, there is a good chance of catching a glimpse of whales from here. The valley which stretches behind the town joins with Noordhoek beach on the Atlantic coast. In recent geological times this was flooded and all the lands towards Cape Point were in fact an island.

Glencairn

It is easy to drive through this coastal resort without realizing you've actually been here, although it does have a small family beach with a tidal pool by the railway station. At low tide you can occasionally see the remains of a steamship, the *Clan Stuart*. She was blown aground on 20 November 1914 while the crew drank in the local hotel, which today is still a popular pub **The Glen**.

Simon's Town

This is the most popular town on False Bay, with a pleasant atmosphere and numerous Victorian buildings lining Main Street. If you want a break from Cape Town, this makes for a good alternative base from which to explore the southern peninsula. It's also a good

Glencairn, Simon's Town & Boulders Beach

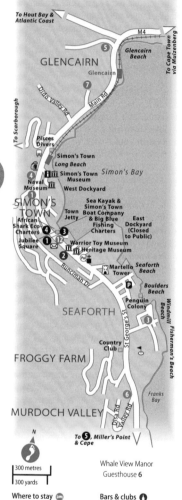

To Hout Bay &
Atlantic Coast

M4

Glencairn
Beach

GLENCAIRN

Glencairn

To Cape Town
via Muizenberg

To Scarborough

Dido Valley Rd

Main Rd

Pisces
Divers

Simon's Town
Long Beach

Simon's Bay

Simon's Town
Museum

Naval
Museum

West Dockyard

SIMON'S
TOWN

African
Shark Eco
Charters

Sea Kayak &
Simon's Town
Boat Company
& Big Blue
Fishing
Charters

Town
Jetty

East
Dockyard
(Closed
to Public)

Jubilee
Square

Warrior Toy Museum

Heritage Museum

Martello
Tower

Runciman Dr

Seaforth
Beach

SEAFORTH

Boulders
Beach

Penguin
Colony

St George's St

Windmill

Fisherman's Beach

Country
Club

FROGGY FARM

Franks
Bay

MURDOCH VALLEY

Dido Rd

Redhill Rd

To 5, Miller's Point
& Cape

N

300 metres
300 yards

place to spot whales in False Bay and notice the statue of a real-size southern right whale on the quayside of the waterfront. For information, there's a **tourist office** ⓘ *Simon's Town Museum (below), T021-786 3046, www.simonstown.com, Mon-Fri 1000-1600, Sat 1000-1300.*

Take some time to wander up the hill away from the main road – the quiet, bougainvillea-bedecked houses and cobbled streets with their sea views are a lovely retreat from the bustling beaches. The main swimming spot is **Seaforth Beach**, not far from Boulders. To get there, turn off St George's Street into Seaforth Road after passing the navy block to the left. The swimming is safe, as there is no surf due to offshore rocks which protect the beach. For children there is a water slide and a wooden raft in the water. Look out for some giant pots, a legacy from whaling days, when they were used for melting whale blubber.

Simon's Town is named after Simon van der Stel, who decided that an alternative bay was needed for securing ships in the winter months as Table Bay suffered from the prevailing northwesterly. However, because of the difficult overland access, the bay was little used in the early years. It was not until 1743 that the Dutch East India Company finally built a wooden pier and some barracks here. In 1768 the town transferred into British hands, and following the end of the Napoleonic Wars in Europe, the British decided to turn Simon's Town into a naval base. It remained as such until 1957 and is now a base for the South African Navy. The two-day **Naval Festival** is held in April each year, when some of the ships are opened to the public.

Just before you hit the town centre, the **Simon's Town Museum** ⓘ *Old Residency, Court Rd, T021-786 3046, Mon-Fri 1000-1600, Sat 1000-1300, entry by donation,* has displays related to the town's history as a naval base for the British and South African navies. Several displays are dedicated to

Just Nuisance, a great dane who became something of a local hero in the 1930s (see box, page 96), who is now Simon's Town unofficial mascot. Also of interest is the **Peoples of Simon's Town Exhibit**, a collection referring to the forcible removal of coloured families from the area in the 1960s and 1970s, photographs, family trees and household goods. The building itself was built in 1777 as the winter residence of the Governor of the Cape.

Nearby, the **South African Naval Museum** ⓘ *Naval Dockyard, St George's St, T021-787 4686, 1000-1600, entry by donation*, includes a collection of model ships, gunnery displays, information on mine-sweeping, a modern submarine control room plus relics from the Martello Tower.

In the centre of town, the **Quayside Centre** is a smart development on St George's Street, next to Jubilee Square in the centre of town, which has greatly enhanced the seafront. Above the shops and restaurants is the comfortable **Quayside Hotel** (see Where to stay, page 97). Cruises in the harbour can be booked here (see page 100).

Just round the corner from Jubilee Square, and worth a quick peek, is the **Warrior Toy Museum** ⓘ *St George's St, T021-786 1395, daily 1000-1600, entry by donation*, a tiny museum with an impressive collection of model cars, trains, dolls and toy soldiers. This is a great little place and definitely worth a stop – nostalgic for adults and fun for kids. New and old model cars are also for sale.

The nearby **Heritage Museum** ⓘ *Amlay House, St George's St, T021-786 2302, Tue-Fri 1100-1600, Sat 1100-1300, entry by donation*, faithfully charts the history of the Muslim community in Simon's Town. The town was designated a 'white' area during the Group Area Act and over 7000 people classified as coloured were relocated. The Amlay family were the last to be forcibly removed from Simon's Town in 1975 and were the first to return in 1995. The exhibition consists mainly of pictures and artefacts dating back to the turn of the 20th century.

Boulders Beach

About 2 km south of Simon's Town is a lovely series of little sandy coves surrounded by huge boulders (hence the name). The attraction here is the colony of African penguins that live and nest between the boulders. **Boulders Visitor Centre** ⓘ *T021-786 2329, www.sanparks.org, Apr-Sep 0800-1700, Oct-Nov and Feb-Mar 0800-18300, Dec-Jan 0700-1930, R60, children (2-11) R30*, has been created to protect the little creatures, and their numbers have flourished. One of the highlights of a visit to Cape Town is watching them happily go about their business of swimming, waddling and braying (their characteristic braying was the reason they were, until recently, known as jackass penguins). This is one of two colonies on mainland Africa, the other being in Betty's Bay (see page 135), and is now a protected area as part of Table Mountain National Park. From the visitor centre a (wheelchair accessible) boardwalk leads you down to viewpoints over the beach. Look out for the little concrete half-moon huts that have been installed for the penguins to nest in and look up from the beach where you're likely to see a single penguin contemplating life from the top of a boulder. Every visitor gets a leaflet telling the story of the colony – it started from just two breeding pairs in 1985 and now numbers some 3000 penguins – and the shop sells all things 'penguiney'. If you want to swim, go to the adjoining Seaforth Beach, which is a lovely sandy cove with a picnic lawn and you may bump into a stray penguin in the water.

Miller's Point

This is the last easy access to the sea on this side of the peninsula. Miller's Point has two sandy coves and a tidal pool. There is a good restaurant, the **Black Marlin** (see Restaurants,

Just Nuisance

An enormous great dane and adored by Simon's Town sailors, Just Nuisance was officially registered as personnel aboard *HMS Afriander* in 1939. His favourite spot was to lie on the deck at the top of the gangplank. No one could easily get past him and he was loathed to move, hence the name. Although he never went to sea, like all new sailors, he underwent a medical examination, which he duly passed, and was declared fit for active duty. He signed his enlistment papers with a paw print. All able seamen were entitled to free travel on the train and Just Nuisance liked nothing better than to make the journey from Simon's Town to Cape Town and he carried his rail pass in his collar. Sometimes, if he found a drunken sailor on the train, he would escort the man back to his bunk in the naval quarters in Simon's Town. However, he was also guilty of several misdeeds. His conduct sheet (on display in Simon's Town Museum along with his collar and official papers), records that he travelled on the train without his pass, went AWOL, lost his collar, resisted eviction from pubs at closing time, and slept on a Petty Officer's bed – for the latter he was deprived of bones for seven days. He died in 1944, and he is the only dog in history to have been given a full military burial and a solemn ceremony included a firing party of Royal Marines and a lone bugler. A simple granite headstone marks his grave on the mountainside above Simon's Town. There's a bronze statue of him on Jubilee Square.

page 99), which is a popular lunch stop for coach tours of the Cape Peninsula. The road then climbs above the sea before rounding the mountains by **Smitswinkel Bay**. On a clear day you can look back to a perfect view of the cliffs plunging into the sea. A short distance from the shore is the Table Mountain National Park entrance to Cape Point.

Beyond Miller's Point be on the lookout for baboons. They are not shy and will approach cars. Wind windows up and remember they can be vicious.

A number of **boat trips** to the Cape of Good Hope originate from Simon's Town harbour. Taking a trip from here allows views of the spectacular coastline and its hinterland from a different angle.

Listings False Bay *maps p78 and p94*

Where to stay

Constantia
The original Cape Dutch homestead and vineyard that gave the area its name is today surrounded by one of Cape Town's most exclusive suburbs, dotted with luxury hotels. All are superb, in lovely settings and with impeccable service, but are firmly in the upper price category.

$$$$ Cellars-Hohenort Hotel
93 Brommersulei Rd, T021-794 2137,
www.collectionmcgrath.com.
One of the most luxurious hotels in Cape Town, set in 2 converted manor houses in 9.5 ha of beautiful gardens on a wine estate with views of False Bay. 49 individually decorated spacious suites, 2 excellent restaurants (see page 98), 3 heated swimming pools, tennis courts, 9-hole golf course and spa.

$$$$ Steenberg Hotel
Tokai Rd, T021-713 2222,
www.steenbergfarm.com.
Country hotel with 24 elegant rooms in converted farm buildings overlooking manicured gardens and working vineyards. Swimming pool, gym, spa, and the beautiful 18-hole golf course has sweeping views of False Bay. The award-winning **Catharina's Restaurant** (see page 98) has an excellent reputation.

$$$ Alphen Boutique Hotel
Alphen Drive, T021-795 6300,
www.alphen.co.za.
Set on an elegant 18th-century Cape Dutch estate, the 19 rooms are decorated with fine antiques and have polished floors and log fires. Gourmet meals in the formal **5 Rooms Restaurant** in the manor house and there's also a bistro, garden bar and swimming pool.

$$$ Glen Avon Lodge
1 Strawberry Lane, T021-794 1418,
www.glenavon.co.za.
A comfortable boutique hotel with characteristic Cape Dutch architecture set in rose gardens, 16 rooms with patio or balcony, some have self-catering facilities, heated pool, lounge with fireplace, romantic candlelit dining room.

Muizenburg

$$-$ Bluebottle Guest House
18 Mount Rd, T021-788 6100,
www.blue-bottle.co.za.
6 neat B&B rooms with floor-to-ceiling glass windows, modern decor with bright colours, self-catering kitchen, bar, gardens planted with indigenous plants. You need to be fit, as there are 131 steps to climb but the sweeping views over False Bay make it worthwhile.

Kalk Bay

$$ Chartfield Guesthouse
30 Gatesville Rd, T021-788 3793,
www.chartfield.co.za.
A turn-of-the-20th-century house with verandas, 13 rooms, DSTV, uncluttered decor of original wooden floors and fireplaces and retro furniture, good harbour views, pool, walking distance to restaurants.

Fish Hoek

$$ Tranquillity Guesthouse
25 Peak Rd, T021-782 2060,
www.tranquil.co.za.
A peaceful option, 600 m above the town, with jaw-dropping views, 4 stylish rooms with huge showers, balconies, nice touches include fruit platters and fresh roses. Watching the sunrise over the mountains on the other side of False Bay is quite special.

Glencairn

$$ Moonglow Guesthouse
7 Bennett Close, T021-786 5902,
www.moonglow.co.za.
6 individually decorated rooms with hand-embroidered percale linen and TV, balconies with fabulous views over Glencairn Beach and False Bay, cosy lounge and bar with library, breakfast room.

$$-$ The Glen
12-14 Glen Rd, T021-782 0315,
www.theglenlodgeandpub.co.za.
Delightful historical hotel in turn-of-the-20th-century building set a short walk from the sea, with 8 good-value rooms with high ceilings, dark polished wood floors, one is a budget room with 4 bunks. Bar and restaurant serving pub meals, seafood and grills.

Simon's Town

$$$-$$ Quayside Hotel
Jubilee Sq, St George's St, T021-786 3838,
www.quayside.ahagroup.co.za.
In a great central location overlooking the harbour, with 26 spacious rooms, bright and sunny marine blue and white decor, good views of False Bay. Buffet breakfasts and

within walking distance of restaurants in Jubilee Sq for other meals.

$$ Central Hotel Guesthouse
96 St George's St, T021-786 3775, www.central hotelguesthouse.com.
The Central first opened in 1828, now restored with an authentic historical feel, 11 rooms with Victorian antiques, characterful old-fashioned dining room with elaborate sideboards and paintings, generous breakfasts that can be taken on the lovely balcony.

$ Simon's Town Backpackers
66 St George's St, T021-786 1964, www.capepax.co.za.
An easy walk from the train station, a 38-bed backpacker joint with small dorms and fairly pleasant doubles, small kitchen, bar, braai on balcony overlooking the main street and harbour, bikes for hire and can organize sea kayaking.

Boulders Beach

$$$ Whale View Manor Guesthouse
402 Main Rd, Murdoch Valley, T021-786 3291, www.whaleviewmanor.co.za.
1 km south of Boulders and across the road from the lovely Fisherman's Beach. 10 stylish rooms with either ocean or mountain views, some with balconies, excellent meals and decadent high tea is served in the garden. There's also a day spa open to non-guests.

$$$-$$ Boulders Beach Lodge
4 Boulders Pl, T021-786 1758, www.bouldersbeachlodge.com.
This friendly, well-run guesthouse is a firm favourite, with 10 double rooms and 2 family rooms, the upstairs rooms have sea views. At night you're likely to see penguins exploring the grounds after everyone has gone home. Good restaurant and the **Curious Penguin** souvenir shop.

Restaurants

Constantia

$$$ Catharina's
Steenberg Hotel, see Where to stay, page 97. Open 1200-1500, 1900-2130.
One of the finest restaurants in the area, where meals are served outside under the oaks or in the contemporarily decorated dining room. The menu features gourmet South African fare such as West Coast mussels, Knynsa oysters and springbok loin, and there's a fine wine list.

$$$ The Greenhouse
The Cellars-Hohenort Hotel, see Where to stay, page 96. Open 0730-2200.
1 of 2 highly rated restaurants at this 5-star hotel, set in a pretty conservatory with white wicker furniture. The Michelin-trained chef produces top-quality fare – mostly modern South African, so expect fish and game. Excellent wine to match.

$$$ La Colombe
At Silvermist (see page 88), Constantia Nek, T021-795 0125, www.lacolombe.co.za. Mon-Sat 1200-1330, 1930-2130.
Perched high up on the mountainside in the Constantia Valley, follow the winding road up through the Silvermist wine estate. French menu with strong Provençal flavours and some Asian influences, and expect the likes of rabbit, duck, fish and game dishes, with emphasis on rich sauces, jus and foams.

Muizenburg
Cafés

Empire Café
11 York Rd, T021-788 1250, www.empirecafe. co.za. Mon-Sat 0700-1600, Sun 0800-1600.
A little tatty but popular with local surfers, this serves eclectic breakfasts including omelettes (try the famous bacon, banana and honey) and specials like line-caught fish or saucy pastas for lunch.

Kalk Bay

$$$ Harbour House
Kalk Bay Harbour, T021-788 4133,
www.harbourhouse.co.za. Open 1200-1600,
1800-2200.
Perched right on the rocks overlooking the
ocean with great views of the jaunty fishing
boats, with bright white decor and wooden
decks, this is well known for its seafood
including grilled crayfish. There's another
branch at Quay 4 at the V&A Waterfront.

$$ Cape to Cuba
Main Rd, T021-788 1566,
www.capetocuba.com. Open 1100-2300.
Atmospheric Cuban restaurant serving
good-value seafood with Caribbean
flavours. Great setting on water's edge with
tables overlooking the harbour. Bar open
till 0200 if there is the demand and cocktails
include mojitos and daiquiris.

$$-$ Brass Bell
By the railway station, T021-788 5455,
www.brassbell.co.za. Open 1000-2300.
A very popular pub and restaurant in a great
location. Downstairs gets packed around
sunset, great for a cool beer outside close
to the waves, serves pub meals and good
pizzas and fish and chips, more expensive
restaurant upstairs serves fresh fish and steak.

Cafés

Kalky's
Kalk Bay Harbour, T021-788 1726.
Open 0800-2100.
Simple seafood and chips at plastic tables,
freshly cooked, counter service and then
listen for your number to be called out. You'll
rub shoulders with Kalk Bay's characterful
fishermen here, and look for seals
in the harbour.

Olympia Café & Deli
134 Main Rd, T021-788 6396.
Open 0700-2100.
A Kalk Bay institution, this laid-back café
serves some of the freshest bread on the

peninsula, plus light lunches, fabulous cakes
and daily specials. Expect to chalk your
name on the blackboard and queue for a
table at weekends.

Simon's Town

$$$ Black Marlin
Miller's Point, 2 km from Simon's Town,
T021-786 1621, www.blackmarlin.co.za.
Open 1200-1600, 1800-2100.
Set in an old whaling station, this place is a
good lunch stop on the way to or from Cape
Point. Fabulous sea views and wide range of
fresh seafood – try the delicious crayfish and
oysters or the signature kingklip skewers. It
can get busy with tour buses in summer so
reservations are essential.

$$ Bertha's
Jubilee Sq, T021-786 2138,
www.berthas.co.za. Open 0700-2200.
Tables at the water's edge are perfect to
enjoy fresh seafood and watch the yachts
and naval ships in the harbour. There's also
a long menu of breakfasts such as French
toast with syrup or eggs Benedict.

Cafés

Salty Sea Dog
Next to Quayside Centre, T021-786 1918.
Mon-Sat 1000-2100, Sun 1000-1630.
Cheap and cheerful place serving fresh
grilled or battered fish and calamari and
chips on trestle tables in the little shack or
on outside tables overlooking the harbour.
Friendly and swift service and sells wine.
Popular with tour groups.

The Sweetest Thing
82 St George's St, T021-786 4200,
www.thesweetestthing.co.za. Mon-Fri
0800-1700, Sat 0900-1700, Sun 0900-1600.
A homely patisserie and café offering sweet
and savoury tarts, muffins and pastries, plus
gooey éclairs, brownies and meringues.
The aromas from the bakery at the back
are wonderful.

Boulders Beach

$$ Boulders Beach Restaurant
Boulders Beach Lodge, see Where to stay, page 98. Open 0800-1115, 1200-1500, 1800-2130.
Relaxed place with wooden floors and broad outside deck, serving good English breakfasts, cocktails (including 'Pickled Penguins'), delicious seafood platters or gourmet salads for a light meal.

Bars and clubs

Simon's Town

Two and Sixpence Tavern
88 St George's St, T021-786 5735, www.twoandsixpencetavern.co.za. Open 1000-2400.
British-style pub serving standard bar food such as burgers, bangers and mash, ploughman's, Sun roasts and curry nights. Has pool tables, occasional live music and 1960-70s sing-alongs on Sun night.

Festivals

Mar South African Navy Festival, Simon's Town, www.navy.mil.za. A weekend celebrating all things maritime when the South African Naval Base is open to the public and many warships and submarines can be visited, plus displays of navy precision drills, and tug boat tours around the harbour.
Oct Cape Town International Kite Festival, Muizenburg Beach, www.capementalhealth.co.za/kite. Africa's biggest celebration of kite-flying with acrobatic kite displays, giant inflatables, craft market, kiddie's rides, kite-making workshop and food stalls. An excellent family day out. Profits go to charity, Cape Mental Health.

What to do

For tour operators running day tours around the Cape Peninsula, see Cape Town, page 72.

Constantia
Golf
Steenberg Hotel, *Tokai Rd, Constantia, T021-713 2222, www.steenberghotel.com.* Beautiful 18-hole course with views of False Bay and the Constantia vineyards, known for its challenging 14th hole, which, at 76 m long, has the largest green in Africa.

Simon's Town
Boat tours
African Shark Eco-Charters, *Quayside Centre, Wharf St, T082-838 2309, www.ultimate-animals.com.* One of the most impressive boat trips in False Bay is to go out towards Seal Island in the hope of seeing great white sharks breaching. It is a hunting technique that the shark uses to surprise and kill its prey, in this case Cape fur seals, and a phenomena that is rarely seen anywhere else in the world. The best time is just before and at sunrise and only for a few months of the year; May-Sep but the best months are Jun-Aug. The trip is a combination of shark breaching and shark cage diving and departs from Simon's Town at 0700 and returns at 12h30: rates start from R1,850.
Sea Kayak Simon's Town, *Simon's Town Jetty, Wharf St, T082-501 8930, www.kayakcapetown.co.za.* A great way to see the penguins at Boulders, and possibly whales in season, is by kayak and 2-hr guided trips are not too strenuous. If the tide is right, it may be able to stop and swim among the rocks. Trips go out daily at 0830, R300, no children under 10. For the adventurous (and fit) kayaking around Cape Point can be arranged from R950.
Simon's Town Boat Company, *Simon's Town Jetty, Wharf St, T082-257 7760, www.boatcompany.co.za.* In whale-watching season, trips go out daily at 1030 and 1400, R850, children (under 12), R500, booking essential. Weather permitting, they also offer fast speed boat rides to Cape Point for R550, children (under 12) R400, and the round 2½-hr trip includes a stop on the seaward

side of Boulders Beach (page 95) to watch the penguins in the water. There are also short boars tours around the harbour area for R50, children (under 12) R30, on the *Spirit of Just Nuisance*, which include entertaining stories about the famous dog (see box, page 96) and the history of Simon's Town, and a visit to the naval dockyard.

Diving
Pisces Divers, *Good's Shed, Simon's Town railway station, Main Rd, Simon's Town, T021-786 3799, www.piscesdivers.co.za.* A PADI dive centre offering shore, reef and kelp forest dives in False Bay and further afield including to several wrecks off Cape Point.

Fishing
Big Blue Fishing Charters, *Simon's Town Jetty, Wharf St, T021-786 5667, www. bigbluefishingcharters.com.* Fishing from *Big Blue*, a 28-ft catamaran with top of the range fishing tackle and equipment catering to both seasoned anglers and novices. The waters around the Cape are home to tuna, yellowtail, snoek, Cape salmon and the occasional marlin.

Golf
Simon's Town Country Club, *St George's St, Simon's Town, T021-786 1233, www. simonstowncountryclub.com.* A 9-hole, 18-tee links course on the seafront, just by the turning for Boulders Beach. This is a narrow course and is a real test for anyone not used to playing in very windy conditions.

This is
Winelands

The Winelands is South Africa's oldest and most beautiful wine-producing area, a fertile series of valleys quite unlike the rest of the Western Cape. It is the Cape's biggest attraction after Cape Town, and its appeal is simple: it offers the chance to sample several hundred different wines in a historical and wonderfully scenic setting.

This was the first region after Cape Town to be settled, and the towns of Stellenbosch, Paarl and Franschhoek are some of the oldest in South Africa. Today, their streets are lined with beautiful Cape Dutch and Georgian houses, although the real architectural gems are the manor houses on the wine estates. While the wine industry flourished during the 18th and 19th centuries, the farmers built grand homesteads with cool wine cellars next to their vines. Most of these have been lovingly restored and today can be visited as part of a Winelands tour – many have even been converted into gourmet restaurants or luxury hotels.

Winelands

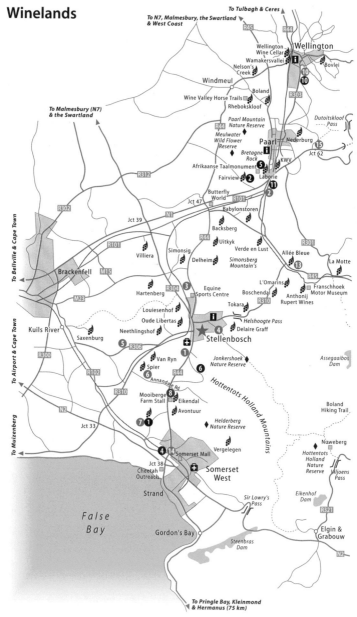

To Tulbagh & Ceres

To N7, Malmesbury, the Swartland
& West Coast

R45

R44

Wellington
Wine Cellar
Wamakersvallei
Wellington

Nelson's
Creek

Bovlei

10
10

Windmeul

R303

Boland

Wine Valley Horse Trails

Rhebokskloof

To Malmesbury (N7)
& the Swartland

Paarl Mountain
Nature Reserve

Dutoitskloof
Pass

R44

Meulwater
Wild Flower
Reserve

Nederburg

Paarl

15

R312

Bretagne
Rock

KWV

Jct 62

Afrikaanse Taalmonument

5

R302

Fairview

Laborie

2

11

Butterfly
World

2

R101

Jct 47

Babylonstoren

Jct 39

N1

R101

Backsberg

R44

Uitkyk

Verde en Lust

R301

Villiera

Simonsig

Delheim

Simonsberg
Mountain's

Allée Bleue

13

La Motte

Brackenfell

M15

R304

3

Equine
Sports Centre

L'Omarins

R45

Franschhoek
Motor Museum

M23

Hartenberg

Boschendal

Anthonij
Rupert Wines

To Bellville & Cape Town

Louiesenhof

Tokara

R310

Kuils River

Oude Libertas

Helshoogte Pass

Delaire Graff

Saxenburg

Neethlingshof

5

R306

Stellenbosch

4

Assegaaibos
Dam

To Airport & Cape Town

R300

Van Ryn

1

Jonkershoek
Nature Reserve

Spier

6

R102

6

Annandale Rd

R44

Mooiberge
Farm Stall

8

Eikendal

Boland
Hiking Trail

R310

Avontuur

7

1

Jct 33

Helderberg
Nature Reserve

Vergelegen

Nuweberg

N2

To Muizenberg

4

14

Somerset Mall

Hottentots
Holland
Nature
Reserve

Viljoens
Pass

Jct 38

Cheetah
Outreach

Somerset
West

Eikenhof
Dam

R321

Strand

Sir Lowry's
Pass

Elgin &
Grabouw

N2

False
Bay

Gordon's Bay

Steenbras
Dam

To Pringle Bay, Kleinmond
& Hermanus (75 km)

Where to stay 🛏
Bellevue Manor **1**
Berg River Resort **2**
Country Guest House **7**
Diemersfontein Wine &
  Country Estate **9**
Franschhoek Country
  House **11**
Lanzerac Manor **4**
L'Avenir Country Lodge **3**
Lekkerwijn **13**
Lord Charles **14**
Palmiet Valley Estate **15**
Spier **6**
Wedgeview Country
  House & Spa **5**

Restaurants 🍴
96 Winery Road **1**
Goatshed **2**
Harvest at Laborie **5**
La Petite Ferme **3**
La Vigna **4**
Monneaux **7**
Mont Marie **6**
Oude Wellington **12**
Seasons **10**
Wilderer's **11**

Bars & clubs 🍷
Thirsty Scarecrow **8**

Essential Winelands

Finding your feet

The N2 highway goes past Cape Town International airport, 22 km east of the city, and then continues along the northern fringes of the Cape Flats, home to the sprawling townships of Mitchells Plain, Nyanga and Khayelitsha. Beyond these the R310 left turning is the quickest route to Stellenbosch, the heart of the Winelands, 16 km from the N2. The N2 continues east splitting the towns of Strand and Somerset West before climbing over the Hottentots Holland Mountains into the Overberg via Sir Lowry's Pass (see page 120). The R44 is an alternative route from Strand to Stellenbosch. Paarl and Wellington are best accessed by the N1 from Cape Town, and Franschhoek by either route.

Metrorail (see page 76) runs from central Cape Town to Somerset West and Strand, and to Wellington via Stellenbosch and Paarl, though these are not advised for visitors as petty theft can be a real concern.

When to go

A year-round destination with a landscape that changes with the seasons. To sip chilled wine and tuck into an alfresco lunch, the best time to visit is between September and March. But during the autumn months of April to June the Winelands look their best as the vines turn an array of gold and deep orange, and the winter months of July and August is when they are at their greenest. Franschhoek's **Bastille Festival** in July, and the **Stellenbosch Wine Festival** in August are popular times to visit but book accommodation ahead during these times.

Essential Winelands

Getting around

The Winelands is generally not well serviced by public transport. Mainline buses run regularly to Somerset West from where passengers have to make their own way to/from the other Winelands towns. Apart from private taxis, the best and cheapest option to get from Cape Town International Airport to the Winelands towns is by shuttle bus; all accommodation in the Winelands can pre-book an airport transfer. Transfers for one to two people (the cost goes down with more) are in the region of R320 from the airport to Somerset West and Strand (32 km); R350 to Stellenbosch (40 km); R480 to Franschhoek (70 km); R440 to Paarl (60 km); and R480 to Wellington (70 km).

Touring the Winelands

The wine estates in the region are far too numerous to list in full, but on an organized tour (see pages 111, 119 and 127) or a self-drive trip (with a designated driver), there is ample opportunity to visit several estates in one day. **Cape Town Tourism**, www.capetown.travel (see page 53), can provide brochures and maps, and the website is a good source of information for the Winelands.

There are also tourist offices in the regional towns. For a list of tour operators offering day tours to the Winelands from Cape Town, see page 72. Wine estates charge a small tasting fee of about R10-30, which often includes a free wine glass.

Although principally an industrial area, Strand is a popular seaside resort and commuter town with an excellent 5-km white-sand beach. It mainly caters for domestic tourists and, despite its proximity to Cape Town, the Winelands and the Whale Coast, it holds little appeal. Further inland, Somerset West is a prosperous town and again a major commuter centre. It has a beautiful location on the slopes of the Helderberg Mountains, with unimpeded views of False Bay and, occasionally, Cape Point, but again there's little interest for visitors. However the unmissable giant 200-shop **Somerset Mall** at the intersection of the N2 and R44, is a useful stop on the way to the Winelands, Whale Coast or Overberg.

Cheetah Outreach
Paardevlei, De Beers Av, from the N2, turn off on to the R44 and head south past Somerset Mall for about 1.5 km, T021-851 6850, www.cheetah.co.za, 0900-1700, Mon-Fri R10, Sat-Sun R5, 30-min tours every half hour, cheetah encounters R130, children (under 14) R80, cheetah cub encounters R220 per person, bat-eared fox encounters R60, children (under 14) R40, café and souvenir shop.

Most of South Africa's remaining wild cheetahs live in unprotected areas of remote farmland in South Africa's northern provinces. They rarely prey on livestock, but when rural farmers lose their animals to other predators they often blame and kill cheetahs. Cheetah Outreach is home to several adult cheetahs, and seasonally cubs, that act as 'ambassadors' for South Africa's free-roaming cheetah to inform the public about the problems they face, and to raise funds for conservation initiatives. These include a breeding and placement programme for Turkish Anatolian Shepherd dogs that are given to farmers to look after their herds, ensuring that predators find other sources of food and farmers can retain their livelihood. The centre is also home to many smaller predators, like meerkats, caracal, serval, bat-eared fox and black-backed jackal – typical animals that share the same habitat as cheetah. Visitors can go on a tour to meet the animals, stroke an adult cheetah and a cute cub (when available), or visit the bat-eared foxes in their enclosure.

Vergelegen Estate
Loursenford Rd, 6 km east of Somerset West, T021-847 1334, www.vergelegen.co.za, 0930-1600, R10, children (under 16) R5, wine tasting R30, cellar tours R20. Camphors at Vergelegen is the formal à la carte restaurant, lunch daily 1200-1500, dinner Fri-Sat 1830-2100, booking essential; Stables at Vergelegen is a café/bistro, 0930-1600. Picnic hampers available Nov-Apr.

This is one of the Cape's finest estates and has a smart wine-tasting room and two restaurants but the highlight is a visit to the magnificent manor house filled with beautiful period furniture and historical paintings, similar to the collection at Groot Constantia. At the front of the house are five **Chinese camphor trees** that were planted by Willem van der Stel between 1700 and 1706. They are the oldest living documented trees in South Africa and are now a national monument. Behind the house is a walled octagonal garden – many of the plants were planted here by Lady Phillips (wife of Sir Lionel Phillips, owner for 25 years from 1917), who wished to recreate a typical English garden, complete with herbaceous border. Look out for the collection of roses next to the main house. The surrounding parkland, much of it similar to an English country estate, is also open for exploration.

Where to stay

$$$ Lord Charles Hotel
Corner of Main Rd and R44, Somerset West, T021-855 1040, www.nh-hotels.co.za.
Pleasant 4-star traditional hotel in expansive beautifully kept grounds with dam and gazebos. 198 smart a/c rooms with good mountain views, full range of facilities including 2 pools, beauty salon, gym, pub and **La Vigna** restaurant (see below).

$$$-$$ The Country Guesthouse
96 Winery Rd, 7 km north of Somerset West off the R44 towards Stellenbosch, T021-842 2945, www.thecountryguesthouse.co.za.
On a working wine estate, with 12 cottages set in immaculate gardens, some have fireplaces, all have private terraces and contemporary decor. Swimming pool, beauty treatments and fine restaurant (see below).

Restaurants

$$$-$ La Vigna
Lord Charles Hotel *(see Where to stay, above). Open 1200-2200.*
Refreshing minimalist decor, lovely garden terrace and you can visit the wine cellar. Long and varied menu including oysters, Indian curries, oriental stir-fries, barbecues and lavish desserts. Also an excellent spot for afternoon teas.

$$ 96 Winery Road
At **The Country Guesthouse** *(see Where to stay, above),* T021-842 2020, *www.96wineryroad.co.za. 1200-1500, 1900-2200, closed Sun evening.*
Pleasant restaurant in an informal farmhouse setting with tables set under oak trees. Very good grills and some fish such as Norwegian salmon, and specials like guinea fowl or duck and cherry pie. Picnics can be pre-booked to enjoy in the gardens next to the farm dam.

Shopping

Somerset Mall, *junction of N2 and R44, T021-852 7114, www.somersetmall.co.za. Mon-Sat 0900-1900, Sun 0900-1700.* The largest shopping mall serving the region with more than 200 shops, restaurants, and a 9-screen Ster-Kinekor cinema.

Transport

Bus
The **Baz Bus** *(www.bazbus.com)* stops in Somerset West at the BP service station next to the Lord Charles Hotel on the corner of Main Rd and the R44. From **Cape Town** it arrives 0900-0915, and from **Port Elizabeth** 2015-2030. For more information see page 207.

Greyhound *(www.greyhound.co.za)*, **Intercape** *(www.intercape.co.za)*, and **Translux** *(www.translux.co.za)* all stop at the Total service station at Somerset Mall on the N2 in Somerset West on the **Cape Town–Durban** route. Times are roughly 1 hr before or after arriving or departing at Cape Town.

elegant tree-lined streets, beautifully restored town houses and an extensive wine route

Stellenbosch, the centre of the Winelands, is the oldest and most attractive town in the region, with a large university giving it a liveliness which is lacking in other nearby towns. The centre has a pleasing mix of architectural styles: Cape Dutch, Georgian, Regency and Victorian houses line broad streets, dappled with shade from centuries-old oak trees, and furrowed with water ditches which still carry water to the gardens. It's a fairly large place but many of the interesting sights are concentrated in a small area along Church, Dorp and Drostdy streets, so it's easy to explore on foot. With its handful of good museums and fun nightlife, Stellenbosch is a perfect base for visiting the wine estates.

Sights

Stellenbosch offers two approaches to sightseeing: walking around the town centre viewing public buildings, oak-lined streets and stately homes; or going on a wine tour, visiting any number of the roughly 200 wineries and private cellars. Spend a couple of days in Stellenbosch and you'll get to do both. No other town in South Africa has such an impressive concentration of early Cape architecture. However many of the earliest buildings were lost to fires in the 18th and 19th centuries; what you see today is a collection of perfectly restored buildings. Following each fire, the destroyed buildings were recreated with the help of photographs, original plans and sketches, although the technology and materials of the day were used. This is perhaps why they appear to have survived in such good condition. This restoration process is not unusual: the town of Tulbagh in the Breede River Valley was completely destroyed by an earthquake in 1969, but today it has the look and feel of an unspoilt quaint Victorian village.

Dorp Street, which runs east–west in the southern part of town, has all the classic features – an avenue of oak trees, running water in open furrows and carefully restored white-walled buildings. In fact the whole street is a national monument and has one of the longest rows of surviving old buildings of any major town in southern Africa. A walk from the Libertas Parva building to the Theological College takes you past some of the best-preserved ones. **Libertas Parva** (No 31), is a beautifully restored classic H-shaped manor house built in 1783, though the present front gable and twin front doors date from the late Georgian period. Continuing east along Dorp Street, you'll pass the famous **Oom Samie se Winkel (Uncle Samie's Store)** ① *No 84, T021-887 0797, 0830-1700*, a Victorian-style general store that is still functioning as a shop today. It became most famous between 1904 and 1944 when the store was owned and run by Samuel Johannes Volsteedt, when he stocked virtually anything and everything the townspeople could possibly need. The shop still sells a wide range of goods and retains it character with items hanging from all corners, and old cabinets full of bits and pieces. Also of particular note on Dorp Street are the town houses just past the junction with Helderberg Street. **Hauptfleisch House** (No 153), **Bakker House** (No 155), **Loubser House** (No 157), and **Saxenhof** (No 159), are regarded as the best-preserved street façades in old Stellenbosch.

Branching off from Dorp Street is Drostdy Street, dominated by a building with a tall tower. Also in this street is the town church, the **Moederkerk**; its current steeple church was designed by Carl Otto Hagen and built in 1862. Inside, it is worth admiring the pulpit and the unusually thick stained-glass windows.

Turn right at the top of Drostdy Street into Van Riebeeck Street to reach the **Botanical Garden** ① *021-808 3054, www.sun.ac.za, 0800-1700, free, Katjiepiering Restaurant, gift and bookshop 1700-1000*. These were established in the 1920s and are part of the University of Stellenbosch, with a fine collection of ferns, orchids and bonsai trees. One of the more unusual plants to look out for is the *Welwitschis* from the Namib Desert.

Heading west back along Van Riebeeck Street brings you to Ryneveld Street, where you'll find the entrance to the engaging **Village Museum** ① *T021-887 2948, www.stelmus. co.za, Mon-Sat 0900-1700, Sun 1000-1600, R30, children (under 16) R5*. The complex currently spreads over two blocks in the oldest part of town. If you follow the guide numbers you will be taken through four houses, each representing a different period of the town's history. The oldest of these is **Schreuderhuis** (1709), one of the earliest houses to be built in Stellenbosch. The simple furniture and collection of household objects are all of the same period. The house was built by Sebastian Schreuder, a German. **Blettermanhuis** (1789) is a perfect example of what has come to be regarded as a typical H-shaped Cape Dutch home. The furnishings are those of a wealthy household between 1750 and 1780. The house was built by Hendrik Lodewyk Bletterman, the last *landdrost* to be appointed by the Dutch East India Company. Notice the contrast in furnishings between Schreuder the messenger and Bletterman the magistrate. The third building in the museum to have been restored is **Grosvenor House** (1803), in Drostdy Street. This is an excellent example of the two-storeyed town houses that once dominated the streets of Cape Town. The

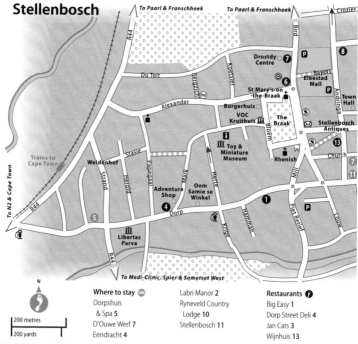

Stellenbosch

To Paarl & Franschhoek
To Paarl & Franschhoek
Crozier
Bird
Du Toit
Bergzicht
Drostdy Centre 7
P
8
Bayers
Koester
Elkestad Mall
P
Andringa
@ 6
Alexander
(Pol)
St Mary's-on-the-Braak
Town Hall
Burgerhuis
VOC Kruithuis
The Braak
Bloem
S
Stellenbosch Antiques
Trains to Cape Town
Weidenhof
Stasie
ℹ
Toy & Miniature Museum
Rhenish
S
13
Church
To N2 & Cape Town
Strand
Herold
Papegaai
Mark
Herte
7
R44
Adventure Shop
Oom Samie se Winkel
1
11
4
Dorp
Krige
Hammann
Piet Retief
P
Louw
Libertas Parva
R44
To Medi-Clinic, Spier & Somerset West

N

200 metres
200 yards

home was built by Christian Ludolph Neethling, a successful farmer, in 1782. The fourth and final house is the fussy **OM Bergh House** (1870), which once had a thatched roof. All four houses are set in neat kitchen gardens which have been recreated to reflect the popular plants of each period. Guides dressed in period clothes are at hand answer any questions and point out interesting details.

Much of the town's activity today takes place around the **Braak**, at the western end of Church Street. This is the original village green and one-time military parade ground. On the western edge by Market Street is the **VOC (Vereenigde Oost-Indische Compagnie) Kruithuis** ① *T021-887 2948, www.stelmus.co.za, Sep-May, Mon-Fri 0930-1300, R5 per person*, or Powder House, built in 1777 as a weapons store. Today it is a military museum. A short distance north, on the corner of Alexander Street, is the **Burgerhuis**, a classic H-shaped Cape Dutch homestead built by Antonie Fick in 1797 that is now the headquarters of the Historical Homes of South Africa Foundation.

Two churches overlook the Braak, **Rhenish Church**, built in 1832 as a training school for coloured people and slaves, which has a very fine pulpit, and **St Mary's-on-the-Braak**, an Anglican church completed in 1852. A little to the west, on Market Street just behind the tourist office, is the **Toy and Miniature Museum** ① *T021-887 2948, www.stelmus.co.za, Mon-Sat 0930-1700, Sun 1400-1700, R20, children (under 16) R10*, a small but fairly diverting collection of antique toys including a working model of the Blue Train, and a set of rooms devoted to miniatures. Most interesting are the tiny replicas of furniture, clothes and household items for dolls' houses that you can buy in the shop.

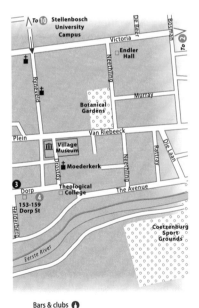

Stellenbosch wine route

Maps and brochures on the wine route can be picked up at the tourist offices in Stellenbosch and Cape Town or visit www.wineroute.co.za. Remember the drink-drive laws in South Africa; when wine tasting, you may be offered up to 15 different wines to sample at each estate, so make sure one of you stays sober.

This was the first wine route to open in South Africa, in April 1971. It was the idea of three local farmers: Neil Joubert, Frans Malan and Spatz Sperling. It has been hugely successful, attracting tens of thousands of visitors every year, and today the membership comprises more than 200 private cellars. It's possible to taste and buy wines at all of them, and the cellars can arrange for wine to be delivered internationally. Most of the estates have excellent restaurants as well as providing very popular picnic lunches with wine – at weekends it is advisable to book in advance – and many also have guest accommodation.

Bars & clubs 🎵
Bohemia 8
Dros **6**
Fandango **7**

Delaire Graff ① *R310, T021-885 8160, www.delaire.co.za, sales and tastings: 1000-1700; restaurants: 1200-1430, 1830-2100.* Owned by Laurence Graff of Graff Diamonds International, this estate sits on the crest of the Helshoogte Pass and has some of the most beautiful views in the valley. There are two restaurants: **Indochine** serves Asian-inspired dishes and the **Delaire Graff Restaurant** is one of the best in the region and has a gourmet bistro menu and stunning outdoor terrace. Much of Graff's personal art collection is on display, a boutique sells diamond jewellery and watches, and there's a luxury lodge and spa (\$\$\$\$).

Delheim ① *Knorhoek Rd, off the R44, T021-888 4600, www.delheim.com, sales and tastings: 0900-1700, cellar tours: 1030 and 1430, restaurant: 0930-1630.* The restaurant has a beautiful setting with views towards Cape Town and Table Mountain, and serves breakfasts, lunches, cheese platters and teas, and offers picnic baskets (October-April) to eat at benches next to the river. Tastings are conducted in a cool downstairs cellar.

Eikendal ① *R44, T021-855 1422, www.eikendal.com, sales and tastings: 0930-1600; cellar tours: Mon-Fri, 1000 and 1430; restaurant: Tue-Sun 1200-1530.* The microclimate on the western slopes of the mountain is ideal for viticulture, and there is a wide selection of both whites and reds. **Cucina di Giovanni's@Eikendal** is the restaurant and unusually (for the Winelands) is Italian with a good choice of gourmet pizza and pasta and tables under the trees overlooking a dam. Two walks have been mapped out among the vines – one an easy half-hour stroll, the other a 1½-hour hike. There are nine comfortable suites for accommodation (\$\$\$-\$\$).

Hartenberg ① *Botterlary Rd, T021-865 2541, www.hartenbergestate.com, sales and tastings: Mon-Fri 0900-1700, Sat 0900-1500, Oct-Easter daily: cellar tours: by appointment; lunches: 1200-1400.* The first vines on this estate were planted in 1692, and today is best known for its Gravel Hill Shiraz. During the summer, lunches are served in the shade and peace of the gardens; come winter the tasting room doubles up as a restaurant with warming log fires. Picnic baskets are available (October-April) to enjoy on the lawns, or picnic backpacks can be taken on a short walking trail through a wetland area on the estate.

Neethlingshof ① *R310, T021-883 8988, www.neethlingshof.co.za, sales and tastings: Mon-Fri 1700-0900, Sat-Sun 1600-1000; cellar and vineyard tours: by appointment; restaurant: Mon-Sun 1600-1000, Tue-Sat 2200-1000.* With its fine Cape Dutch buildings and grand pine avenue (which features on the labels of the wines), this estate is a very pleasant one to visit. The first vines were planted here in 1692 and the manor house was built in 1814 in traditional Cape Dutch H-style. Today this has been converted into the **Lord Neethling Restaurant** renowned for its venison and veal, which has outside tables on the terrace with beautiful views of the gardens.

Saxenburg ① *Polkadraai Rd, T021-903 6113, www.saxenburg.co.za, sales and tastings: Mon-Fri 1700-0900, Sat 1630-1000, Sun 1600-1000; restaurant: Wed-Sun 1600-0900.* Saxenberg has a long history, starting in 1693 when Simon van der Stel granted land to a freeburgher, Jochem Sax. Sax planted the first vines and built the manor house in 1701, and the estate has been producing ever since. It produces a small number of cases each year; its Private Collection of red wines is very good. The **Guinea Fowl** restaurant is in part of the original wine cellar and accommodation is in three self-catering apartments on the estate (\$\$).

BACKGROUND
Stellenbosch

In November 1679, Governor of the Cape Simon van der Stel left Cape Town with a party of soldiers in order to explore the hinterland. There was already a great need for additional land to be brought under cultivation to supply both Cape Town and passing ships calling for fresh supplies. On the first night the group camped beside a stream they named the Kuilsrivier. The stream turned out to be a tributary of a much larger river, the Eersterivier. As they followed the Eersterivier towards the mountains they found themselves in a fertile alluvial valley. There was no sign of human habitation, the waters were cool and clean and everything seemed to grow in abundance – exactly the type of land Van der Stel had been sent to discover. Several days after entering the valley the group camped under a large tree on an island formed by two branches of the Eersterivier. The camp was named Van der Stel se Bosch (Van der Stel's Wood).

Six months later, in May 1680, eight families from Cape Town moved into the area, tempted by the offer of as much free land as they could cultivate, and by the summer of 1681 Stellenbosch was a thriving agricultural community. This became the first European settlement in the interior of southern Africa. By the end of 1683 more than 30 families had settled in the valley, a school had been built and a *landdrost* (magistrate) had been appointed. Throughout his life, Simon van der Stel maintained a close interest in the development of the town. One of his greatest legacies was to order the planting of oak trees along the sides of every street. Canals were also built to bring water to the town gardens. Today, a number of the original oaks are still standing and some have been proclaimed national monuments.

It is difficult to picture it today, but at the end of the 17th century this new settlement was a frontier town. For the next 100 years the magistracy had dealings with the explorers, hunters, adventurers and nomadic peoples who lived beyond the Cape, and the authority extended over 250,000 sq km. In the meantime, the town prospered as an agricultural centre and also emerged as a place of learning. In 1859 the Dutch Reformed Church started a Seminary which in 1866 became the Stellenbosch Gymnasium, renamed Victoria College in 1887. After the creation of the Union of South Africa in 1910, there was pressure on the new government to establish a single national university. By this stage Victoria College had emerged as a respected Afrikaner school, and Stellenbosch itself was regarded as an important centre of Afrikaner culture. In 1915 a local farmer, Johannes Marais died and left £100,000 towards higher education in Stellenbosch. This bequest finally persuaded the government to yield to public pressure and in April 1918 the Victoria College became the University of Stellenbosch.

Spier ① R310, T021-809 1100, www.spier.co.za, sales and tastings: 1000-1630; restaurants 1000-1630. This is the Winelands' most commercial and family-friendly estate. The impressive tasting room features a 370-kg chandelier made from recycled bottles, and wine can be paired with olives, cheeses, soup or chocolate, while children can taste grape juices with an activity sheet about how insects play a role in the vineyards. There's also a bird of prey centre, craft market, children's play areas and beautiful grounds dotted with lakes and streams. **Eight** is the formal restaurant, **Eight-to-Go** is the deli where you can create a picnic, or pre-book a ready-made picnic to collect on arrival, and accommodation is at the **Spier Hotel**, see Where to stay, page 115.

Simonsig ① *Kromme Rhee Rd, M23, T021-888 4900, www.simonsig.co.za, sales and tastings: Mon-Fri 0830-1700, Sat 0830-1600, Sun 1100-1500; cellar tours: Mon-Sat 1100; restaurant: Tue-Sat 1200-1500, Sun 1200-1400.* This large estate has been in the Malan family for 10 generations, and among some exceptionally fine whites and reds, it is known for producing Méthode Cap Classique (South Africa's version of champagne). There is an attractive outdoor tasting area with beautiful views out over the Simonsberg Mountain, and **Cuvée**, the restaurant, has a more modern menu than most and a terrace under oak trees.

Listings Stellenbosch *maps p104 and p110*

Tourist information

Stellenbosch Tourist Office
36 Market St, T021-887 9150, www. stellenbosch.travel, Mon-Fri 0800-1800, Sat 0900-1700, Sun 1000-1600 (in Jun and Aug the office opens 1 hr later and closes 1 hr earlier).
A professional and helpful office, which provides a *Stellenbosch on Foot* map and can help with accommodation bookings, tour information and wine routes.

Where to stay

In town

$$$ Dorpshuis & Spa
22 Dorp St, T021-883 9881, www.proteahotels.com.
A smart Victorian townhouse with 27 individually decorated a/c rooms with antiques, marble-clad bathrooms and private patios, heated swimming pool and the **Oak Leaf** à la carte restaurant.

$$$-$$ D'Ouwe Werf Hotel
30 Church St, T021-887 4608, www.ouwewerf.com.
Converted Georgian house with 44 a/c rooms an 5 apartments with kitchenettes, all individually decorated with Cape-style furniture and DSTV. Good-sized pool and

vine-shaded terrace where breakfast and lunch are served. The **1802** restaurant has a good reputation.

$$$-$$ Labri Manor
71 Victoria St, T021-886 5652, www.labrimanor.co.za.
A fine Victorian house with 10 luxury rooms with DSTV, polished wooden floors, huge 4-poster beds, subtle yellow walls and dark wood antiques. Spa room, cobbled courtyard, dinner and picnic baskets on request.

$$ Eendracht
161 Dorp St, T021-883 8843, www.eendracht-hotel.com.
Housed in a reconstruction of what was one of Stelllenbosch's oldest houses, this boutique hotel has 12 rooms with modern understated decor and luxuries like silk-filled duvets, pool, bar and the small restaurant serves traditional South African dishes such as *water-blommetjiebredie.*

$$ Ryneveld Country Lodge
67 Ryneveld St, T021-887 4469, www.ryneveldlodge.co.za.
Friendly B&B in a beautiful late 19th-century house full of antiques with breakfast room, shady terrace and small pool, 10 a/c rooms, some in more expensive cottages have additional kitchenettes and are suitable for families.

$$ Stellenbosch Hotel
162 Dorp St, T021- 887 3644,
www.stellenboschhotel.co.za.
Central hotel with 32 a/c rooms and 6 self-catering apartments in buildings with restored façades dating to 1815. Although small with plain decor, good value and centrally located. Friendly bar popular with locals, bright dining room with tables on terrace overlooking the street (see Restaurants, page 116).

Out of town

$$$$ Lanzerac Manor
Jonkershoek Rd, 2 km from town centre
T021-887 1132, www.lanzerac.co.za.
Very expensive but fittingly luxurious hotel set around an 18th-century Cape Dutch manor house on a wine estate, tastings and cellar tours on offer. 48 spacious and plush suites with private patios and all mod cons, 2 restaurants: the formal **Governor's Hall**, and the more relaxed **Lanzerac Terrace** for alfresco dining during summer. There's an extensive spa with a separate pool overlooking the vines which is also popular with non-guests for a day of pampering.

$$$ Spier Hotel
Spier Wine Estate (see page 113),
T021-809 1100, www.spier.co.za.
Condo-style buildings set around courtyards with private pools for each section, 153 large rooms with stylish decor in strong colours and polished concrete floors, beautiful bathrooms stocked with aromatherapy products, restaurant, wine bar and spa.

$$$ Wedgeview Country House & Spa
The Bonniemile, 5 km south of town,
T021-881 3525, www.wedgeview.co.za.
Set in 1.5 ha of attractive grounds surrounded by vineyards with 13 garden thatched suites, main house has snooker room, bar, lounge and breakfast room, 2 swimming pools and beauty spa. Rates are for B&B, restaurant for light lunches and snacks and 3-course dinners on request.

$$$-$$ L'Avenir Country Lodge
5 km north of Stellenbosch off the R44
towards the N1 and Paarl, T021-889 5001,
www.lavenirestate.co.za.
A peaceful setting on a smart wine farm that produces award-winning pinotage with 11 a/c rooms with contemporary African decor, good views of the farm dam, pool. Price includes breakfast and wine tasting, meals arranged on request.

$$ Bellevue Manor
5 km south of Stellenbosch on the R44, T021-880 1086, www.bellevuestellenbosch.co.za.
Peaceful farm with 8 purpose-built a/c thatched B&B cottages in Cape Dutch style with pleasant country-style furnishings, TV, fireplace, private terrace, good-sized pool with braai area.

Restaurants

As well as the restaurants in town, eating at a wine estate is especially nice for lazy lunches in a picturesque setting. Some of these are also listed separately under details of the individual estates on the Stellenbosch wine route (see page 111).

$$$ Rust en Vrede
Annandale Rd, off the R44, 12 km south of Stellenbosch, T021-881 3757, www.rustenvrede.com. Tue-Sat from 1830.
Superb gourmet restaurant on a beautiful wine estate and overseen by John Shuttleworth, one of South Africa's most celebrated chefs. Dinner is a 4-, 6- or 10-course event, and the wine list is nothing short of an encyclopedia (there are 6 pages devoted to just champagne/Méthode Cap Classique) but a sommelier is on hand to help diners pair wine with the spectacular food.

$$$-$$ Mont Marie
Blaauwklippen Rd, T021-880 0777, www.montmarie.co.za. Wed-Sun 0830-1500, Thu-Sat 1830-2100.
In another gorgeous wine estate setting, the menu at this acclaimed restaurant changes regularly according to the availability of fresh

produce. Expect refined dishes of South African, Asian and European cuisine. Also open for gourmet breakfasts.

$$ The Big Easy
95 Dorp St, T021-887 3462, www. thebigeasyrestaurant.co.za. Mon-Fri 0730-1000, 1200-2200.
Brasserie-style restaurant owned by successful South African golfer Ernie Els featuring memorabilia and photos, set in a historic building dating from 1798. Farm breakfasts, tapas like oysters and game carpaccio, and mains including seared tuna and steaks, more than 170 Stellenbosch wines on the wine list.

$$-$ Jan Cats
At the Stellenbosch Hotel, see Where to stay, page 115. Open 0700-2200.
Casual hotel restaurant with cosy interior and street-side terrace on Dorp St, with good-value pub-style meals like steak chips plus local favourites like West Coast mussels or Cape Malay curry.

$$-$ Wijnhuis
Corner of Church and Andringa Streets, T021-887 5844, www.wijnhuis.co.za. Open 0800-2300.
Bustling wine bar and wine shop in characterful historic building, pretty outside eating in a courtyard. Breakfasts served until noon, and menu offers steak, some seafood and venison, delicately presented, and over 20 wines available by the glass.

Cafés

Dorp Street Deli
56 Dorp St, T021-886 8807. Mon-Sat 0700-2300.
Delicious range of breakfasts, creative sandwiches and light lunches such as quiche and pasta. The deli sells imported cheese and ham and freshly baked bread and pastries. Open late and is licensed.

Bars and clubs

Bohemia
1 Victoria St, T021-882 8375. Mon-Fri 1100-0200, Sat-Sun 1200-0200.
As the name suggests, bar with bohemian decor and laid-back atmosphere in an old Stellenbosch tin-roofed house with veranda, popular with students, the stage often hosts up-and-coming bands.

Dros
Corner of Bird and Alexander Streets, T021-886 4856, www.dros.co.za. Open 0800-2400.
A large bar-cum-restaurant serving standard pub fare such as burgers, steaks, ribs and pizza and the noisy bar livens up with students later.

Fandango
Drostdy Centre, T021-887 7506, www.fandango.co.za. 0930-0100.
Café and bar with a good-value all-day food menu, tables outside on the square, popular for after-work cocktails, occasional live music. Also rents out bicycles.

Thirsty Scarecrow
Corner of R44 and Annandale Rd, 9 km south of town, T021-881 3444. Wed-Sun 1130-2300.
Pub and craft beer outlet at the colourful Mooiberge Farmstall, with a long deck and eclectic bar with stools made from tractor seats. Snacks include a trio of German sausages (bockwurst, bratwurst and wiener with sauerkraut and mustard) or try the beef and ale pie, burgers or pizzas.

Entertainment

Theatre
Endler Hall, *Victoria St, T021-808 2340, www. sun.ac.za.* As part of the university music faculty, this venue with its mighty organ and celebrated acoustics hosts some 40 concerts (Feb-Nov) of classical, choral and chamber music and they start at either 1630 or 2000. Tickets are booked through **Computicket** (see page 66).

Oude Libertas Amphitheatre, *on the wine estate of the same name, 4 km west of the centre off the R310, T021-808 7473, www.oudelibertas.co.za*. Outdoor events from Nov-Mar in an attractive outdoor amphitheatre surrounded by lawns where patrons can have a picnic and bottle of wine beforehand. Again tickets are booked through **Computicket** (see page 66). There's a farmers market here every Sat 0900-1400.

Festivals

Jan   **Stellenbosch Wine Festival**, at the Coetzenburg Sport Grounds over the last week of Jan, www.stellenboschwinefestival.co.za. Visitors can taste over 200 different wines, along with food and wine pairings from the estate restaurants, and there are activities like grape-stomping or barrel-rolling and performances by some of South Africa's most popular musicians.

Shopping

Stellenbosch's most famous shop and a tourist attraction in its own right is **Oom Samie se Winkel** (see page 109). Also along historic Dorp St are plenty of arts, crafts and gift shops, jewellers, clothing boutiques and art galleries.

Eikestad Mall, *between Bird and Andringa Sts, T021-886 6267, www.eikestadmall.co.za. Mon-Sat 0900-1800, Sun 0900-1400*. Stellenbosch's most centrally located shopping mall with the usual South African chain stores, supermarkets, cafés and takeaways, plus a 5-screen Ster-Kinekor cinema.

Stellenbosch Antiques, *17 Andringa St, T021-883 3917, www.stellenboschantiques.co.za. Mon-Fri 0900-1700, Sat 0900-1300*. A 40-year-old shop and a relative treasure trove of antiques and collectables, including oriental carpets, jewellery, silver and copper ware, ceramics and Victorian and art deco furniture.

What to do

Bicycle hire

Cycling between the wine estates is a pleasurable way of exploring the Winelands. Expect to pay about R170 per day for bike and helmet hire.

Adventure Shop, *Black Horse Centre, corner of Dorp and Mark Streets, T021-882 8112, www.adventureshop.co.za*. They'll drop off bikes at hotels or you can arrange to pick them up at the office. Alternatively join their 4- to 5-hr guided tour which departs for the office at 0900, goes for a ride around town and into the countryside for wine tasting: R580. Also the office for the **Vine Hopper** (see below) and can organize other activities including guided hiking.

Fandango, see Bars and clubs, page 116. This bar also rents out bicycles.

Horse riding

Equine Sport Centre, *4 km north of Stellenbosch on the R44, T082-463 3139, www.equinesportcentre.co.za*. Horse trails go through the wine farms on the R44 between Stellenbosch and Klapmuts including Delvera, Warwick, Remhoogte, Morgenhof and Knorhoek. Short rides start from R150, with wine tasting from R250-595 depending on how many estates are visited and if a picnic is supplied. Beginners welcome, children over 8.

Transport

It's 50 km to Cape Town (via the N2), 33 km to Franschhoek, 35 km to Paarl and 20 km to Somerset West.

The town is served by the suburban Metro railway from **Cape Town**, but for safety reasons, this is best avoided. Hiring a car is the best way of getting here as you then have the freedom to explore the surrounding wine estates. The trip from Cape Town takes about 1 hr, either along the N1 or the N2. Alternatively many Cape Town tour operators organize day trips to the Winelands, see page 72.

Vine Hopper, *T021-882 8112, www. vinehopper.co.za, or book at the Adventure Shop (above).* Once in Stellenbosch, if you don't have a car (or don't want to drive), this useful hop-on, hop-off bus goes between the town centre and some of the estates.

There are 2 routes on alternative days – 1 to the north and 1 to the south – and 6 estates on each are visited. Allow an additional R20-45 or so for wine tasting at each estate. R250 for a 1-day ticket and R440 for a 2-day ticket, pickups 0900-1630.

Franschhoek

charming, sophisticated Winelands village and the country's culinary capital

This is the most pleasant of the Wineland's villages, with a compact centre of Victorian whitewashed houses backed by rolling vineyards and the soaring slopes of the Franschhoek Mountains. The town was founded 300 years ago when French Huguenots fleeing religious prosecution in France were granted land in the area. They brought their traditions – and their expertise in the production of wine – and the town still boasts a strong French character today. Visitors will notice the frequent use of French words like auberge (inn) or vigneron (winemaker) and the **Bastille Festival** in July (see page 124) is well worth making time for. The quaint main street is made up of restaurants, craft shops and galleries, and the more than 40 outlying wine estates all have their individual appeal. Additionally, Franschhoek is famed for its cuisine and dubs itself the 'gourmet capital of South Africa', so a visit here should guarantee an excellent meal accompanied by a fine glass of wine.

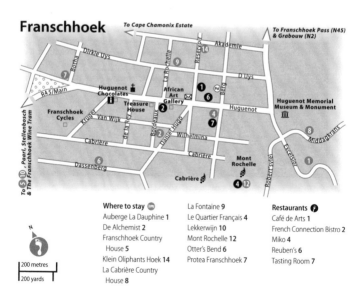

Where to stay
Auberge La Dauphine 1
De Alchemist 2
Franschhoek Country
  House 5
Klein Oliphants Hoek 14
La Cabrière Country
  House 8

La Fontaine 9
Le Quartier Français 4
Lekkerwijn 10
Mont Rochelle 12
Otter's Bend 6
Protea Franschhoek 7

Restaurants
Café de Arts 1
French Connection Bistro 2
Miko 4
Reuben's 6
Tasting Room 7

200 metres
200 yards

BACKGROUND
Franschhoek

Although the first Huguenots arrived at the Cape in 1688, the village of Franschhoek only took shape in 1837 after the church and the manse had been built. The first immigrants settled on farms granted to them by Simon van der Stel along the Drakenstein Valley at Oliphantshoek in 1694. Franschhoek is built on parts of La Motte and Cabrière farms. The village became the focal point of the valley but the oldest and most interesting buildings are to be found on the original Huguenot farms and estates.

Sights The **Huguenot Memorial Museum** ⓘ *T021-876 2532, www.museum.co.za, Mon-Sat 0900-1700, Sun 1400-1700, R10, children (under 16) R5*, is housed in two buildings either side of Lambrecht Street. The main building, to the left of the Huguenot Monument, is modelled on a house designed by the French architect, Louis Michel Thibault, built in 1791 at Kloof Street, Cape Town. The displays inside trace the history of the Huguenots in South Africa. There are some fine collections of furniture, silverware and family bibles, but the most interesting displays are the family trees providing a record of families over the past 250 years. One of the roles of the museum today is to maintain an up-to-date register of families, so that future generations will be able to trace their ancestors.

Next door to the museum is the rather stark and unattractive **Huguenot Monument**, a highly symbolic memorial built to mark 250 years since the first Huguenots settled in the Cape. It is set in a peaceful rose garden with the rugged Franschhoek Mountains providing a contrasting background. The three arches represent the Trinity, and the golden sun and cross on top are the Sun of Righteousness and the Cross of Christian Faith. In front of the arches, a statue of a woman with a bible in her right hand and a broken chain in her left symbolizes freedom from religious oppression. If you look closely at the globe you can see objects carved into the southern tip of Africa: a bible, harp, spinning wheel, sheaf of corn and a vine. These represent different aspects of the Huguenots' life, respectively their faith, their art and culture, their industry and their agriculture. The final piece of the memorial, the curved colonnade, represents tranquillity and spiritual peace after the problems they had faced in France.

Franschhoek wine route
Maps and information can be picked up at the tourist office or visit www.franschhoek.org.za.

Also known as the Vignerons de Franschhoek, there are 42 wine estates on the route lying along the Franschhoek Valley. Again many have their own excellent restaurants and several also offer luxury accommodation. Maps and information on all the estates are available at the tourist office. Not many of the tour operators in Cape Town offering Winelands tours include Franschhoek, so hiring a car is the most convenient way to get there, but the **Franschhoek Wine Tram** (see page 124) can arrange transfers from Cape Town for the day.

Anthonij Rupert Wines (formerly L'Ormarins) ⓘ *R45, T021-874 9000, www.rupertwines. com, sales and tastings: Mon-Sat 1000-1630*. The original land was granted to the Huguenot, Jean Roi, in 1694, who named the farm after his village in the South of France. The present homestead was built in 1811 – from its grand marble halls and staircases you look out across an ornamental pond and neat gardens. Cheese platters and high teas are served

One of the popular recommended day drives from Cape Town is known as the Four Passes route. This takes you through the heart of the Winelands, and, as the name suggests, over four mountain passes. It is a wonderful day out from Cape Town, especially if combined with fine wine and gourmet food in Franschhoek. The first stop on the drive is Stellenbosch. From here you take the R310 towards Franschhoek. Driving up out of Stellenbosch you cross the first pass – **Helshoogte Pass**. After 17 km you reach a T-junction with the R45: a left turn would take you to Paarl, 12 km, but the route continues to the right. This is a pleasant drive up into the Franschhoek Valley. The road follows a railway line and part of the Berg River. After passing through Franschhoek, take a left in front of the Huguenot Monument and climb out of the valley via the **Franschhoek Pass**. This pass was built along the tracks formed by migrating herds of game centuries earlier, and was originally known as the Olifantspad (elephant's path). One of the more surprising aspects of this drive is the change in vegetation once you cross the lip of the pass, 520 m above the level of Franschhoek. As the road winds down towards Theewaterskloof Dam, you pass through a dry valley full of scrub vegetation and fynbos – gone are the fertile fruit farms and vineyards.

Take a right across the dam on the R321 towards Grabouw and Elgin. An alternative but much longer route back to Cape Town is to take a left here, onto the R43. This is the road to Worcester, 50 km, the principal town in the Breede River Valley. From Worcester follow the N1 back to Cape Town.

The Four Passes Route continues across the Theewaterskloof Dam and then climbs **Viljoens Pass**, the third of four. To the right lies the Hottentots Holland Nature Reserve, a popular hiking region. The country around here is an important apple-growing region. At the N2 highway turn right and follow the road back into Cape Town. The fourth and most spectacular pass is **Sir Lowry's Pass**, which crosses the Hottentots Holland Mountains. From the viewpoint at the top you will be rewarded with a fine view of the Cape Flats with the brooding Cape Peninsula behind.

on the veranda. Among the classic range of wines, is the Italian varietal range, Terra del Capo. Also here is the **Franschhoek Motor Museum** ⓘ *Mon-Fri 1000-1600, Sat-Sun 1000-1500, T021-874 9000, www.fmm.co.za, R60, children (3-12) R30, under 3s free,* which has over 80 vintage and classic cars on display plus other vehicles such as an 1898 tricycle. Any car enthusiast will enjoy a visit here and the valuable cars are displayed in chronological order from pre-1900 models up to a 2003 Ferrari.

Boschendal ⓘ *R310, T021-870 4272, www.boschendal.com, sales and tastings: 0830-1630; vineyard and cellar tours: 1030, 1130 and 1500 by appointment.* Boschendal has been producing wine since 1687 and is today one of the most popular and beautiful estates in the region, not least for its excellent food and pleasant wine-tasting area underneath a giant oak. The restored H-shaped manor house (1812) is one of the finest in South Africa, and is open as a museum to the public. **The Werf Restaurant** serves excellent gourmet country cuisine (Wednesday-Sunday 1200-1430, Friday-Saturday 1800-2100), **Le Pique Nique** (1215-1330) offers picnic hampers in the gardens between September and May, and the **Farmshop & Deli** (0800-1700) has light meals and afternoon teas.

Mont Rochelle ① *Dassenberg Rd, T021-876 2770, www.virginlimitededition.com/mont-rochelle, sales and tastings: 1900-1000; cellar tours: Mon-Fri 1230 ,1100 and 1500; restaurant 1800-1200.* This estate was established in 1715 by Jaques de Villiers, one of the original Huguenots that came to the valley in 1688 and is now owned by Virgin boss Richard Branson. It has one of the most attractive settings in the region with beautiful views of the valley and it produces some good full bodied red wines and a couple of whites. Tastings can be combined with wine-pairing lunches at the Country Kitchen restaurant in the wine-tasting centre and picnic baskets are available. The estate is also home to the hotel with the **Miko** restaurant (see Where to stay, page 122, and Restaurants, page 123).

La Motte ① *R45, T021-876 3119, www.la-motte.co.za, sales and tastings: Mon-Sat 0900-1700; cellar tours by appointment.* The original manor house was built in 1752 and the grand old cellars can be viewed through glass walls from the tasting room. The museum and gallery has interesting exhibits on Cape Dutch architecture and some valuable local art. The smart **Pierneef à La Motte** restaurant (Tuesday-Sunday 1100-1700, Thursday-Saturday 1830-2230) has a good choice of traditional South African dishes, and the **La Motte Farm Shop** (0900-1700) has tables on the stoep or in the garden and offers high tea and deli fare. There's a 5-km circular hiking trail on the estate which takes about two hours to complete, and monthly classical music concerts are presented in the historic cellar.

Vrede en Lust ① *R45, T021-874 1611, www.vnl.co.za, sales and tastings: 1000-1700; cellar tours by appointment: restaurant Mon-Sat 0730-1700, Sun 0800-1600 and Wed and Fri for dinner until 2200.* Set in a spectacular setting in the Franschhoek Valley against the slopes of the Simonsberg between Franschhoek and Paarl, this estate was established in 1688 and today produces prize-winning wines. One of the less formal estates, wine tasting can be accompanied by an artisan bread platter from the **LUST Bistro & Bakery**, which also offers early breakfasts, lunches and daily blackboard specials. Booking is essential for Lust's Sunday buffet lunch. Accommodation is in five rooms in the manor house or three vineyard cottages ($$$).

Listings Franschhoek *maps p104 and p118*

Tourist information

Franschhoek Wine Valley Tourist office
62 Huguenot Rd, T021-876 3603, www.franschhoek.org.za, Mon-Fri 0800-1700, Sat 0900-1700, Sun 0900-1600.
Helpful staff with a good knowledge of accommodation and restaurants. The office also has the Franschhoek wine route (Vignerons de Franschhoek) desk (see page 119).

Where to stay

In town

$$$$ Le Quartier Français
16 Huguenot Rd, T021-876 2151, www.lqf.co.za.
A superb hotel and impeccable service with 17 enormous luxury rooms with fireplaces, plush furnishings and views over the pool and peaceful, shady courtyard, some have private splash pools and lofts for

children. **The Screening Room**, is a private cinema, and **The Treatment Room**, an intimate spa. The **The Tasting Room** (see Restaurants, page 123) is considered one of Franschhoek's best.

$$$$ Mont Rochelle
Dassenberg Rd, T021-876 2770,
www.virginlimitededition.com.
Part of Richard Branson's **Virgin Limited Edition** hotels, 24 luxury suites and rooms set in the main manor house or in garden units, elegantly decorated with enormous bathrooms, superb restaurant (see page 123), cigar bar, swimming pool, gym and sauna, attentive service, good mountain views and pleasant rolling gardens.

$$$ La Cabrière Country House
Park Lane, off Middagkrans Rd,
T021-876 4780, www.lacabriere.co.za.
Small luxurious and stylish guesthouse set just outside town in formal lavender and herb gardens, 6 a/c rooms with Provençal decor, limed-wood furniture, views of vineyards and mountains, swimming pool.

$$$-$$ De Alchemist
28 Van Wijk St, T021-876 3767,
www.dealchemist.co.za.
A beautifully restored house dating from 1861 with 9 rooms furnished with period pieces including Victorian claw-foot baths, lounge with open fire in winter, neat gardens with pool, country-style breakfasts, walking distance to restaurants.

$$$-$$ Klein Oliphants Hoek
14 Akademie St, T021-876 2566,
www.kleinoliphantshoek.co.za.
A fine guesthouse close to the centre of Franschhoek which was originally a missionary hall built in 1888, with 8 small but comfortable a/c rooms. The vast, high-ceilinged lounge, once the original meeting hall, has a fireplace and is filled with antiques, and there's a veranda for afternoon tea overlooking pretty gardens.

$$$-$$ La Fontaine
21 Dirkie Uys St, T021-876 2112,
www.lafontainefranschhoek.co.za.
One of the finest guesthouses in Franschhoek with 14 rooms set in a Victorian house near the village centre, elegant decor with antiques, polished wooden floors and Persian rugs, some rooms are set in the garden around the pool and the stables have been converted into a family unit.

$$ Auberge La Dauphine
At La Dauphine Wine Estate off Excelsior Rd,
T021-876 2606, www.ladauphine.co.za.
One of the most peaceful locations in the valley, with 5 luxury a/c B&B rooms each with a spacious lounge and patio in a carefully restored wine store, plus 3 self-catering farm cottages sleeping 4, surrounded by beautiful gardens and vineyards. Large swimming pool and fishing in the farm dam can be arranged.

$$ Protea Hotel Franschhoek
34 Huguenot Rd, T021-876 3012,
www.proteahotels.co.za.
A quality offering from Protea and in an excellent location right in the village centre, parts of which date from the 1880s. The 30 individually decorated rooms are arranged around the swimming pool, and there's a decent restaurant and bar.

$ Otter's Bend
Dassenberg Rd, T021-876 3200,
www.ottersbendlodge.co.za.
Budget accommodation in 5 small en suite log cabins, and a self-catering flat sleeping 4 in a lovely wooded spot around a swimming pool. Communal fully equipped kitchen with fireplace and braai. Breakfast extra.

Out of town

$$$$-$$$ Franschhoek Country House
Huguenot Rd, 1 km east of town,
T021-876 3386, www.fch.co.za.
Very elegant boutique hotel with 14 rooms and 12 suites, some with fireplace, private verandas, the newer suites are 100 sq m

and very luxurious with French-style furniture, dramatic drapes and candelabras, 2 swimming pools, spa, lovely fountains in the grounds, excellent restaurant.

$$ Lekkerwijn
R45, just before the junction with the R310 to Stellenbosch, T021-874 1122, www.lekkerwijn.com.
A fine B&B in park-like gardens with peacocks and guinea fowl, with 6 rooms plus a self-catering cottage suitable for a family of 4. The bedroom wing was designed by Herbert Baker and is arranged around a private pillared courtyard, tastefully furnished lounge and swimming pool.

Restaurants

Franschhoek is dubbed 'gourmet capital of South Africa', and for good reason. Booking ahead, especially at the weekends, is advised. For a full list of more than 40 restaurants in the area, visit www.franschhoek.org.za/franschhoek-restaurants.

$$$ La Petite Ferme
On Franschhoek Pass Rd, T021-876 3016, www.lapetiteferme.co.za. Daily for lunch 1200-1600.
Spectacular views over the Franschhoek Valley from this smart 'boutique' winery. Well known for its wholesome country fare like baby chicken with lemon stuffing, or hearty braised rabbit with parsnips.

$$$ Miko
Mont Rochelle Hotel (see Where to stay, page 122). Sat-Sat 1230-1500, Mon-Sat 1900-2130.
Small, formal restaurant at the ultra-smart Mont Rochelle in a perfect setting overlooking the vineyards, excellent gourmet menu with a contemporary South African theme. Also arranges picnics on the estate and **The Country Kitchen** is a bistro adjacent to the wine cellar.

$$$ Monneaux
At Franschhoek Country House (see Where to stay, page 122). Open 0800-1000, 1200-1430, 1900-2100.
Highly rated, serving contemporary fusion cuisine, attractive outdoor terrace and cosy dining room. To whet your appetite consider bacon-wrapped fish with almond cream or chicken breast marinated in ginger and beetroot.

$$$ Reuben's
19 Huguenot Rd, T021-876 3772, www. reubens.co.za. Open 1200-1500, 1800-2200.
Run by one of South Africa's best-known celebrity TV chefs, there's another branch in Cape Town's **One&Only** luxury hotel (see page 57). A faultless experience with sculptured cuisine that is presented like works of art. To whet the appetite think double-baked gruyère soufflé with honey truffle dressing or herb-buttered mussels with celery purée and bouillabaisse sauce. Book at least 2 weeks in advance.

$$$ The Tasting Room
At Le Quartier Français (see Where to stay, page 121). Tue-Sat 1900-until meal ends.
Consistently rated as one of the best restaurants in South Africa run by an award-winning **Relais & Chateaux** Grande Chef. Formal 8-course gourmet dinners are a taste-sensation and a theatrical experience and take about 3½ hrs. Justifiably, advance bookings are essential.

$$ The French Connection Bistro
48 Huguenot Rd, T021-8764056, www. frenchconnection.co.za. Open 1200-1530, 1830-2145.
French bistro serving refreshingly unfussy food such as steamed mussels, steak frites or Toulouse sausages and mash. Good food and generous portions at sensible prices.

Cafés

Café des Arts
*7 Reservoir St, T021-876 2952,
www.cafedesarts.co.za. Tue-Sat 0800-1700,
Wed, Fri-Sat 1830-2100.*
A small art gallery and cosy informal place
with log fire, open kitchen, garden tables,
and a daily changing chalkboard menu for
breakfast and lunch, and on some nights
dinner. Well-liked for its hearty-style plates –
Franschhoek is more often associated with
haute cuisine.

Festivals

Jul Franschhoek Bastille Festival, www.
franschhoekbastille.co.za, usually the 2nd
week of Jul. There's the opportunity to don
a beret and join Franschhoek's residents
to celebrate Bastille Day, with a food and
wine marquee, barrel rolling and chefs and
waiter races, a French film festival and a
masked ball.

Shopping

African Art Gallery, *42 Huguenot Rd, T021-
876 2165, www.africanartgallery. co.za. Open
0900-1730.* Series of rooms on 2 storeys
selling local arts and crafts, including antique
furniture, Massai jewellery, woven baskets,
fabrics and batiks.
Huguenot Chocolates, *62 Huguenot St
(next to the tourist office), T021-876 4096,
www.huguenotchocolates.com. Mon-Fri
0800-1730, Sat-Sun 0930-1700.* A chocolaterie
making fine Belgian chocolates, sold in
elegant boxes tied up with ribbon. You can
watch them being made and the aromas
are irresistible.
The Treasure House, *3 Bordeaux St,
T021-876 2167, www.treasurehouse.co.za.
Tue-Sun 1000-1700.* With over 10,000 rare,
antiquated, out-of-print and contemporary
books, as well as paintings and vinyl

records, this is worth a browse and they can
organize international shipping.

What to do

Bicycle hire
Franschhoek Cycles, *Mont View Building,
13 Fabriek St, T021-876 4956, www.
franschhoekcycles.co.za. Mon-Fri 0830-
1730, Sat 0830-1300.* A range of bikes for
hire for self-tours of the village and wine
farms including mountain bikes, hybrids, a
tandem, children's bikes and bikes with baby
seats. Rates start from R150 per hr to R385
for a guided tour including wine tasting
and a picnic.

Horse riding
Paradise Stables, *outside the village on
the Robertsvlei Rd, T021-876 2160, www.
paradisestables.co.za.* Guided trails through
the vineyards with stops at 2 estates for wine
tasting for R750 (including tastings) or hourly
rides for R200. Beginners welcome, children
over 12.

Transport

It's 71 km to **Cape Town** (via the N1), 26 km to
Paarl and 31 km to **Stellenbosch**. There is no
regular public transport so you will need a car
or visit as part of a Winelands tour.
The Franschhoek Wine Tram, *Franschhoek
Square, 32 Main Rd/R45, at the entrance of
the village, T021-300 0338, www.winetram.
co.za.* This hop-on hop-off option works
in a similar way to the **Vine Hopper** in
Stellenbosch (see page 118) except in an
open-side tram and open-air tram-bus and
goes between the village and some of the
estates. The **Blue Line** visits 8 estates and the
Red Line visits 7, and departures are every
15 min 1000-1730, R200, children (2-17) R85,
under 2s free; allow an additional R20-45 or
so for wine tasting at each estate. Transfers
can be arranged from Cape Town.

While Paarl is home to two of South Africa's better-known wine estates, **KWV** and **Nederburg** (see page 128), the town itself is fairly staid and is not as interesting as Stellenbosch or as fashionable as Franschhoek. All of the attractions and restaurants are strung out along Main Street at the base of Paarl Mountain. When the first European arrival, Abraham Gabbema, saw this mountain in October 1657 it had just rained; the granite domes sparkled in the sunlight and he named the mountains *paarl* (pearl) and *diamandt* (diamond). The first settlers arrived in 'Paarlvallei' in 1687 and, shortly afterwards, the French Huguenots settled on four farms, **Laborie**, **Goede Hoop**, **La Concorde** and **Picardie**. The town grew in a random fashion along an important wagon route to Cape Town. Several old buildings survive, but they are spread out rather than concentrated in a few blocks as in Stellenbosch.

Sights
The 1-km walk along Main Street will take you past some of the finest architecture in Paarl. Here you'll find one of the oldest buildings, the **Paarl Museum** ⓘ *303 Main St, T021-876 2651, Mon-Fri 0900-1600, Sat 0900-1300, R5, children (under 16) free.* This 18th-century U-shaped Cape Dutch former parsonage houses a reasonably diverting collection of Cape Dutch furniture and kitchen copperware plus some more delicate silver. There is also a small section outlining Paarl during Apartheid, although the fact that Nelson Mandela spent his final years in prison near Paarl is barely mentioned. Only a few hundred metres away, in Gideon Malherbe House, the **Afrikaans Language Museum** ⓘ *11 Pastorie St, T021-872 3441, www.taalmuseum.co.za, Mon-Fri 0900-1600, Sat 0900-1300, R25, children (under 16) R10, under 6s free,* gives a detailed chronicle of the development of the Afrikaans language and the people involved. The house itself was built in 1860 by a wealthy wine farmer of the same name and the downstairs rooms have been decorated with period furniture donated by his descendants.

Paarl Mountain Nature Reserve
ⓘ *Jan Philips Mountain Drive, T021-872 3658, Nov-May 0700-1900, Apr-Oct 0700-1800, free.*
Paarl runs along the eastern base of Paarl Mountain, a giant granite massif, which in 1970 was declared the Paarl Mountain Nature Reserve. Within the 1900-ha reserve is a network of footpaths, a circular drive and a couple of dams. The vegetation differs from the surrounding countryside because of the bedrock – the granite mass is not as susceptible to veld fires and many of the fynbos species grow exceptionally tall. The domed summit is easy to climb, and near the top is an old cannon dating from the early days of the Cape Colony. Just below the summit a mountain stream flows through the **Meulwater Wild Flower Reserve**. This garden was created in 1931, and contains specimens of the majority of flowers found around Paarl Mountain including 15 species of protea.

Set high on the slopes of Paarl Mountain amongst granite boulders and indigenous trees stands the controversial **Afrikaanse Taalmonument** ⓘ *Gabbema Doordrift St, follow signs off Main St just after the R45 enters the south of town from the N1, T021-863 0543, www.taalmuseum.co.za, 0800-1700, Oct-Mar 0800-2000, coffee shop and visitor centre 0800-1645, R25, children (under 16) R10, under 6s free,* three concrete columns linked by a low curved wall. This is the Afrikaans Language Monument, inaugurated in October 1975 and designed by Jan van Wijk. Built to celebrate 100 years of Afrikaans being declared as a different language from Dutch, it is thought to be on the only monument in the world dedicated to a language. Each column represents different influences in the language. The phrase *Dit is ons erns*, roughly meaning 'this is our earnestness' is inscribed on the pathway leading up to the monument. There are excellent views across the Berg River Valley from

Paarl

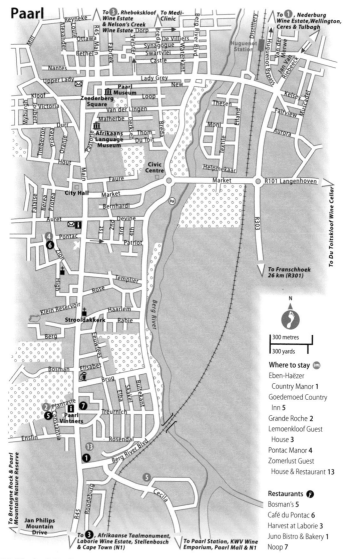

300 metres
300 yards

Where to stay 🏠
Eben-Haëzer
  Country Manor 1
Goedemoed Country
  Inn 5
Grande Roche 2
Lemoenkloof Guest
  House 3
Pontac Manor 4
Zomerlust Guest
  House & Restaurant 13

Restaurants 🍴
Bosman's 5
Café du Pontac 6
Harvest at Laborie 3
Juno Bistro & Bakery 1
Noop 7

here, and on a clear day you can see False Bay, Table Mountain and all the vineyards. As well as light meals, the coffee shop organizes cheese platters and picnic baskets to take on walks; phone ahead, T021-863 2800.

Those with little children in tow may wish to visit **Butterfly World** ① *on the R44 at junction 47 of the N1, T5628 875-021, www.butterflyworld.co.za, 1700-0900, R65, children (16-3) R37, under 3s free, family of 4 ticket R167*, the largest such park in South Africa, with butterflies flying freely in colourful landscaped gardens. They are at their most active on sunny days. There are also spiders, scorpions, chameleons, tortoises and meerkats to see and you can buy packets of seeds for children to feed the goats, ducks and chickens in the garden. There is a craft shop and the **Jungle Leaf Café** on site.

Paarl wine route
① *Maps and information can be picked up at the tourist office or visit www.paarlwine.co.za.*
The route was set up in 1984 and today there are some 30 members and again some of the estates have opened their own restaurants and accommodation. Paarl is often called the 'Red Route' for its legendary red wines including Cabernet Sauvignon, Shiraz and port, although each estate also produces a significant amount of whites.

Babylonstoren ① *Klapmuts/Simondium road, off the R45, T021-863 3852, www. babylonstoren.com, sales and tastings: 0900-1700; cellar tours 1200; Babylonstoren Garden, 0900-1700 or pre-book a garden tour for 1000, R10; Babel Restaurant Wed-Sun 1000-1600.* Between Paarl and Franschhoek, this lovely historic Cape Dutch farm dates to 1777, and the present owners have both preserved some original features and introduced some stylish design elements. Wine tasting is in the Wine Shed, once a stable, while the stunning all-white and glass **Babel Restaurant** is in a former cattle shed. Do not miss walking around the Babylonstoren Garden where over 300 varieties of the plants are edible and used in the restaurant. It's divided into 15 clusters such as vegetables, orchards, berries, bees, indigenous plants, ducks and chickens and includes a prickly pear maze. Accommodation is in 12 immaculately restored labourers' cottages ($$$$).

Backsberg ① *off the R45 between Paarl and Franschhoek, T5141 875-021, www.backsberg. co.za, sales and tastings: Mon-Fri 1700-0800, Sat 1630-0930, Sun 1630-1030; cellar tours by appointment; restaurant: 1530-0930.* This very pleasant estate located along the lower slopes of the Simonsberg Mountain is where the Back family has been producing wine since the 1920s. Lunches are served under the oaks and the menu features traditional South African home-style meals, picnic platters are also available, and on Sunday afternoons in summer there's a set lunch with a lamb on the spit and you can laze on the green lawns and listen to a local band.

Fairview ① *Suid-Agter–Paarl Rd, off the R101, T021-863 2450, www.fairview.co.za, wine and cheese sales and tastings and restaurant: 0900-1700.* This popular estate has a rather unusual attraction in the form of a goat tower, a spiral structure which is home to two pairs of goats. In addition to a variety of good wines (look out for the popular 'Goats do Roam' label – a humorous dig at French wines) visitors can taste delicious goat cheeses, which are now produced from a herd of over 700 goats and sold in South African supermarkets. Their Camembert consistently wins awards as the best in the world at the annual World Cheese Awards. Meals are served in **The Goatshed** restaurant (see Restaurants, page 130).

The Laborie ⓘ *Taillefer St, T021-807 3390, www.laboriewines.co.za, sales and tastings: 0900-1700, Sun 1100-1500; restaurant: 1200-1500, Wed-Sat 1830-2130.* Part of **KWV** (see below), this is a beautifully restored original Cape Dutch homestead – in many ways the archetypal wine estate, and developed with tourism firmly in mind. It's an attractive spot, with a tasting area overlooking rolling lawns and vineyards, and a highly rated restaurant (see Restaurants, page 130). As well as a good range of wines they produce an award-winning brandy. Accommodation is in seven B&B rooms in restored farm buildings ($$) and one deluxe room in the manor house ($$$).

KWV Wine Emporium ⓘ *Kohler St, T021-807 3007, www.kwvwineemporium.co.za, sales and tastings: Mon-Sat 0900-1630, Sun 1100-1600; cellar tours: Mon-Sat 1000, 1015 (in German), 1030, 1415, Sun 1100; café; Mon-Sat 0930-1600.* A short distance from the Laborie estate is the famous **KWV Cellar Complex** which contains the five largest vats in the world. The **Ko-operative Wijnbouwers Vereniging van Zuid-Afrika** (Cooperative Wine Growers' Association) was established in Paarl in 1918 and is responsible for exporting many of South Africa's best-known wines. They are also well known for their brandy and tastings are served with Belgian chocolates.

Nederburg ⓘ *Sonstraal Rd, T021-862 3104, www.nederburg.com, sales and tastings: Mon-Fri 0900-1700, Sat 1000-1600, Nov-Mar Sun 1000-1400; cellar tours Mon-Fri 1030 and 1500, Sat-Sun 1100; restaurant: Mon-Sat (and Sun Oct-Apr) 1100-1600.* This is one of the largest and best-known estates in South Africa. Their annual production is in excess of 650,000 cases and their wines win countless annual awards. As such a large concern they are involved in much of the research in South Africa to improve the quality of the grape and vine. Every April the annual Nederburg Auction attracts buyers from all over the world and is considered one of the top five wine auctions in the world. The estate's 1000-sq-m auction hall also doubles up as the kitchen and studio for the popular TV show MasterChef South Africa™. The homestead was built in 1800, and today is a National Monument and home to the bistro-style restaurant which has a terrace with fine views of the Drakenstein Mountains. Picnic baskets are available to enjoy on the lawns.

Rhebokskloof ⓘ *Northern Agter–Paarl Rd, T021-869 8386, www.rhebokskloof.co.za, sales and tastings and restaurant: Mon-Fri 0900-1700, Sat-Sun 1000-1500.* This old estate is now a thoroughly modern outfit. Informal tastings are accompanied by cheese and biscuits and the terrace café is popular with tour groups and on Sundays they offer a family buffet lunch. There are occasional music concerts on summer weekends (check the website for the programme) and the stage is set up on the lawns next to the estate's dam; picnic baskets are available. The estate is also home to **Wine Valley Horse Trails** (see page 130).

Tourist information

Paarl Tourist Office
216 Main St, T021-872 4842, www. paarlonline.com, Mon-Fri 0800-1700, Sat-Sun 1000-1300.
Helpful, with information on touring the wine route.

Where to stay

In town

$$$$ Grande Roche
Plantasie St, T021-863 5100, www.granderoche.com.
A T-shaped manor house dating to 1707 which has established itself as one of the top hotels in South Africa, with 35 luxury a/c suites set in a collection of restored farm buildings in peaceful gardens surrounded by vineyards, 2 floodlit tennis courts, 2 swimming pools, gym. **Bosman's** restaurant is regarded as one of the best in the country (see Restaurants, page 130).

$$$ Pontac Manor Hotel
16 Zion St, T021-872 0445, www.pontac.com.
Elegant Victorian manor house with manicured gardens full of oak trees that are home to an army of squirrels. 22 spacious a/c rooms with antiques and fine fabrics, some with kitchenettes. Smart bar, comfortable lounges with fireplaces and a quaint daytime café (see Cafés, page 130).

$$ Goedemoed Country Inn
Cecilia St, T021-863 1102, www.goedemoed.com.
Close to town but in a farm-like setting centered around a manor house that dates to 1818, 9 spacious rooms either in the house or garden chalets with vine-covered verandas and Paarl Mountain views, bar, breakfasts and swimming pool.

$$ Lemoenkloof Guest House
396a Main St, T021-872 3782, www.lemoenkloof.co.za.
Country house on northern edge of town, with 30 a/c rooms with floral fabrics, fresh flowers and black-and-white tiled bathrooms, grouped in several historical buildings dating to the early 1800s. Pleasant gardens, palm-shaded pool and sunny breakfast room.

$$ Zomerlust Guest House & Restaurant
193 Main St, T021-872 2117, www.zomerlustrestaurant.co.za.
A restored historic house in the centre of town with 14 rooms, some in converted stables, courtyard, terrace, swimming pool, library, wine cellar. The cosy restaurant (Mon-Sat 1000-2300) offers breakfasts as well as daily local specials for lunch and dinner such as eisbein, waterblommetjie bredie or farm pies.

Out of town

$$$ Palmiet Valley Estate
1 km north of junction 62 on the N1, T021-862 7741, www.palmietvalleyestate.co.za.
A restored 1642 historic Cape Dutch homestead located on a wine estate with 10 spacious doubles and 1 honeymoon suite, each decorated with antiques, private balconies or terraces, neat garden, swimming pool, massages available, very good food served in the dining room or on the terrace.

$ Berg River Resort
5 km out of town towards Franschhoek on the R45, south side of the N1, T021-863 1650, www.bergriverresort.co.za.
Self-catering chalets of varying comfort sleeping 2-6, caravan and camping sites with electric points, pool, mini-golf, petting farmyard, canoes, tractor rides, kiosk for

snacks and drinks, nice spot next to the river and ideal for families.

Restaurants

$$$ Bosman's
At the Grande Roche Hotel, Where to stay, page 129). Open 0700-1030, 1200-1400, 1830-2100.
Award-winning international cuisine in a grand vineyard-fringed setting. Popular 3-course set lunch, but the real treat is the celebrated 5-course menus (R580), offering superbly created Cape cuisine. A sommelier talks you through the wine.

$$ Harvest at Laborie
Taillefer St, off the R45 south of town, T021-807 3095, www.harvestatlaborie.co.za. Daily 1200-1530, Wed-Sun 1830-2130.
Relaxed and family-friendly restaurant on wine estate with pleasant seating under giant oak trees. Delicious Mediterranean dishes, as well as Cape specialities like bobotie and Karoo lamb burgers, and uses vegetables and herbs from the estate's own gardens.

$$ Noop
127 Main St, T021-863 3925, www.noop.co.za. Mon-Sat 1100-2300.
Set in a restored heritage building with outside tables on the stoep, this unpretentious restaurant has a varied menu from local venison burgers to prawn tempura. Make room for the traditional malva pudding.

$$ Wilderer's
Wilderer's Distillery, 3 km outside Paarl on R45 on the south side of the N1, T021-863 3555, www.wilderer.co.za. Tue-Sun 1100-1700.
Relaxed lunchtime continental restaurant in a schnapps distillery. The speciality is *lammkuchen*, a type of pizza from Strasbourg, and they also serve pasta, veal and fish dishes. Finish off with a shot of their pear or fynbos schnapps. Live jazz on the 1st Sun of the month.

$$-$ The Goatshed
Fairview (see page 127), T021-863 3609, www.goatshed.co.za. Open 0900-1700.
At the popular wine and cheese farm, which can sometimes be overrun with tour groups, but don't let that put you off as the food is excellent. Cheese platters with freshly baked bread are the highlight, but the mains of duck, lamb, veal and trout will appeal to the hungrier. Naturally the baked cheesecake is superb.

Cafés

Café du Pontac
Pontac Manor Hotel, see Where to stay, page 129. Open 0700-1700.
Old-fashioned tearoom with quaint sideboards, high back chairs, chandeliers and tables on the pretty veranda of this 17th-century manor house. Breakfast buffets (0700-1000), filled baguettes, salads, pastas and high teas.

Juno Bistro & Bakery
191 Main Rd, T021-872 0697, www.junowines. com. Mon-Wed 0700-1830, Thu-Sat 0730-2100.
The café and deli of Juno Wines offering uncomplicated, delicious dishes, and the only place in Paarl to buy freshly baked baguettes, ciabattas and rye loaves. Also an art gallery and wine shop and the wine itself is produced along fair-trade principles.

What to do

Horse riding
Wine Valley Horse Trails, at *Rhebokskloof Wine Estate (see page 128), T021-869 8687, www.horsetrails-sa.co.za.* Rides through the vineyards on the estate and into the Paarl Nature Reserve, from R400 for 1 hr to R950 for half a day with wine tasting. Quad-bikes and carriage rides for non-riders are also on offer. Beginners welcome, children over 8.

Wellington

Wellington, 11 km north of Paarl on the R301, like the other Winelands towns, is surrounded by beautiful countryside and has a number of fine historic buildings, with the added bonus of far fewer tourists thronging the streets. Nevertheless, there is little in the town to keep visitors for long – there are a few wine estates in the surrounding area, but the town is best known for its dried fruit. To the north, the countryside opens up into the rolling Swartland, an important wheat region.

The shady **Victoria Park** in Church Street is notable for its roses. Look out for the archway which was built to commemorate the coronation of King Edward VII in 1902. The fountain in **Joubert Square** was unveiled in 1939 as a memorial to the Huguenot settlers in the valley. The **Wellington Museum** ① *Church St, T021-873 4710, Mon-Fri 0900-1700, Oct-Feb, Sun 0900-1300, R5, children (under 16) free*, has a small collection on the history of the town and the Huguenot farms in the district. The archives of the Huguenot Seminary are kept here. Oddly, there are a few ancient Egyptian relics on display.

Listings Wellington district *map p104*

Tourist information

Wellington Information Office
*14 Burger St, T021-864 1378, www.
wellington.co.za, Mon-Fri 0800-1700,
Sat-Sun 1000-1300.*
A friendly office that can also provide information about the 21-member wine route and the **Wellington Wine Walk** (www.winewalk.co.za), a 3- to 4-day guided walk through the Wellington Winelands staying in B&B accommodation on historic Huguenot farms.

Where to stay

$$$-$$ Diemersfontein Wine and Country Estate
*Van Riebeck Drive, off the R303,
T021-864 5050, www.diemersfontein.co.za.*
A classic country house set in beautifully tended gardens on a wine estate, with 30 rooms, either in the main house or in restored farm buildings, some with kitchenettes, traditional, plush furnishings, elegant teak-panelled lounge, swimming pool, very good restaurant (see Restaurants, below) and horse riding.

Restaurants

$$ Seasons
At the Diemersfontein Wine and Country Estate (see above). Open 0800-1100, 1215-1530, 1830-2100.
Contemporary restaurant with tables overlooking the farm dam and mountains. Light lunches such as tomato and goat's cheese tart or warm trout salad, and heavier dishes for dinner such as crusted salmon or pork belly.

$$-$ Oude Wellington
*R301, Bain's Kloof Pass, 5 km east of town,
T021-873 1008, www.kapwein.com.
Open 0800-2000.*
Lovely spot on the Kapwein wine and brandy estate in an old whitewashed farmstead dating to 1795 with outside seating in the grounds with dogs, peacocks and ostriches roaming around. Wholesome country-style cooking using produce from the farm. There is also farm cottage accommodation ($$-$).

This is
Whale Coast

The evocatively named Whale Coast lives up to its title from July to November, when large numbers of whales seek out the sheltered bays along the coast for breeding. Whales can be seen close to the shore from False Bay all the way east to Mossel Bay, but by far the best place for whale spotting is Hermanus as the whales favour the sheltered Walker Bay, and daily sightings are guaranteed in August and September.

The most beautiful and exhilarating stretch of this coast is between Gordon's Bay and Hermanus, where the mountains plunge into the ocean forming a coastline of steep cliffs, dangerous headlands and natural harbours. This route is often compared to the spectacular Chapman's Peak Drive on the Cape Peninsula, and rightly so. This is an area of much beauty and also botanical significance and, along with Table Mountain National Park, is part of the UNESCO-declared Cape Floral Kingdom. It's known for its fynbos and over 9600 plant species have been recorded here. Elsewhere along the coast there are opportunities to see the fearsome great white shark, and the seaside towns feature miles of sandy beaches and rock pools. The region makes both an interesting day trip from Cape Town and an ideal stopover to and from the Garden Route.

Gordon's Bay, Rooiels and Pringle Bay

After leaving the N2 at Somerset West, the first town immediately on the R44 is Gordon's Bay, a popular family seaside resort with two sandy beaches, **Bikini** (which has been awarded Blue Flag status) and **Main**, both of which are safe for swimmers. The rocky shoreline, a short walk from the seafront, is popular for fishing. The most likely catch includes mackerel, steenbras and kabeljou. The beach road is lined with a number of seafood restaurants and this is a popular lunch spot for people from Cape Town.

Following the R44 south, the next coastal resort after Gordon's Bay is **Rooiels** (19 km), a cluster of holiday homes at the mouth of a small river. The beach has a strong backwash, so be wary if children are swimming. There's a large troop of chacma baboons in this region that move between Rooiels and Betty's Bay and they can sometimes be seen on the beach. Continuing towards Hermanus, the road leaves its precipitous course and climbs the hills inland. After 5 km turn right to **Pringle Bay**, which is dominated by a large

Essential Whale Coast

Finding your feet

It's easiest to rent a car and self-drive from Cape Town south along the Whale Coast. It takes about 1½ hours to drive the 122 km inland route from Cape Town to Hermanus via the N2 and then the R43 from Bot River. But the more pleasurable alternative is along the R44 that leaves the N2 at Somerset West at the base of Sir Lowry's Pass and follows the headland at the eastern end of False Bay. It goes via the coastal villages in the lee of the Hottentots Holland Mountains and joins the R43 after Kleinmond. This route is just over 140 km from Cape Town to Hermanus and takes a leisurely 2½ hours.

Best places to stay

The Marine, page 142
Auberge Burgundy, page 142
Grootbos Private Nature Reserve, page 147

None of the three major coach companies runs a coastal service via Hermanus, although the hop-on hop-off Baz Bus (www.bazbus.com, see page 207) runs along the N2 and stops at Bot River, which is 23 km from Hermanus.

If you don't have a car, the Baz Bus comes into its own when you head further east along the Garden Route (see page 148) as the N2 hugs the coast, collecting and dropping off passengers at their chosen hostel.

Best restaurants

Bientang's Cave, page 143
Fisherman's Cottage, page 143
Mogg's Country Cookhouse, page 143

When to go

The whale-viewing season is July to November, with almost guaranteed sightings in Walker Bay during September.

Time required

Can be driven on a long day trip from Cape Town. For a more leisurely pace, stay overnight in Hermanus.

rock outcrop known as the Hangklip, 454 m. This is the rock you see when standing by the lighthouse at Cape Point looking across False Bay. Hangklip was formerly known as 'Cabo Falso' ('false cape'), because of its resemblance to Cape Point. It prompted sailors from the east to turn north earlier than they should have done into what is now known as False Bay. The gravel loop road around **Cape Hangklip** is a scenic distraction; another track leads to Hangklip. The road rejoins the R44 just before Silver Sands.

Betty's Bay

This small holiday village, midway between Somerset West and Hermanus, is known for its penguin colony and botanical garden. The community was named after Betty Youlden, the daughter of a local businessman who had plans to develop the Cape Hangklip area in the 1930s. Fortunately little came of the idea and today the village remains an untidy collection of holiday homes in a beautiful location. At Stony Point there is a **reserve** ⓘ *0900-1700, R10 per person*, to protect a colony of African penguins, one of only two shore-based breeding colonies in South Africa with the more famous and larger breeding colony at Boulders Beach near Simon's Town (see page 95). A boardwalk allows visitors good views of the penguins without disturbing them. White-breasted and Cape cormorants may be spotted too. Also here are the remains of a whaling station plus the hulk of a whaler, the *Balena*. The station was operational between 1913 and 1930 when blubber was shipped to Europe where it was used for lubricating machinery.

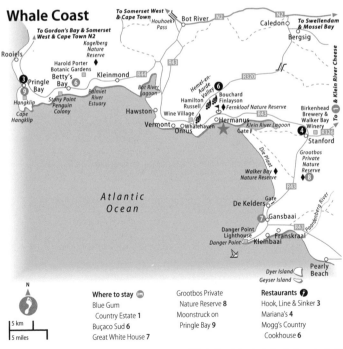

Whale Coast

Where to stay
Blue Gum
  Country Estate **1**
Buçaco Sud **6**
Great White House **7**

Grootbos Private
  Nature Reserve **8**
Moonstruck on
  Pringle Bay **9**

Restaurants
Hook, Line & Sinker **3**
Mariana's **4**
Mogg's Country
  Cookhouse **6**

5 km
5 miles

Harold Porter Botanic Gardens

On the corner of Clarence Drive and Broadwith Rd, off the R44, T028-272 9311, www.sanbi.org, Mon-Fri 0800-1630, Sat-Sun 0800-1700, R18, children (6-16) R10, under 5s free, Red Disa Restaurant.

Behind the village this garden, lying between mountains and coast, is worth a visit if time permits and was originally acquired in 1938 by Harold Porter, a keen conservationist. In his will he bequeathed the grounds to the nation. There are 10 ha of cultivated fynbos garden and a further 191 ha of natural fynbos which has been allowed to flourish undisturbed. (Fynbos is the term given to a type of vegetation that is dominated by shrubs and comprises species unique to South Africa's southwestern and southern Cape.) The reserve incorporates the whole catchment area of the Dawidskraal River. The garden has many fynbos species, including proteas, ericas, legumes, buchus and brunias. Another draw is the chance of seeing red disa flowering in its natural habitat – this usually occurs from late December to late January. More than 88 species of bird have been identified; of special interest are the orange-breasted sunbird and the rare protea canary, which is only seen in fynbos environments.

Kleinmond, Vermont and Onrus

Kleinmond is a popular summer resort in Sandown Bay that has been frequented by the wheat farmers of the interior since 1861 and is today a sizeable resort. Exercise caution when swimming at Kleinmond as the sandy beach is steep; children should be watched at all times. The name Kleinmond refers to the 'small mouth' of the Bot River lagoon. Information is available from the helpful **Hangklip-Kleinmond Tourism Bureau** ⓘ *signposted, Protea Centre, Main Rd, T028-271 5657, www.ecoscape.org.za, Mon-Fri 0830-1700, Sat 0900-1400, Sun 1000-1400.* Just before you reach Kleinmond you will see the sign for **Kogelberg Nature Reserve** ⓘ *3 km from the R44, T028-271 5138, www.capenature.co.za, 0730-1900, R40, children (3-12) R20.* Considered the heart of the Cape Floral Kingdom, Kogelberg features high mountain peaks, steep kloofs, valleys and several tributaries of the pristine Palmiet River. It presents perhaps the finest example of mountain fynbos in the Western Cape, especially in spring when the proteas flower. The broader Kogelberg Biosphere Reserve was South Africa's first registered biosphere reserve (in 1998) and it encompasses the entire coastal area from Gordon's Bay to the Bot River vlei, and inland to Grabouw and the Groenland Mountain. The Kogelberg does not have many large animals although leopards have been sighted and the Cape clawless otter may be seen in or near the Palmiet River. Smaller antelope include grey rhebuck, klipspringer and grysbok, while baboons, porcupine, mongoose, dassies and hares are fairly common. There are a number of day and overnight hikes and Cape Nature has some stunning self-catering eco-cabins here.

To the east of the town is the Bot River Lagoon, a popular sailing and canoeing area. Where the Bot River meets the sea is a large marsh which is home to thousands of waterfowl, especially at low tide. The more common species are spoonbills, herons, pelicans, gulls, terns, kingfishers and geese and a pair of fish eagles breed at the lagoon. There is also a small herd of wild horses that roam the marshlands; they are thought to be descendants of horses hidden in the vlei during the Anglo Boer War and after several attempts to cull them in the 1950s, they are now protected.

After Kleinmond the R44 joins the R43, which then continues along the coast to the next sizeable settlements of Vermont and Onrus, these days more or less suburbs of Hermanus, before arriving in Hermanus proper. **Vermont**, named after the American state, was founded by CJ Krige who became the first speaker of the South African parliament. The beach here is sheltered by high dunes and is safe for children. **Onrus**, meaning 'restless', lying on the east bank of the mouth of the Onrus River, was named by the first European settlers because of the perpetual noise made by the waves along the rocky coastline. The Onrus River forms a small lagoon with a short sandy beach which is also safe for children to swim from. The beach is popular with surfers too.

Listings Gordon's Bay to Hermanus *map p135*

Where to stay

Gordon's Bay

$$ Celtic Manor
22 Suikerbossie Drive, T021-856 1907,
www.celticmanor.co.za.
High up on the hill above Gordon's Bay with sweeping views of False Bay, boutique guesthouse with 6 rooms and 1 self-catering apartment sleeping 4, guests share dinner around a large dining table, comfortable lounge and bar, pool and spa treatment room.

Pringle Bay

$$ Moonstruck on Pringle Bay
264 Hangklip Rd, T028-273
8162, www.moonstruck.co.za.
Intimate guesthouse with large windows overlooking the ocean and mountains, 4 spacious rooms, stylish decor, balconies and fireplaces, pool with wooden deck, 100 m from the beach reached by a private path through the fynbos.

Betty's Bay

$$ Buçaco Sud
Clarence Drive, T028-272 9750,
www.bucacosud.co.za.
Spanish-style villa with 6 tastefully decorated rooms, terracotta tiles, fireplaces in public areas, all rooms have either mountain or coastal views, breakfast served in attractive courtyard with pool.

Restaurants

Gordon's Bay

$$$-$$ Harbour Lights
Old Harbour, Beach Rd, T021-856 1830
www.harbourlightsrestaurant.co.za.
Open 1200-1500, 1800-2200.
Popular place, especially with families in the holidays, with great views of the yacht basin at night, serving linefish and seafood platters, plus there's a sushi bar, a good wine list and a collection of rare whiskies.

$$-$ Bertie's Moorings
Harbour Island, T021-856 3343, www.berties.
co.za. Sun-Thu 1000-2200, Fri-Sat 1000-2400.
Lively pub serving light meals and good seafood on the waterfront, also a venue for local live bands at the weekends, the furniture and the bar are made from wine barrels.

Pringle Bay

$$ Hook Line & Sinker
382 Crescent Rd, T028-273 8688. Tue-Sun,
lunch 1200, dinner 1900.
Lunch is beer-battered hake and chips wrapped in newspaper, while dinner is a chalkboard menu of seafood cooked by charismatic owner and chef Stephan in the open-plan kitchen. On Wed and Sun nights he also cooks steak. Only seats 26 people and very popular with Cape Town people so reservations are essential.

★Hermanus and around

smart seaside resort and whale-watching capital of South Africa

Hermanus has grown from a rustic fishing village to a much-visited tourist resort famed for its superb whale watching. It is the self-proclaimed world's best land-based whale-watching site, and indeed Walker Bay is host to impressive numbers of whales during the calving season (July to November). However, don't expect any private viewings – Hermanus is very popular and has a steady flow of binocular-clutching visitors. While this means it can get very busy, there is also a good range of accommodation and restaurants, and while you may find it far too crowded at Christmas or during the whale season, at other times it reverts to its small-town calm.

Sights

The **Old Harbour** is a national monument and a focal point for tourist activities. A ramp leads down the cliff to the attractive old jetty and a group of restored fishermen's cottages, including the **Old Harbour Museum** ① *T028-312 1475, www.old-harbour-museum.co.za, Mon-Sat 0900-1300, 1400-1700, R20, children (under 12) R10*. The displays are based on the local fishing industry and include models of fish, a whale skeleton, some shark jaws, fish tanks and early fishing equipment. One of the most interesting features is the recordings of calls between whales. There are also telescopes to watch the whales further out. An information plaque helps identify what you see. Outside the museum on

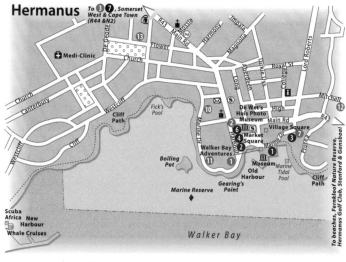

Hermanus

Where to stay			
Auberge Burgundy 1	Quarters 2	Bientang's Cave 1
Hermanus Backpackers 13	Windsor 10	Burgundy 2
Marine 7	Zoete Inval 3	Fisherman's Cottage 4
Misty Waves 11		Mogg's Country
Mitchell St Village 12	**Restaurants** ❼	Cookhouse 7
	Annie se Kombuis 6	Pavilion 3

400 metres
400 yards

Whale watching

The WWF acknowledges Hermanus as one of the 12 best places in the world to view whales. It is the ideal destination if you wish to see whales from land without bobbing around in a boat. The town promotes itself as the 'heart of the Whale Coast', and during the season most visitors should not be disappointed. The town's advantage is that whales can come very close to the shore. The combination of low cliffs and deep water at the base of the cliffs means that you are able to look down from above into clear water and see the outlines of whales from as close as 10 m.

To add to the excitement there is a whale crier who between 1000 and 1600 during September and October strolls around the town centre blowing a kelp horn to announce the arrival of each whale in Walker Bay. The whale crier is easily identified: he wears a giant Bavarian-style hat and carries a sandwich board which records the daily sightings of whales from different vantage points around Walker Bay.

The first southern right whales start to appear in Walker Bay from June onwards. By the end of December most have returned to the southern oceans. The whales migrate north to escape heavy winter storms in the oceans around Antarctica. In August and September most of the calves are born in the calm sheltered bays, where the cows then stay with their young for a further two months. They can travel up to 2000 km to and from Antarctica on this continuous annual cycle. Out of an estimated world population of only 7000 southern right whales, up to 80 have been recorded mating and calving in Walker Bay. The best months are September and October when daily sightings are almost guaranteed. You would be unlucky not to see some sign of whale action during this period, though of course they are just as likely to be in the middle of the bay as up close to one of the vantage points along the cliff path.

The southern right whale is distinguished from other whales by its V-shaped 'blow', produced by a pair of blowholes, and callosities which appear randomly on and around the oval head. The callosities are growths of tough skin in patterns which help to identify individuals. Southern right whales are basically black with occasional streaks of grey or white on the back. Their flippers are short, broad and almost square. They are thought to live for up to 100 years, and a fully grown adult can weigh as much as 80 metric tonnes.

They are so-named because they were regarded as the 'right' whale to catch. The carcass yielded large quantities of oil and baleen, and the task of collecting the booty was made all the more easy by the fact that the whale floated in the water when killed. The northern right whale is virtually extinct, and the southern right has shown only a slight increase in numbers since international legislation was introduced to protect the species. The South African coastline is the most likely place in the world to see them in coastal waters.

BACKGROUND
Hermanus

The town is named after Hermanus Pieters, an old soldier who set up camp in the bay while looking for better pastures for his animals during the hot summer months. The presence of a freshwater spring persuaded him to spend the summer here. Soon other farmers arrived with their families from the interior. Almost by accident it became a holiday destination – the herds required little attention, so the men turned their attention to fishing while the women and children enjoyed themselves on the sandy beaches. When the farmers returned inland to the winter pastures, it was the fishermen who remained and settled here.

In the 1920s the town gained a reputation as an excellent location for convalescing, and even doctors from Harley Street in London were recommending the 'champagne air' of Hermanus. As it became popular with the gentry, so suitably smart hotels were built to accommodate them. After the Second World War the construction of a new harbour stimulated the expansion of the fishing industry and there are now three canning factories in Walker Bay.

the harbour ramp is a collection of small restored fishing boats, the earliest dating from 1855. Also on show are the drying racks for small fish and cement tables which were once used for gutting fish.

The **De Wet's Huis Photo Museum** ⓘ *Market Sq, T028-313 0418, Mon-Fri 0900-1300, 1400-1700, Sat 0800-1300, 1400-1600, entry fee to the Old Harbour Museum covers this, and you can also pay the fee here,* houses an interesting collection of photography depicting the historical development of Hermanus. The building is interesting in itself as it was a Sunday school next to the Dutch Reformed Church, and it was carefully dismantled stone by stone and re-erected in Market Square.

Outside the old harbour is a memorial to those who died in the First World War. Set in the stonework is a barometer and the words "to help to protect the lives of present and future fishermen". Either side of the beehive-shaped monument are two ship's cannons.

Walks around Hermanus

The excellent **Cliff Path** starts at the new harbour in Westcliff in the west and follows the shore all the way round Walker Bay to Grotto Beach in the east, a distance of just over 12 km. Between cliffs the path goes through stands of milkwood trees and takes you around the sandy beaches. The most popular viewpoints are Dreunkrans, Fick's Pool, Gearing's Point, the Old Harbour, Die Gang, Siever's Punt, Kwaaiwater and Platbank. On an ideal day allow at least a morning for the walk and it is accessible from many points along the route. Bench seats are provided at the prime viewpoints, which make them good spots for a picnic. The path from the **Windsor Hotel** to beyond the **Marine Hotel** and from Kraal Rock to the Mossel River is wheelchair friendly.

Beaches

There are some good beaches a short distance in either direction from the town centre. The best beaches to the west are found at Onrus and Vermont (see page 137). Heading east towards Stanford and Gansbaai, there are long, open beaches or secluded coves with patches of sand and rock pools. **Grotto Beach** is the largest, best developed and most popular for swimming and is one of South Africa's many Blue Flag beaches. The fine white sands stretch beyond the Klein River Lagoon, and there are changing facilities, a restaurant and a beach shop. Slightly closer to the town centre is **Voëlklip Beach**, a little run down, but with well-kept lawns behind the sand. Conditions are good for swimming and surfing. The most popular spot for surfers is **Kammabaai** next door to Voëlklip Beach. There are braai facilities under the shade of some milkwood trees.

Fernkloof Nature Reserve

① T028-313 8100, www.fernkloof.com, 24 hrs, free. The visitor centre, 500 m from the entrance, has a display of the most common plants you are likely to see when walking in the reserve. All the hiking trails start from here.

Set in the hills behind Hermanus, the reserve has a 60-km network of trails through an area rich in protea and coastal fynbos. Access is from the east end of Hermanus – just before the Main Road crosses Mossel River, turn up Fir Street. The reserve gates are just beyond the botanical society buildings. The diversity of plants in the reserve is due to the long period it has been under protection, plus its range of elevation from 60m to 850 m. With such a varied plant population, there is also a wide range of bird and animal species including mongoose, dassie and baboon. Higher up in the mountains, look out for breeding black eagles. Small patches of indigenous forest remain in some of the moist ravines.

Hermanus wine route

Hidden away in the **Hemel-en-Aarde Valley** behind Hermanus are a few vineyards producing some surprisingly good wines, mostly Burgundy varieties based around Pinot Noir and Chardonnay grapes. Rarely crowded, there are several vineyards open to the public and have tastings in their cellars. Most are along the R320, and their details and a map can be found at www.hermanuswineroute.com. **Hamilton Russell Vineyards** *① T028-312 3595, www.hamiltonrussellvineyards.com, sales and tastings: Mon-Fri 0900-1700, Sat 0900-1300,* is the oldest and one of the more picturesque estates along the route and dubs itself both the most southerly wine estate in Africa and the closest to the sea. The cellar and tasting room are set beside a small trout lake. To get there follow the R43 out of Hermanus towards Cape Town, after 2 km turn towards Caledon, R320, then turn right 5 km along this gravel road. For those short of time, **Wine Village** *① at the entrance to the Hemel-en-Aarde Valley, the corner of the R43 and the R320, T028-316 3988, www.winevillage.co.za, Mon-Fri 0900-1800, Sat 0900-1700, Sun 1000-1500,* offers tastings and sells wine from over 700 Cape estates and is very informative about cultivators and blends. It can also organize international shipping.

Tourist information

Hermanus Tourism
Old Station Building, Mitchell St, T028-312 2629, www.hermanus.co.za, Mon-Fri 0800-1800, Sat 0900-1700, Sun 0900-1500 (shorter hours in winter).
Extremely helpful and has lots of information on the surrounding area, plus an accommodation booking service.

Where to stay

There are dozens of accommodation options in Hermanus; these are just a few. For a full listing, Hermanus Tourism runs an accommodation booking service; www.hermanusaccommodation.co.za. Be sure to book well ahead during whale season and school holidays, when room rates are also at their highest.

$$$$ The Marine
Marine Drive, T028-313 1000, www.collectionmcgrath.com/marine.
A historic hotel and one of the finest in the country with 42 luxurious rooms, some with stunning ocean views, all with exceptionally fine furnishings – silk curtains, plush carpets, 4-poster beds and marble bathrooms. Also has a spa, heated pool, shop, restaurants and bars.

$$$ Quarters
5 Harbour Rd, T028-313 7700, www.quarters.co.za.
Contemporary boutique hotel overlooking the old harbour and ocean, 18 smart rooms with a/c, Wi-Fi and DSTV, most with balconies and some with kitchenettes, rooftop wooden deck and pool, spa treatments in rooms, breakfast and an easy stroll to restaurants.

$$$-$$ Auberge Burgundy
16 Harbour Rd, T028-313 1201, www.auberge.co.za.
Provençal-style villa in the heart of Hermanus. 17 rooms with private terraces or balconies, some with fine views across Walker Bay, the penthouse can sleep 6, all set around a sumptuous inner courtyard with a pool.

$$$-$$ Misty Waves
21 Marine Drive, T028-313 8460, www.hermanusmistybeach.co.za.
Spacious modern 4-star hotel on 2 levels with ample decks and roof terraces, suites have ocean views and spa baths, pool, restaurant, the annex next door offers elegant B&B accommodation with 4-poster beds and chandeliers.

$$ Mitchell St Village
56-60 Mitchell St, T028-312 4560, www.56mitchellstreet.co.za.
A block back from the sea with 11 individually decorated rooms, some have private courtyards or balconies and fireplaces, 2 swimming pools, attractive lounge with honesty bar, spa treatment facilities, short walk to restaurants.

$$ Windsor Hotel
49 Marine Drive, T028-312 3727, www.windsorhotel.co.za.
Large and popular, this is Hermanus's oldest hotel built in 1896, set on cliffs overlooking the ocean, with 70 rooms with TV, pay more for the ones with sea views. Excellent views across Walker Bay from the glazed lounge, though a slightly plain restaurant. Frequently used by tour groups.

$ Hermanus Backpackers
26 Flower St, T028-312 4293, www.hermanusbackpackers.co.za.
Well positioned behind Main Rd, dorms, doubles/twins with or without bathrooms, vibey atmosphere, bar with pool table, TV lounge with DVD library, nightly braai, pickup from Baz Bus for a small fee, will book all activities and give out maps of the area.

$ Zoete Inval
23 Main Rd, T028-312 1242,
www.zoeteinval.co.za.
Friendly budget choice with 9 B&B double
and family rooms, and dorms in a converted
loft, self-catering facilities, pleasant TV
lounge, sunny deck with jacuzzi. Will meet
the Baz Bus at Bot River Hotel for a small fee.

Restaurants

$$$ The Burgundy
Market Sq, Marine Drive, T028-312
2800, www.burgundy restaurant.co.za.
Open 0830-1700, 1900-2200.
Restored rural cottage set back from the old
harbour. One of the top restaurants in town
but relaxed, with tables spilling onto a shady
terrace outside. Excellent seafood including
superb grilled crayfish and good poultry too
like chicken stuffed with dates or duck with
orange sauce.

$$$ The Pavilion at the Marine
See page 142, Tue-Sat 1900-2130.
Superb award-winning establishment with
a glamorous monochrome interior and
sweeping views over Walker Bay. The menu
offers gourmet seafood including crayfish
and scallops as well as quail, duck, venison
and prime beef. The wine list is excellent and
includes plenty of fish-friendly whites.

$$ Annie se Kombuis
Warrington Arcade, 8 Harbour Rd,
T028-313 1350, www.anniesekombuis.co.za.
Lunch Tue-Sun 1100-1430, dinner Mon-Sat
1800-2130.
A great place to try traditional South African
dishes like *smoorsnoek* pâté with crusty farm
bread, *waterblommetjie*, babotie, oxtail,
chicken pie, ostrich, venison and seafood,
served up in a homely atmosphere with
farm-style furnishings.

$$ Bientang's Cave
Access is via steps from the car park on
Marine Drive, between Market Sq and The
Marine, T028-312 3454, www.bientangscave.
com. Open 0900-1600, whale season (Jul-
Nov) 1900-2130.
The name doesn't lie, it's an actual cave
with an extended deck overlooking the
waves. Superb spot for whale watching
during season. Excellent seafood buffets and
famous bouillabaisse soup, simple wood
benches and long tables. Very popular,
book ahead.

$$ Fisherman's Cottage
Corner of Harbour and Main roads, T028-
312 3642, www.fishermanscottage.co.za.
Mon-Sat 1000-2100.
Tiny place set in a charming old thatched
cottage with thick whitewashed walls
and run by a Belgian chef. Try the seafood
bouillabassie or steak tartare with capers and
save room for the very good crème brûlée
and brandy tart.

$$-$ Mogg's Country Cookhouse
Hemel-en-Aarde Valley, 11 km from
Hermanus off the R320 towards Caledon,
T076-314 0671, www.moggscookhouse.com.
Wed-Sun 1230-1400.
Lovely rustic setting in an old farm labourer's
cottage and great spot for lunch if you're
visiting the vineyards. Every dish is home
made using herbs and veggies from the
garden and likely choices include barley and
oxtail soup, kudu pie with pumpkin fritters,
or parmesan, artichoke and spinach tart.

Festivals

Aug Hermanus Food and Wine Festival,
www.winevillage.co.za. Wine tasting from
over 50 vineyards, plus craft beer, cheese,
olives and handmade chocolates in the
gourmet food tent.
Sep Hermanus Whale Festival, T028-313
0928, www.whalefestival.co.za. Primarily
an arts festival which attracts theatre and
singing acts along with children's events and
a craft market, and also the best time of the
year to spot whales in Walker Bay.

Shopping

As befits a popular tourist town there are plenty of curio shops and speciality boutiques. Market Square has a small, daily craft, curio and clothes market.

Village Square, *T028-312 2761, www. village-square.co.za. Mon-Sat 0900-1700, Sun 1000-1500.* Right in the heart of things and adjacent to Market Square and Marine Drive, 60 shops, plus restaurants, most of which have outdoor seating with views of Walker Bay.

What to do

Boat trips

Hermanus Whale Cruises, *office at the New Harbour, T028-313 2722, www.hermanus-whale-cruises.co.za.* 2-hr whale-watching cruises in season (Jun-Dec), at 0900, 1200, 1400 and 1600, R700, children (6-13) R300, under 5s free, including snacks and soft drinks. For a small extra fee will pick up from hotels. As a permit holder, they are allowed to get the boat within 50 m of the whales.

Southern Right Charters, *office at the New Harbour, T082-353 0550, www. southernrightcharters.co.za.* Again, and for the same prices, boat-based 2-hr whale watching Jun-Dec, 0900, 1200 and 1500, and also permitted to get within 50 m of the whales.

Walker Bay Adventures, *office at the Old Harbour, T082-739 0159, www. walkerbayadventures.co.za.* 2-hr sea-kayaking trips from the old harbour for R350, but it is prohibited to get closer than 300 m to whales. Also organizes canoe trips on the Klein River Lagoon; the 5-hr trip, R450 including lunch, is good for birdwatching and there are more than 130 species around the lagoon, while the 3-hr 'wine tour', R550, stops at **Mosaic Private Sanctuary** for snacks and wine tasting.

Diving

Scuba Africa, *New Harbour, T028-316 2362, www.scubaafrica.com.* Equipment hire, dive courses (NAUI) and daily organized dives from R400. In addition to coral reef and kelp forest dives, there are 3 stimulating wreck dives between Hermanus and Arniston.

Golf

Hermanus Golf Club, *Main Rd, Eastcliff, T028-312 1954, www.hgc.co.za.* A beautiful 18-hole par-73 course in the lee of the mountains with heather-lined fairways, some holes have sea views, visitors welcome, green fees from R200.

Swimming

Below The Marine (see page 142) is the **Marine Tidal Pool**, which always has plenty of sea life and fish. Along Westcliff Rd is a smaller pool known as **Fick's Pool**, which is a sheltered spot and has the bonus of a sandy bottom.

Stanford

The next town along the R43, 17 km east of Hermanus, Stanford is a peaceful Victorian village set inland from the Atlantic, which has become a popular centre for artists and craftsmen. It is an attractive spot, with some well-restored Victorian thatched cottages and a beautiful setting on the Klein River. **Stanford Tourism** ⓘ *13 Queen Victoria St, T028-341 0340, www.stanfordinfo.co.za, Mon-Fri 0830-1630, Sat 0900-1600, Sun 1000-1300*, is in the courtyard of the old Stanford Hotel. Some of the more notable buildings include **Bachelor's Hope** at 19 Morton Street, which was built in 1902. In the 1930s it was dubbed Bachelor's Hope because it was home to the village's lady teachers and many a local bachelor found his wife there. The **Anglican Church** on the corner of Longmarket and Morton streets dates from 1872. The **Dutch Reformed Church** on the corner of Queen Victoria and Church streets was built in 1926 but was replaced in the 1960s by the present hall. However, the original church tower, clock and organ remain and have been restored.

Just out of the village off the R326 towards Caledon, the **Birkenhead Brewery & Walker Bay Winery** ⓘ *T028-341 0013, www.walkerbayestate.com, 0800-1700, restaurant Wed-Sun 1100-1700*, produces both beer and wine and is worth a stop for wine tasting the Chardonnays and Cabernet Sauvignons and sample the six craft beers that are brewed; the tastiest is Birkenhead Premium Lager, a slow-brewed beer using rich malted two-rowed barley and aromatic Hallertau and Saaz hop cones. You can take a tour of the hop garden before a tasting and perhaps have a meal in the pub.

Klein River Cheese ⓘ *T028-341 0693, www.kleinrivercheese.co.za, Mon-Fri 0900-1700, Sat 0900-1300, picnics mid-Sep to mid-May, 1100-1500*, is another popular place to stop. The factory specializes in making Gruyère and other cheeses using Jersey and Ayrshire milk. Visitors can watch cheese being made, taste the produce in the shop, or enjoy a delicious picnic lunch on the banks of the Klein River. To get here from the R43, take the left turn onto the R326 opposite the turning to Stanford and follow the signposts.

To the west of the village is the **Walker Bay Nature Reserve** ⓘ *T028-314 0062, www.capenature.co.za, 0700-1900, R40, children (2-13) R20*, which stretches from the Klein River estuary to De Kelders just before Gansbaai and covers about 1000 ha with a coastline of 17 km. It features a long beach, known as **Die Plaat**, with white sands and rocky limestone outcrops. Vegetation is coastal fynbos and along the Klein River Lagoon are tracts of milkwood trees. Offshore, whales and numerous species of seabirds, including the striking African black oystercatcher, can be spotted. Visitors can explore the coast on hikes though swimming is not recommended as the sea can be rough. There are two entrances, one to the west of Stanford on a back road, and one further south off the R43 just north of De Kelders.

Gansbaai

The R43 reaches Gansbaai 22 km south of Stanford. This popular fishing bay dates back over a century and was named by fishermen who used it for protection against large storms. The original name gansgat ('goose hole') refers to the colony of Egyptian geese, which used to nest in the reeds that surrounded a natural spring in the bay. These days the village is a prosperous fishing harbour with a modern deep-water wharf and several fish-canning factories. It has, however, managed to retain the character of a small community and busy fishing harbour, albeit with strong ties to the tourist industry. It is the principal

Shark-cage diving

Offshore from Gansbaai, Dyer Island is named after Samson Dyer, a black American who lived on the island collecting guano around 1806. The Portuguese first named it Isla de Fera ('Island of Wild Animals') and the name is still applicable. Today the island is an important breeding spot for African penguins and many other sea birds. On nearby Geyser Island there is a breeding Cape fur seal population thought to number 50,000. Both are protected by Cape Nature and you are not allowed on to the islands. The area between the two islands is known as Shark Alley, as great white sharks are attracted to the breeding seals. One of the most popular activities here is cage diving to see the sharks, and viewing a great white at such close quarters is certainly an amazing experience. Several companies offer trips, and you do not need any scuba training or qualification. Most boats depart from the harbour in Kleinbaai (4 km south of of Gansbaai), and they generally spend about three to five hours at sea (depending on sea conditions and shark activity); expect to be in the cage for about 20 minutes. All diving equipment, including a wetsuit, is provided. Costs are in the region of R1600 including a light breakfast or lunch, plus around R400 for return transfers from Cape Town, and R350 for a DVD. Children under 12 are not permitted in the cage.

Great White Shark Tours, T083-300 2138, www.sharkcagediving.net.
Marine Dynamics Shark Tours, T079-930 9694, www.sharkwatchsa.com.
Shark Diving Unlimited, T082-441 4555, www.sharkdivingunlimited.com.
Shark Lady, T028-313 2306, www.sharklady.co.za.
White Shark Diving Co, T082-559 6858, www.sharkcagediving.co.za.

base for shark-cage diving and a number of Capetonians have second houses along this coast. Like Hermanus, there are some excellent vantage points along the cliffs and beaches for whale watching. **Gansbaai Tourism** ⓘ *Great White Junction, Kapokblom St, T028-384 1439, www.gansbaaiinfo.com, Mon-Fri 0900-1730, Sat 0900-1600, Sun 1000-1600,* has information on the shark-cage diving operators and maps of the coastline showing the area's walking routes.

To the southwest of Gansbaai, a gravel road runs 8 km along the rugged coast to the most southerly point of Walker Bay marked by the 18-m-tall **Danger Point Lighthouse** ⓘ *Mon-Fri 1000-1500, R14, children (under 12) R7,* is an octagonal white masonry tower and the lighthouse keeper will give visitors a tour. In May 1852 the *HMS Birkenhead* sank offshore here with a loss of 445 lives, though every woman and child on the ship escaped unharmed in the lifeboats and this is where the phrase 'women and children first' was thought to have been originated. It took the sinking of a further 20 ships before the lighthouse came into operation in 1895.

Where to stay

$$$$ Grootbos Private Nature Reserve
Off the R43, 13 km south of Stanford,
T028-384 8000, www.grootbos.com.
There are 2 luxury lodges on this 1750
ha private reserve: **Forest Lodge** has 16
free-standing steel- and glass-suites set
in a milkwood forest with stunning views
over Walker Bay, the **Garden Lodge** has 11
stone- and thatch-rooms set on a hillside
surrounded by fynbos. Facilities include
restaurants, bars, pool and spa, guided
beach and flower walks and horse riding.

$$$-$$ Blue Gum Country Estate
7 km from Stanford on the R326, xz,
www.bluegum.co.za.
Set on a working farm which the Klein River
runs through, the 12 rooms are in the manor
house or garden cottages with colonial
decor, wooden floors, DSTV, 4-poster beds
and private verandas, restaurant, lots of
walks around the farm and a pool.

$$-$ The Great White House
5 Geelbek St, Gansbaai, T028-384 3273,
www.thegreatwhitehouse.co.za.
Across the road from the harbour, thatched
house with 3 cottage-style rooms that
sleep 2-4, fireplaces and wooden floors,
good restaurant and pub (see Restaurants,
below) used by the shark dive companies
to do their briefings, and there's a tidal pool
opposite for those brave enough to swim in
the Atlantic.

Restaurants

Stanford

$ Mariana's at Owls Barn
12 Du Toit St, T028-341 0272.
Thu-Sun 0900-1600.
Deli stocked with local products, cheeses,
stuffed olives and chutneys. Also serves
bistro-style meals on the vine-shaded
stoep. The cheese soufflé or mussels are
particularly good. Much of the produce is
grown in the vegetable and herb garden.

Gansbaai

$ The Great White House
See Where to stay, above. Open 0800-2000.
Serves filling breakfasts, light lunches and
snacks, in a historic cottage with a skeleton
of a southern right whale hanging from the
ceiling or on the veranda overlooking the
harbour. This is where sea-shaken shark-cage
divers warm up in front of the fireplace after
their excursion.

Shopping

Gansbaai

For details of shark-cage diving
see box, opposite.
Dyer Island Cruises, *T082-801 8014, www.*
whalewatchsa.com. 2½-hr boat trips to Dyer
and Geyser Islands to see penguins and seals.
All cruises depart from Kleinbaai harbour
near Gansbaai and, during the season,
whales and sharks may be spotted too, R950,
children (6-12) R650, under 5s free.

This is
Garden Route

One of South Africa's most celebrated regions, the Garden Route is a 200-km-long stretch of coast separated from the interior by the Tsitsikamma and Outeniqua mountains. The ocean-facing slopes are covered with luxuriant greenery, in contrast to the dry and treeless Karoo in the interior, and it is this dramatic change in landscape that occurs over a distance of no more than 20 km, that prompted the name.

With long stretches of sand, nature reserves, leafy forests and tourist-friendly seaside towns, few visitors to Cape Town miss it. Officially the route runs from Heidelberg in the west to Tsitsikamma in the east, though most visitors drive from Cape Town along the N2 highway over the Hottentots Holland Mountains and through the Overberg to Mossel Bay and beyond.

The larger towns, such as Plettenberg Bay and Knysna, are highly developed tourist resorts, while other areas offer untouched wilderness and wonderful hikes, including one of the most famous in the country, the Otter Trail. If hiking isn't your scene, the beaches are stunning, there are numerous activities from bungee jumping to mountain biking, and various attractions from craft markets to wildlife sanctuaries hug the N2 to distract the motorist.

Essential Garden Route

Finding your feet

The Garden Route is served by George Airport (see page 165) at the western end and Port Elizabeth Airport at the eastern end. Flights link both these with Cape Town and Johannesburg. The options here are to fly into one, hire a car to explore the Garden Route and return the car to the other. Alternatively, drive there from Cape Town and drop off a car in Port Elizabeth and fly back or onwards from there.

By road, the most direct route from Cape Town to the Garden Route is along the N2; it's an easy 385-km drive to Mossel Bay via the Overberg and you can break your journey for lunch in the attractive town of Swellendam. Alternatively, if you have the extra time there is the option of travelling from (or back to) Cape Town either via the Whale Coast (see page 132) or along Breede River Valley/Route 62.

Best places to stay

Garden Route Game Lodge, page 156
Fancourt Hotel and Country Club, page 164
Moontide Guest Lodge, page 174
Phantom Forest Eco-Reserve, page 182
Tsala Treetop Lodge, page 191
The Plettenberg, page 192

Best restaurants

Cruise Café, page 184
East Head Café, page 184
Ile de Pain Bread & Café, page 184
Nguni Restaurant, page 193
Zinzi at Tsala Treetop Lodge, page 193
Bramon Wine Estate, page 199

Getting around

To get the most out of the Garden Route you really need a car; many of the attractions are in between the major resorts so it's good to have the flexibility to stop when you want. The Baz Bus offers a very adequate service and drops and picks up at Garden Route backpackers' hostels every day. Mainline

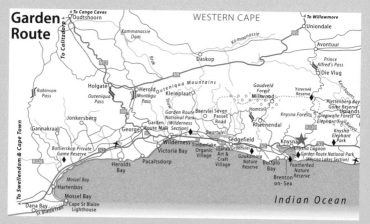

buses also operate a daily service, but most departures and arrivals are in the middle of the night and it's not as economical as the Baz Bus.

Touring the Garden Route

There are a number of organized tours for exploring the Garden Route which start and finish in Cape Town. For those on a budget and short of time, the **Bok Bus**, T082-3201979, www.bokbus. com, offers comprehensive three- to seven-day budget tours of all the major attractions along the Garden Route.

Accommodation is in hostels or you can upgrade to a guesthouse. Prices start at R3850 for the standard five-day tour and includes breakfasts, most dinners and entrance fees. There are numerous other coach and minibus operators running short scheduled tours from Cape Town along the Garden Route that appeal to a wide range of age groups and offer a variety of accommodation alternatives depending on budget. These include: **African Eagle**, T021-464 4266, www. daytours.co.za; **Cape Rainbow**, T021-551 5465, www.caperainbow.com; **Hylton Ross**, T021-506 2575, www.hyltonross.

Best activities
Golf at Fancourt or Pezula, pages 165 and 186
Boat cruise to see the Knysna Heads, page 186
Bloukrans Bungee Jump, page 197
The Otter Trail, page 200
Tsitikamma Canopy Tour, page 203

co.za; and **Springbok Atlas**, T021-460 4700, www.springbokatlas.co.za.

When to go

The area's popularity means that good-value accommodation is difficult to find, and gets booked up months in advance, especially during peak season. It is advisable to avoid the area during the two weeks over Christmas and the New Year, and at Easter. For the rest of the school holidays most of the self-catering accommodation might be fully booked, but hotels and bed and breakfasts should have a free room – call in advance to be sure. For more information about the Garden Route visit **www.gardenroute.co.za**. The regional towns have tourist offices, and the branches of **Cape Town Tourism** can provide comprehensive information (see page 53). The **Knysna Oyster Festival** takes place in July, while April sees the colourful **Pink Loerie Mardi Gras**. Over Easter, Sedgefield celebrates all things slow in its **Slow Festival**.

Time required

Although the full length of the Garden Route could be driven in a day, four to five days is required to see the main highlights. A week would allow a more leisurely pace with time for hiking or the beach. Most visitors either choose a base for exploring the area, or spend a day or two in a couple of places along the way.

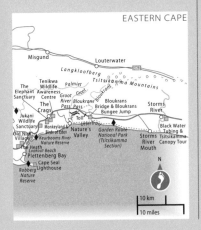

attractive region of rolling wheat, sheep fields and quiet country towns

Having climbed the spectacular Sir Lowry's Pass from Somerset West into the Hottentots Holland Mountains, the N2 highway cuts east across the interior of the Overberg towards Mossel Bay. In the early days of settlement, people would refer to the area beyond the Hottentots Hollands as 'over the berg'. The landscape is immediately very different on this side of the mountains – the road passes through forested hills before opening onto endless dry, orange plains. Most of the towns en route are quiet farming centres, and were some of the first areas settled by white farmers as they ventured east of Cape Town. It is easy to pass quickly through the region without taking much in, and if you are keen to get to the Garden Route, Mossel Bay can be reached in three hours; but there are several sights worth lingering over on the way.

East to Caledon

Some 10 km from Sir Lowry's Pass is a turning signposted Villiersdorp, R321. This takes you back into the heart of the Winelands, or north to the Breede River Valley. A short loop takes you to the undistinguished twin towns of Grabouw and Elgin, although Grabouw has the notoriety of being the centre of South Africa's apple industry and is where the popular fizzy drink Appletizer is made. Regional information is available from **Elgin Valley Tourism** ① *T021-848 9838, www.elginvalley.co.za, 0900-1700*, at the Peregrine Farm Stall on the N2; worth a stop for refreshment at the charming **Red Tractor Café** and a farm stall has been here since the 1960s. Continuing east, the N2 crosses the Houhoek Pass and then reaches Bot River where there is the turning for Hermanus (35 km). It is a further 23 km on the N2 to Caledon.

Caledon

The regional capital of the Overberg, 120 km from Cape Town, lies just off the N2 at the foot of the Swartberg Mountains. It is a typical rural town – small and quiet, and the prosperity of the town and the region is based on agriculture. Look out for the endangered blue crane which is found on open farmland in the area – 75% of South Africa's blue cranes, the national bird, are found in the Overberg.

The town is famous for its hot springs, which produce over 800,000 litres per day. The water has a high ferrous carbonate content. Not surprisingly the first European settler, Ferdinandus Appel, sought to develop the springs. He was granted an 18-ha freehold, on the condition that he built baths and accommodation. Word of the water's healing powers spread quickly and distinguished guests from the Dutch East India Company frequented the springs. Today, the **Caledon Hotel** (see opposite), harnesses the springs, and day visitors can use the spa's facilities (1000-1900). The pool at the top is the hottest, with water temperatures averaging 40°C, and there are additional saunas, cold pool, steam room and a café.

Listings Overberg *map p135*

Where to stay

$$ Houw Hoek Inn
Off N2 12 km past Grabouw, T021-284 9646, www.houwhoekinn.co.za.

The oldest licensed hotel in South Africa on the site of Dutch East India Company toll gate; the oldest section dates from 1779, the upstairs was built in 1860, while there's a newer block of modern rooms. 50 rooms, restaurant in a converted farm building, and lovely gardens with pool dominated by large old oak and blue gum trees.

$$ Old MacDaddy
Off N2 5 km after Grabouw, on the right and then 8 km on a gravel road, T021-844 0241, www.oldmac daddy.co.za.
The rural retreat of the artistic hotels, **Grand Daddy**, and **Daddy Long Legs**, on Long St in Cape Town (see pages 53 and 54). Like the **Grand Daddy**, this also has a collection of 10 vintage Airstream trailers to sleep in with interiors themed and designed by an artist but in a farm environment in the Elgin Valley. Communal barn area with restaurant, bar, lounge with fireplace, pool and deck.

$$$-$$ The Caledon Hotel
Spa & Casino, 1 Nerina Av, Caledon, T028-214 5100, www.the caledoncasino.co.za, 1 km out of town just off the N2.

Unattractive modern complex with 95 a/c rooms but with a good range of facilities based around the hot springs (see page 152). Flashy casino, 3 restaurants, pub, extensive gardens, a spa, and horse riding.

Restaurants

$ Dassiesfontein
On the N2 halfway between Bot River and Caledon, T028-214 1475, www.dassies.co.za. Open 0830-1730.
Country restaurant and farm stall selling home-made bread (they grind their own flour), cheese and biltong, tables in cottage decorated with antiques, local dishes such as bobotie and bredie, buffet lunch on Sun.

Swellendam
elegant historical town with Cape Dutch architecture and an appealing museum

Founded in 1745, Swellendam is the third oldest European town in South Africa (after Cape Town and Stellenbosch), and it is also one of its most picturesque with an appealing, quiet atmosphere. The main centre bears witness to its age with an avenue of mature oak trees and whitewashed Cape Dutch homesteads. Combined with the rural setting and beautiful views, it's a very pleasant spot to spend a day or two, or at the very least pull in from the N2 for lunch given that it is roughly halfway between Cape Town and the Garden Route.

Sights
Of all the old Cape buildings in town the **Drostdy Museum** ⓘ *18 Swellengrebel St, T028-514 1138, www.drostdymuseum.com, Mon-Fri 0900-1645, Sat-Sun 1000-1500, R25, children (6-16) R5 under 6 free*, which covers entrance to a number of buildings, is the most impressive and is often described as one of the country's great architectural treasures. The main building dates from 1747, built as the official residence and seat for the local magistrate or landdrost. Originally built in the shape of a T, the addition of two wings changed the form to an H. Inside, some of the floors have been preserved; what was the lounge has a lime-sand floor, while the kitchen floor is made from cow dung, which helps keep the room cool. The museum concentrates on local history, with a well-preserved collection of 18th- and 19th-century furniture. Within the grounds is a restored Victorian cottage, Mayville, which has an antique rose garden plus the original gazebo and is today home to a coffee shop.

Close by is an open-air display, on the **Crafts Green**, of many of the early farm tools, charcoal burners, wagons and a horse-driven mill complete with threshing floor. Opposite the museum is the **Old Gaol**, which housed both prisoners and local government officials, including the jailer who was also the postmaster. In the middle of all the cells was one without windows, known as the 'black hole'. Today, this is a local arts and crafts centre, with a good café.

Not far from the town centre are more restored buildings from the town's early days. The **Oefeningshuis** (1838) first served as a place for the religious instruction of freed slaves; it now houses the tourist office. Note the painted plaster clock face, which reads 1215, set above a working clock. This was designed for illiterate churchgoers – if the painted face was the same as the clock's, it was time for service. Worth a look is the fine, domineering **Dutch Reformed church**. This large whitewashed building has a tall central clock tower and a mix of architectural styles. Just next to the church, on **Church Square**, are some fine examples of early two-storey town houses built by wealthy farmers who used to visit the town for holy communion. The square had to be large enough to hold their ox wagons. Another grand town house is the **Auld House** dating from 1802 which for many years was the family home for the Overberg trader, Joseph Barry. Inside is some furniture, originally fitted on a steamer which used to sail between Cape Town and Port Beaufort. Also worth a visit is the small **Church of St Luke** built in 1865. Finally, look out for the shop **Buirski & Co**, built in 1880. It has one of the finest examples of Victorian wrought-iron balconies and fittings in the town.

Bontebok National Park
2 km east of Swellendam towards Mossel Bay, the turning off the N2 is clearly signposted, and then it's 3.7 km on a gravel road to the Die Stroom Gate, T028-514 2735, www.sanparks.org, Oct-Apr 0700-1900, May-Sep 0700-1800, R90, children (under 16) R45.

This park can be visited for a few hours or there is accommodation (see page 156), and is a good place to spot several species of antelope in a pleasant setting on the Breede River. There are two loop roads for drives, and some short walking trails from the rest camp where there is also a swimming spot in the river.

At the beginning of the 20th century the bontebok was the rarest species of antelope in Africa. It had been hunted and driven off its natural habitat by the early settlers in the Overberg. Fortunately, something even scarcer came to their rescue – a group of local conservation-minded farmers, who recognized the need to set up a protected area to save the remaining animals (rumoured to be fewer than 20). In 1931 the first reserve was established, but it was not until the herd was moved to a more suitable environment beside the Breede River in 1960 that the numbers started to recover significantly. This has proved to be a success but, although no longer endangered, there are still not many places where the bontebok can be seen in the wild. Today, there are about 200 bontebok in the park and other antelope indigenous to the Overberg have been introduced to the reserve, including red hartebeest, steenbok and duiker plus the rare Cape mountain zebra. Furthermore, the Breede River provides a perfect setting for the Cape clawless otter. Bird species number about 200, and include blue crane, spurwing goose, secretary bird, Stanley's buzzard, and sunbirds and cuckoos may be seen around the office and rest camp.

Heidelberg to Albertinia
Continuing east from Swellendam along the N2, the road passes several small agricultural towns. **Heidelberg**, 58 km from Swellendam, is dominated by its Dutch Reformed church

BACKGROUND
Swellendam

Swellendam started as a trading outpost for the Dutch East India Company. The new settlement was named after Governor Hendrik Swellengrebel and his wife, Ten Damme. Once established, all sorts of characters passed through looking for their fortunes or more land. One of the most successful was Joseph Barry who, in the 1800s, had a virtual monopoly on all trade between Cape Town and the new settlements in the Overberg and Little Karoo.

In 1795 a particularly strange event took place. Just at the point when British soldiers were bringing an end to Dutch rule in the Cape, the burghers of Swellendam declared themselves to be an independent republic, in a reaction to the maladministration and corruption of the Dutch East India Company.

Hermanus Steyn was president from 17 June to 4 November 1795 but, once the British had set up a new regime in Cape Town, the republic was quietly forgotten about. During the 19th century the town prospered and grew as the agricultural sector gradually expanded. This came to an abrupt halt in May 1865, when a fire that started in a baker's destroyed 40 of the town's finest old buildings. Even greater harm was caused by a prolonged drought and when, in 1866, the influential Barry Empire was declared bankrupt the whole region's fortunes declined. Today the town is a prosperous community, and many of the old buildings are still standing, or have been restored.

on the banks of the Duivenhoks River, and was named Heidelberg after the city in Germany in 1855. After another 34 km, **Riversdale** is a small farming centre based around wheat, wool and potatoes. The small **Julius Gordon Africana Museum** ⓘ *Long St, T028-713 8053, Mon-Fri 0800-1300, free*, outlines the lives of several local characters and is home to some paintings by Irma Stern, Thomas Bowler and Peter Wenning. Around the town are no fewer than 15 stone churches, the oldest being the St Matthew's Anglican Church, built in 1856. The **tourist office** ⓘ *T028-713 1996, www.riversdale.co.za, Mon-Fri 0830-1730, Sat 0900-1200*, is on the N2 as you drive through.

Abertinia is another 39 km along the N2 and has a pretty backdrop formed by the smooth foothills and sharp peaks of the Langeberg Mountains. A product collected around Albertinia is the juice from aloe plants, *Aloe ferox*, which is an important ingredient in medicine and cosmetics. You can visit the **Alcare Aloe Factory** ⓘ *T028-735 1454, www.alcare. co.za, 0900-1700*, on the N2 just outside town. They conduct free tours and sell a variety of aloe skincare products and there's a coffee shop. Mossel Bay is 53 km from Albertina.

Garden Route Game Lodge ⓘ *7 km east of Albertinia off the N2, T028-735 1200, www. grgamelodge.co.za, day visitors 0730-1630, 2-hr game drives 1100 and 1400, R425, children (6-12) 50% discount, (3-5) 75% discount, under 3s free*, is a private game lodge that has been stocked with a number of species of large game including giraffe, white rhino, lion, elephant, kudu, zebra, wildebeest and buffalo. It's a popular excursion from Cape Town and one of the nearest places to the city for wildlife viewing. Transfers from Cape Town can be arranged. There is luxurious accommodation (see page 156), and day visitors are welcome for game drives, which must be pre-booked, and breakfast and lunch are available in the à la carte restaurant for extra. There is also a cheetah-breeding centre and reptile encounters are on offer where the resident herpetologist (reptile man) will share his knowledge of snakes, crocodiles and other cold-blooded creatures.

Listings Swellendam

Tourist information

Swellendam Tourism
Oefeningshuis, Voortrek St, T028-514 2770, www.swellendamtourism.co.za, Mon-Fri 0900-1700, Sat 0900-1200.
This office produces a leaflet called Swellendam Treasures, which outlines the interesting Cape Dutch buildings still standing today.

Where to stay

$$$ De Kloof
8 Weltevreden St, T028-514 1303, www.dekloof.co.za.
Elegant thatched Cape Dutch homestead (1801), 7 doubles and 1 family suite with contemporary African and Asian decor, bar and lounge with fireplace, 12-m swimming pool, champagne breakfasts included and evening meals on request.

$$$ Shoone Oordt Country House
1 Swellengrebel St, T028-514 1248, www.schooneoordt.co.za.
A striking Victorian manor house with lattice balconies surrounded by landscaped gardens with pool, 10 rooms decorated with antiques, some with claw-foot baths and 4-poster beds, lovely conservatory restaurant serving 4-course dinners.

$ Old Mill Guest House
241 and 243 Voortrek St, T028-514 2790, www.oldmill.co.za.
A beautiful listed building in a spacious garden with a stream flowing through, 6 characterful rooms set in outbuildings such as the old watermill, superb meals served in the restaurant.

$ Swellendam Backpackers
5 Lichtenstein St, T028-514 2648, www.swellendambackpackers.co.za.
Popular hostel with a dorm in the main house, plus individual double or triple Wendy houses in secluded corners around the garden, lots of camping space, internet, kitchen, home-cooked meals. Can arrange local tours, hiking in the mountains and visits to the nearby Bontebok National Park. **Baz Bus** stop.

Bontebok National Park

$$ Lang Elsie's Kraal Rest Camp
Reservations through SANParks, T012-428 9111, www.sanparks.org.
For cancellations and bookings under 72 hrs, and campsite reservations, contact reception, T028-514 2735. Pleasant location next to the Breede River, 10 self-catering chalets sleeping 4, 2 of which are wheelchair accessible, good views of the Langeberg Mountains from the outside terraces. Shady camping and caravan sites ($) along the river, some with electric points. Buy provisions in Swellendam.

Albertinia

$$$$-$$$ Garden Route Game Lodge
7 km east of Albertinia off the N2, T028-735 1200, www.grgamelodge.co.za, see page 155.
Accommodation in main lodge or in secluded thatched chalets, decorated with an African theme, restaurant and bar with wooden decks, spa, swimming pool, special activities for children. Rates include game drives and meals and transfers from Cape Town can be arranged.

Restaurants

$$$ Herberg Roosjie van de Kaap
5 Drostdy St, T028-514 3001,
www.roosjevandekaap.com.
Tue-Sun 1900-2130.
Opposite the Old Drostdy and Swellendam's
original inn, with cosy atmosphere in
a candlelit room with thick walls and a
low reed ceiling, superb gourmet South
African fare, steaks and seafood. Also has 12
comfortable B&B rooms (**$$**) around a pool.

$$ Koornlands
5 Voortrek St, T028-514 3567,
www.koornlandsrestaurant.co.za.
Mon, Wed-Sun 1200-2200.
A historic Cape Dutch cottage serving local
food such as crocodile steaks, ostrich fillets,
loin of kudu, guinea fowl and freshwater
trout. Desserts include a delicious Cape
brandy tart.

Cafés

La Belle Alliance
1 Swellengrebel St, T028-514 2252.
Open 0800-1700.
Under the trees by the Koornlands River, the
building used to be Swellendam's Masonic
Lodge, giant breakfasts, good sandwiches,
and afternoon tea with Belgian chocolate
cake and lemon meringue pie.

Old Gaol
Church Sq, Drostdy Museum, T028-514 3847,
www.oldgaolrestaurant.co.za.
Breakfasts, light meals such as bobotie or
chicken pie, hot soup in winter, home-made
lemonade, and best known for *melktert*
cooked in a copper pan over coals.

What to do

Canoeing
Felix Unite River Adventures, *T021-670
1300, www.felixunite.co.za*. Runs trips from
Cape Town for canoeing on the Breede River,
with overnight stays in bush camps, restored
Voortrekker ox wagons, or A-frame houses.
Umkulu, *T021-853 7952, www.umkulu.co.za*.
Another operator that will take you to the
Breede River from Cape Town for a day's
float, some wine tasting, and an overnight
stay at a local lodge.

Golf
Swellendam Golf Club, *Andrew White St,
T028-514 1026*. 9-hole 72-par course in the
lee of the Langeberg Mountains with views
across town.

Horse riding
Two Feathers Horse Trails, run by
Swellendam Backpackers (see page
156). Offers 1- to 2-hr scenic rides through
forests along the foothills of the Langeberg
Mountains for all levels of riders. There's also
the option of an overnight ride and sleeping
in a mountain hut.

Transport

It's 240 km to **Cape Town**, 225 km to
George, 560 km to **Port Elizabeth**,
270 km to **Knysna**.

Bus
Buses stop at the Swellengrebal Hotel on
Voortrek St. **Greyhound**, **Intercape** and
Translux all stop here daily on the Cape
Town–Durban route. **Cape Town** (2 hrs),
Port Elizabeth (9 hrs), **Durban** (24 hrs).
   Towards **Cape Town** the **Baz Bus** arrives
in Swellendam 1800-1815, towards **Port
Elizabeth**, 1145-1200, and drops off at
Swellendam Backpackers.
   For more information, see Getting around,
page 207.

Mossel Bay
port and industrial town but also a bustling holiday resort at the start of the Garden Route

Built along a rocky peninsula which provides sheltered swimming and mooring in the bay, Mossel Bay is one of the larger and less appealing seaside towns along the Garden Route. Nevertheless, during the school holidays, the town is packed with domestic visitors. A fact often overlooked in promotional literature is that since the discovery of offshore oil deposits, Mossel Bay is also the home of the ugly Mossgas natural gas refinery and a multitude of oil storage tanks. The town has a number of Portuguese flags and names dotted around, thanks to the first European to anchor in the bay – Bartolomeu Dias, who landed in February 1488, followed by Vasco da Gama, who moored in the bay in 1497. The bay's safe anchorage and freshwater spring ensured that it became a regular stopping-off point for other seafarers, and today many of the local attractions relate to the sea and reflect the bay's importance to the early explorers. The town was named by a Dutch trader, Cornelis de Houtman, who in 1595 found a pile of mussel shells in a cave below the present lighthouse.

Sights
Bartolomeu Dias Museum Complex ① *T044-691 1067, www.diasmuseum.co.za, Mon-Fri 0900-1645, Sat-Sun 0900-1545, R20, children (6-18) R5, under 5s free.* Here you'll find the

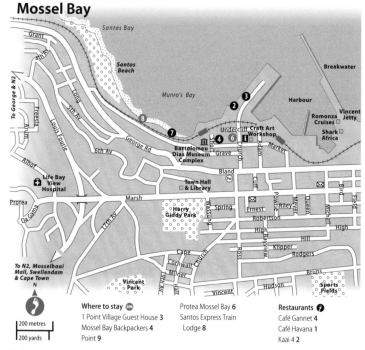

Mossel Bay

Where to stay		Protea Mossel Bay **6**	Restaurants
1 Point Village Guest House **3**		Santos Express Train	Café Gannet **4**
Mossel Bay Backpackers **4**		Lodge **8**	Café Havana **1**
Point **9**			Kaai 4 **2**

Culture Museum, the Shell Museum, an Aquarium, the Maritime Museum, some Malay graves, and the original freshwater spring that attracted the early sailors and which still flows into a small dam. There's also a tea shop on site in a restored 1830s cottage. The displays in the Maritime Museum are arranged around a full-size replica of Bartolomeu Dias's caravel (which you can climb aboard for an extra fee; R20, children R5). Also here is a tree with a fascinating past, the **Post Office Tree**, a giant milkwood situated close to the freshwater spring. History relates that in 1500 a letter was left under the tree by a ship's captain. A year later it was retrieved by the commander of the Third East India Fleet en route to India. Messages were also left carved in rocks and left in old boots tied to the branches. The tree has been declared a national monument and it is still possible to send a postcard home from here – all mail dispatched from the Post Office Tree is franked with a special commemorative stamp and makes a great souvenir.

In the middle of the bay is **Seal Island** which can be visited by cruises departing from the harbour. The island is inhabited by colonies of African penguins and Cape fur seals (the best month to see seal pups is November). Between September and November the warm waters of the bay are often visited by southern right, humpback and Brydes whales while calving. Another vantage point for viewing whales and dolphins is **The Point** at the end of Marsh Street. Close by is the 20-m-high **Cape St Blaize Lighthouse** ⓘ *Montague St, T044-690 3015, Mon-Fri 1000-1500, R15, children (under 12) R7*, built in 1864, one of only two remaining continuously manned lighthouses in South Africa.

St Blaize Trail

The St Blaize Trail is a perfect introduction to the stunning coastline that you are likely to encounter along the Garden Route. This is a 13.5-km walk along the cliffs and rocky coast west from Mossel Bay. The official trail starts from Bats Cave, just below the lighthouse; the path is marked by the white image of a bird in flight. As you walk further from the town the scenery becomes more and more spectacular. You can leave the coast at Pinnacle Point, and follow a path inland to Essenhout Street. This cuts about 5 km off the walk. The path ends by a group of houses in Dana Bay. From here you will have to organize your own transport back into town, so it helps to have a mobile phone to call a taxi from Mossel Bay. A helpful map is available from the tourism office. You are rightly warned to be careful in places during strong winds, as there are some precipitous and unprotected drops from the cliff tops.

Mossel Bay

Huckle
Daley
Beach
Lazaretto
Cemetery
Bland
Lower Cross
Marsh
Upper Cross
Montagu
Point
Cape St Blaize
Lighthouse
Bats Cave
Cape
St Blaize
The
Point
St Blaize Trail
Indian Ocean

Pavilion **7**
Sea Gypsy Café **3**

Botlierskop Private Game Reserve

T044-696 6055, www.botlierskop.co.za. To get there turn off the N2 on to the R401 to the northeast of Mossel Bay, the Klein Brakrivier turn-off, and follow signs for 25 km.

This private reserve is situated on a 2400-ha game farm, which is home to 24 different species of animals and a wide variety of birds. A former farm, the land has been restocked and wildlife includes the rare black impala, rhino, elephant, lion, buffalo, giraffe, mountain zebra and eland. Activities include game drives, nature walks, picnics and horse riding. The most exciting activity is elephant riding, which costs from R590 per person, no children under six. Luxurious accommodation is available (see Where to stay, below) or you can visit for the day, though booking is essential. Check out the website for prices and programmes.

Listings Mossel Bay *maps p150 and p158*

Tourist information

Mossel Bay Tourism Bureau
*Corner of Church and Market Sts,
T044-691 1067, www.visitmosselbay.co.za,
Mon-Fri 0800-1800, Sat-Sun 0900-1600.*
Provides information and acts as a central reservations office for accommodation.

Where to stay

$$$ The Point
*Point Rd, T044-691 3512,
www.pointhotel.co.za.*
Large, ugly construction but in an unbeatable location, right on the rocks below the lighthouse. All 52 rooms have sea views and balconies, but could do with a refurb. **The Lighthouse** restaurant and bar caters for most. The rock pool just outside is good for swimming.

$$$-$$ Protea Hotel Mossel Bay
*corner of Church and Market Sts,
T044-691 3738, www.oldposttree.co.za,
www.proteahotels.com.*
This is part of the museum complex and was formerly known as the **Old Post Office Tree Manor**, with 31 comfortable rooms in a smart manor house dating to 1846, making it the third-oldest building in Mossel Bay. Meals at **Café Gannet**, see Restaurants, page 161, with views across the bay, small swimming pool.

$$ 1 Point Village Guest House
*Bland St East, T044-690 7792,
www.pointguesthouse.co.za.*
Good location near the Point, neat guesthouse with 7 rooms, some with sea views, individually decorated in fresh colours. Heated swimming pool in courtyard, generous breakfasts, also rents out good-value self-catering holiday cottages nearby.

$ Mossel Bay Backpackers
*1 Marsh St, T044-691 3182,
www.mosselbayhostel.co.za.*
Dorms and doubles, breakfasts and dinners available, kitchen, pool, convenient location 300 m from the beach and close to some bars, travel centre can organize activities, such as shark-cage diving. **Baz Bus** stop.

$ Santos Express Train Lodge
*Santos Beach, T044-691 1995,
www.santosexpress.co.za.*
A string of 5 train carriages set 30 m from the sea, with tiny but cheap cabins sleeping 2-4 on bunks, shared hot showers, sun deck and an onboard pub and restaurant serving seafood, spit-roasts and braais. **Baz Bus** stop.

Botlierskop Private Game Reserve

$$$$ Botlierskop Private Game Reserve
T044-696 6055, www.botlierskop.co.za.
19 luxury tented suites on wooden platforms, good views over river and mountains, some have private jetties for fishing, decorated in a

colonial theme with 4-poster beds swathed in mosquito nets. Rates include game drives, walks and all meals.

Restaurants

$$ Café Gannet
Bartolomeu Dias Museum Complex (page 158), Market St, T044-691 1885, www.cafegannet.co.za. Open 0700-2300.
Well-established seafood restaurant, popular all year round since the tour buses stop here, also grills and wood-fired pizzas, bay views from the shady outdoor terrace.

$$ Café Havana
38 Marsh St, T044-690 4640, www.cafehavana.co.za. Open 1200-2200.
Cuban-inspired decor, quirky mirrors and mosaic tables, long tapas and cocktail menu, and unusual mains such as Cuban pork and bean stew or steak with rum and cream. The lively bar stays open until late.

$$ Kaai 4
Quay 4, at the harbour, T084-258 1713, www.kaai4.co.za. Open 1200-1500, 1830-2200, but phone ahead as it's weather dependent.
Open-air restaurant concept that first become popular on the West Coast, with rustic tables in the sand or under canvas on the harbour wall, with an excellent range of traditional South African food such as potbread, *potjiekos*, fish braais, lamb on the spit, and koeksisters for dessert.

$$-$ Sea Gypsy Café
Quay 4, at the harbour, T044-690 5496, www.seagypsy.co.za. Open 0900-2200.
Some meat dishes, but the seafood has literally just been pulled out of the sea. Good-value platters and combos and excellent hake and sole and chips, crayfish in season. The quirky wooden deck decorated with fishing nets and buoys is perfect for sundowners.

$ Pavilion
Santos Beach, T044-690 4567. Open 1000-2300.
Historic seaside pavilion built in 1916 and the ideal spot for lunch, just stroll up straight from the beach onto the old wooden veranda and enjoy a light lunch while watching the boats in the bay.

Entertainment

Theatre
The Barn in Mossel Bay, *7 km west of Mossel Bay off the N2, T044-698 1022, www.thebarns. co.za.* A rustic country theatre showing comedy, tribute bands and live music. Guests sit at wooden tables around the stage and can order a picnic platter.

Shopping

Arts and crafts
Craft Art Workshop, *3 Market St, next to the tourist office, T044-691 1761, www.mosselbayart.co.za. Mon-Fri 0900-1700, Sat 0900-1500.* Sells African curios, many made by local disadvantaged communities, and you can watch artists at work. The **Spinning Cup Coffee Shop** offers lunches, cakes, muffins, scones and traditional melktert.

Shopping malls
Mosselbaai Mall, *Louis Fourie Rd, T044-693 0965, www.mosselbaaimall.co.za. Mon-Fri 0900-1800, Sat 0900-1700, Sun 0900-1400.* Easily accessible from the N2, has more than 60 shops, including a **Checkers** supermarket.

What to do

Boat trip
Romonza, *from Vincent Jetty at the harbour, T044-690 3101, www.mosselbay.co.za/romonza.* Runs daily pleasure cruises, the most popular being outings to Seal Island in the bay. 1-hr boat trips depart on the hour 1000-1600, R145, children (under 12) R65; 2-hr sunset cruise (Dec-Apr) R300, children (under 12) R150 and there's a cash bar. **Romonza** also offers the only licensed boat-based whale watching in Mossel Bay (Jul-Nov), 3 hrs, R660, children (under 12) R400.

Diving

Electro Dive, *Quay 4 at the harbour, T082-561 1259, www.electrodive.co.za*. Can organize equipment hire and boat charters and offers PADI courses. Close to Santos Beach are 4 recognized dive sites that can be reached from the shore, and the Windvogel Reef is 800 m off Cape St Blaize.

White Shark Africa, *Quay 4 at the harbour, T044-691 3796, www.whitesharkafrica.com*. Offers cage diving and snorkelling in pursuit of a great white shark on a 15-m catamaran aptly named *Shark Warrior*. The trip costs R1450 and is 4-5 hrs long and includes lunch and drinks.

Fishing

Mossel Bay Deep Sea Adventures, *T083-260 2222, www.deepseaadventures.co.za*. Full- or half-day deep-sea fishing charters including all equipment, can take children from 8.

Surfing

Billeon, *T082-971 1405, www.billeon.com*. Offers 2-hr surfing lessons at The Point from R350 and rents out boards to experienced surfers. Also runs 3-hr sandboarding trips to Dragon Dune from R380.

Transport

It's 394 km to **Cape Town**, 55 km to **George**, 116 km to **Knysna**, 80 km to **Oudtshoorn**, 206 km to **Tsitsikamma**, 375 km to **Port Elizabeth**. The N2 bypasses Mossel Bay, almost halfway between Cape Town and Port Elizabeth.

Bus

All buses stop at the Shell Truckport at Voorbaai on the N2, 7 km from Mossel Bay; the **Baz Bus** is the only service that goes right into town. Arrange a taxi from your hotel, but remember that some buses pass through in the early hours. **Greyhound**, **Intercape** and **Translux** all stop here daily on the Cape Town–Durban route. **Cape Town** (6 hrs), **Durban** (19 hrs) via **Port Elizabeth** and **East London** (13 hrs). **Intercape** and **Translux** also have a daily service between Mossel Bay and **Johannesburg** and **Tshwane** (**Pretoria**) (16 hrs).

Towards **Cape Town** the **Baz Bus** arrives in Mossel Bay 1530-1545, towards **Port Elizabeth**, 1345-1415. It drops and picks up at all the hostels.

For more information, see Getting around, page 207.

George and around

commercial centre and transport hub, popular with golfers

Often referred to as the capital of the Garden Route, George owes this status to the fact that it has an airport. It is also an important junction between the N2 coastal highway and the N12 passing through the Outeniqua Pass into the Karoo. It lies in the shadow of the Outeniqua Mountains, but unlike the majority of towns along the Garden Route, it is not by the sea. The town itself is a mostly modern grid of streets interspersed with some attractive old buildings and churches. While it is pleasant enough, it has little appeal compared to other towns along the coast; the main reason overseas visitors come here is en route to Oudtshoorn, the capital of the Little Karoo, known for its ostrich farms and the Cango Caves (see page 172), and to play golf. George has several outstanding golf courses and has previously hosted the President's Cup.

BACKGROUND
George

The first settlement appeared here in 1778 as a forestry post to process wood from the surrounding forests. In 1811 it was formally declared a town, and named after King George III. It was at this time that its wide tree-lined streets – Courtenay, York and Meade – were laid out. For the next 80 years the town remained the centre for a voracious timber industry. Much of the indigenous forest was destroyed supplying wood for wagons, railway sleepers and mine props. Some of the trees, which are endemic to South Africa, came to be known as **stinkwoods** because of their odour when freshly cut. Few remain today, although they are slow growing back.

Sights

Within the town itself there are only a few sights of interest. On the corner of Cathedral and York streets, **St Mark's Cathedral**, consecrated in 1850, has an unusually large number of stained-glass windows for its size; many were designed by overseas artists of limited fame. In 1911 a bible and royal prayer book were given to the church by King George V. The interior of the **Dutch Reformed Mother Church** at the north end of Meade Street reflects the town's early history as a centre for the timber industry. The pulpit is carved out of stinkwood and took over a year to create. The ceiling was built from yellowwood, and six yellowwood trunks were used as pillars. The mountains create an impressive backdrop to the church when viewed from the corner of Courtenay and Meade streets.

The small 12-ha **Garden Route Botanical Garden and Southern Cape Herbarium** ① *49 Caledon St, T044-874 1558, www.botanicalgarden.org.za, Sep-Apr 0700-1900, May-Aug 0730-1800, free, tea garden Mon-Fri 1000-1600*, has a wide variety of indigenous trees, flowerbeds, fynbos and succulent plants with the Outeniqua Mountains as a backdrop. It was established on land where two dams were built in the 1800s to send water down into George via a series of stone-lined furrows. The dams are still there: one has become a shallow wetland while the other is a lovely stretch of open water' both attract a number of birds.

In front of the tourist office, housed in the King Edward VII library, is an ancient oak tree known as the **Slave Tree**. It is one of the original trees planted by Adrianus van Kervel in the early 1800s and has been declared a national monument. The tree acquired its name because of the chain embedded in the trunk with a lock attached to it. The story of the chain can be traced back to when a public tennis court was in use next to the library (now the information office), and the court roller was secured to the tree to prevent playful children from rolling it down the street. Housed in the old Drostdy, the **George Museum** ① *Courtenay St, T044-702 3523, Mon-Fri 0900-1630, Sat 0900-1230, entry by donation*, has displays on the timber industry as well as musical instruments and a collection of old printing presses. In the Sayer's Wing is an exhibition devoted to former President PW Botha, who was a member of parliament for George for 38 years. The **Outeniqua Transport Museum** ① *2 Mission Rd, just off Knysna Rd, T044-801 8289, Sep-Apr, Mon-Sat 0800-1700, May-Aug, Mon-Fri 0800-1600, Sat 0800-1400, R20, children (4-12) R10, under 3s free*, has an interesting display outlining the history of steam train travel including 13 steam locomotives, a 1947 Royal Mail coach, and a room dedicated to model railways, as well as a collection of vintage cars and flight memorabilia.

Victoria Bay

If you are based in George and wish to spend a quiet day by the sea, this small resort is only 9 km or 15 minutes' drive away. Victoria Bay, 2 km off the N2, is an excellent place to surf during the winter. It has a narrow cove with a broad sandy beach, a grassy sunbathing area, and a safe tidal pool for children. There's only one row of houses with some of the best-positioned guesthouses in the region.

Listings George and around *map p150*

Tourist information

George Tourism
124 York St, T044-801 9299,
www.georgetourism.org.za,
Mon-Fri 0800-1700, Sat 0900-1300.
Has a wide range of information on the Garden Route.

Where to stay

$$$$ Fancourt Hotel and Country Club
R404, 6 km north of George Airport,
T044-804 0010, www.fancourt.com.
An upmarket resort and one of the world's leading golf destinations, set on 500 ha, with 4 18-hole golf courses, 2 of which were designed by Gary Player. There are 150 rooms in the 19th-century manor house or garden suites, spa, gym, tennis courts, 2 outdoor pools, 1 indoor heated pool, and 3 superb restaurants. Rates drop significantly in low season (1 Apr-31 Aug).

$$ Oakhurst Hotel
Corner of Meade and Cathedral Streets,
T044-874 7130, www.oakhursthotel.co.za.
Centrally located quality town inn in the design of a classic Cape Dutch house with thatched roof, 25 smart, individually decorated rooms, large restaurant, lounge, bar and pool.

$$ Protea Hotel King George
King George Drive, T044-874 7659,
www.proteahotels.com.
Smart country hotel situated close to George Golf Course, with 109 comfortable a/c rooms set in a mock Victorian villa, some

with balconies. Good **Fairway Restaurant** and wood-panelled **Rex Tavern** pub, 2 swimming pools in spacious grounds.

$ Outeniqua Backpackers
115 Merriman St, T082-216 7720,
www.outeniqua-backpackers.com.
Good set-up with dorms and doubles, braai area, breakfasts, DSTV and Wi-Fi. Rents out bikes and they'll drop you off at the top of Montagu Pass for the 15-km ride back down. **Baz Bus** stop and free pickups from George Airport.

Victoria Bay

$$-$ Sea Breeze
300-m walk to the beach, T044-889 0098,
www.seabreezecabanas.co.za.
Modern development of 36 bright and airy self-catering 2- to 4-bed flats and chalets with DSTV and braai. The beach has a safe tidal pool, good for families.

Restaurants

As well as the town restaurants, **Fancourt Hotel and Country Club** (see above) has several superb top-range restaurants open to non-guests.

$$$-$$ La Locanda
124 York St, T044-874 7803, www.la-locanda.
co.za. Mon-Fri 1100- 2200, Sat 1700-2200.
Home-style cooking from Italian chefs who make their own pasta and cure their own cold meats, and there's a long menu of over 60 dishes using well-researched recipes from Italy. South African and Italian wine.

$$ Kafé Serefé
60 Courtenay St, T044-8742046
www.kafeserefe.co.za. Mon-Fri 1130-2230,
Sat 1800-2230.
Elegant interiors with Persian rugs and Arabic lamps, this Turkish restaurant serves a range of mezzes, some melt-in-the-mouth kebabs and aged steaks, and for breakfast, bacon and egg shwarmas. Diners are entertained by a belly dancer on Wed and Sat nights.

$$ Old Town House
Corner of Market and York Streets, T044-874 3663. Mon-Fri 1200-1500, Mon-Sat 1800-late.
Housed in one of George's oldest buildings (1848), which was the original town meeting hall, local specialities include springbok shank and kudu steak, plus seafood and grills, and excellent home-made desserts.

Shopping

Shopping malls
Garden Route Mall, *out of town on the junction with the N2, T044-887 0044, www. gardenroutemall.co.za. Mon-Fri 0900-1800, Sat 0900-1700, Sun 0900-1500.* A 125-store mall with all the usual South African chain stores, restaurants, and a multi-screen Ster-Kinekor cinema. On the opposite of the N2 from the mall, the **Outeniqua Farmers' Market** has 125 food and craft stalls and is held on Sat 0800-1400.

What to do

Golf
Fancourt Hotel and Country Club, *R404, 6 km north of George Airport, T044-804 0030, www.fancourt.com.* 4 gold courses including the par-71, 5935-m, championship links course designed by Gary Player.
George Golf Club, *Langenhoven St, T044-873 6116, www.georgegolfclub.co.za.* Par-72, 18-holes, 5852-m course surrounded by trees. Visitors welcome except Wed and Sat afternoon.

Tour operators
Outeniqua Adventure Tours, *T044-8711470, www.outeniquatours.co.za.* Minibus tours to sights along the Garden Route or Klein Karoo, can also organize cycling tours.

Transport

George is on the N12, 6 km north of the N2, and 55 km south of Oudtshoorn over the Outeniqua Pass. The N2 continues from George to Wilderness, but the alternative route back from the Garden Route to Cape Town is from Oudtshoorn via the scenic Route 62 east to Worcester and then the N1; a distance of roughly 450 km. If you're short of time, or not returning to Cape Town, the easiest access is to Oudtshoorn is from George.

It's 420 km to **Cape Town**, 320 km to **Port Elizabeth**, 61 km to **Knysna**, 55 km to **Mossel Bay**, 93 km to **Plettenberg Bay**, 151 km to **Tsitsikamma**, 60 km to **Oudtshoorn**.

Air
George Airport *(T044-876 9310, www.acsa. co.za)* is 10 km southeast of the town centre. It has ATMs, restaurants and car rental desks. You'll need to pre-arrange a shuttle with your hotel or take a taxi, **Eden Taxis** *(T044-587 8490)*. The main car rental companies have desks in the terminal building (see below).

FlySafair and SAA have daily flights between George and **Cape Town** (1 hr), and **Johannesburg** (1 hr 45 mins). **Kulula** and **Mango** have daily flights between George and **Johannesburg** (1 hr 45 mins).

Airline offices All air tickets can be booked online at www.computicket.com. **FlySafair** *(www.flysafair.co.za)*, **Kulula** *(www. kulula.com)*, **Mango** *(www.fly mango.com)*. **South African Airways** *(SAA, www.flysaa.com)*. For further details, see pages 205 and 206.

Bus
All buses stop at the old railway station at the east end of Market St. **Greyhound**,

Intercape and **Translux** run daily to **Cape Town** (6 hrs) and **Durban** (18 hrs) via **Knysna** (1 hr), **East London** (9 hrs) and **Port Elizabeth** (4 hrs). **Translux** and **Intercape** also have a daily service between George and **Johannesburg** (14 hrs) and **Tshwane** (**Pretoria**) (16 hrs) via **Bloemfontein** (9 hrs).

Towards **Cape Town** the **Baz Bus** arrives in George 1430-1450; towards **Port Elizabeth**, 1515-1530; and drops off at **Outeniqua Backpackers** (see page 164).

For more information, see Getting around, page 206.

Car hire
The car hire companies all have desks at the airport. **Avis** *(T044-876 9314, www. avis.co.za)*; **Budget** *(T044-876 9204, www. budget.co.za)*; **Hertz** *(T044-801 4700, www. hertz.co.za)*; **Tempest** *(T044-876 9250, www. tempestcarhire.co.za)*.

Oudtshoorn
appealing ostrich-farming capital in a fertile valley surrounded by high peaks

By far the largest settlement in the Little Karoo, this is a pleasant administrative centre which still retains much of the calm of its early days. It is a major tourist centre and the two major reasons for coming here are the countless ostrich farms that surround the town and the superb Cango Caves. There are also several nature reserves and scenic drives, which are introductions to the diversity of the landscape. Oudtshoorn itself is appealing, with broad streets, smart sandstone Victorian houses, many of which are now B&Bs, and a good choice of restaurants. The centre of town is compact and it is easy to find your way about on foot, but you'll need transport to see the outlying sights such as the Cango Caves and ostrich farms.

Sights
Within the town limits there is little to see aside from appreciating the sandstone Victorian buildings. There are several **ostrich palaces** in town, which unfortunately are not open to the public, but are still worth a look from the outside for their ornate exteriors. Most examples are in the old part of town on the west bank of the Grobbelaars River. Look out for **Pinehurst**, on St John Street, designed by a Dutch architect, and **Gottland House**, built in 1903 with an octagonal tower. Other buildings of note include **Mimosa Lodge**, **Oakdene** and **Rus in Urbe**. Unfortunately, many fine Victorian buildings were demolished in the 1950s.

The **Catholic Cathedral**, on Baron von Rheede Street, is a fascinating modern cruciform building with splendid stained-glass windows and a chapel beneath the main altar. The cathedral houses two notable works of art: the first is a painting given by Princess Eugenie in memory of her brother – the last of the Bonapartes, who died fighting with the British against the Boers. The second is a replica of a Polish icon incorporating childhood items from refugee children sent to Oudtshoorn during the Second World War; the children returned bearing the gift to celebrate the 50th anniversary of their evacuation.

In the centre of town, the **CP Nel Museum** ⓘ *3 Baron van Rheede St, T044-272 7306, www.cpnelmuseum.co.za, Mon-Fri 0800-1700, Sat 0900-1300, R20, children (under 16) R5*, is a fine sandstone building with a prominent clock tower and was originally built as a boys' high school. The masons who designed the building had been brought to Oudtshoorn by the 'feather barons' to build their grand mansions. The displays include a reconstructed trading store, synagogue and chemist, plus an interesting section on the history of the ostrich boom and the characters involved. The rest of the collection of historic objects was bequeathed to the town by CP Nel, a local businessman. A short walk away is **Le Roux Town House** ① *146 High St*, which is part of the CP Nel Museum and the entry fee covers both. This classic town house was built in 1908 and provides a real feel for how the wealthy lived in the fine ostrich palaces of Oudtshoorn. The interior and furnishings are in art nouveau style and the furniture was shipped from Europe between 1900 and 1920. During the summer, teas are served in the garden. **Arbeidsgenot** ① *Jan van Riebeeck Rd*, is the former home of Senator Cornelius Langenhoven, a leading figure in the history of the Afrikaans language who wrote the old national anthem of South Africa.

Listings Oudtshoorn maps p150 and below

Tourist information

Oudtshoorn Tourist Bureau
Baron van Rheede St, T044-279 2532, www.oudtshoorn.com, Mon-Fri 0800-
1800, Sat 0830-1300.
Has a well-informed, enthusiastic and helpful team and is worth a visit for details on accommodation and the less well-known sights of the Karoo.

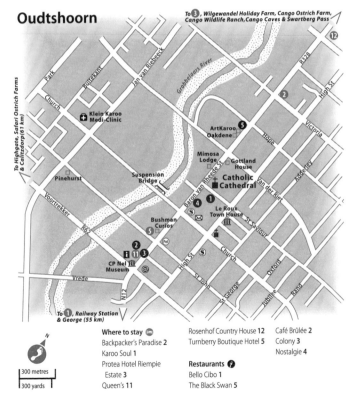

Oudtshoorn

Where to stay	Rosenhof Country House 12	Café Brûlée 2
Backpacker's Paradise 2	Turnberry Boutique Hotel 5	Colony 3
Karoo Soul 1		Nostalgie 4
Protea Hotel Riempie	**Restaurants**	
Estate 3	Bello Cibo 1	
Queen's 11	The Black Swan 5	

Where to stay

$$$ Queen's Hotel
5 Baron van Rheede St, T044-272 2101,
www.queenshotel.co.za.
Elegant and historic central hotel (1880) next
to the CP Nel Museum, with 40 a/c stylish
and comfortable rooms, impressive marble
foyer, excellent restaurant, café and deli (see
Restaurants, below), bar, pool in courtyard.

$$$ Rosenhof Country House
264 Baron van Rheede St, T044-272 2232,
www.rosenhof.co.za.
Victorian house (1852) with 12 a/c upmarket
rooms, 2 suites have their own splash
pools, beautiful rose garden, spa, gym,
pool, fine food in the restaurant, pub, and
cosy lounge with fireplaces decorated with
valuable artwork.

$$ Protea Hotel Riempie Estate
Baron van Rheede St, 3 km north of town,
T044-272 6161, www.proteahotels.com.
Well-run Protea with easy access to the
ostrich farms on the R328. 29 a/c rooms in
comfortable thatched rondavels opening up
to the mature shady gardens, the restaurant
offers tasty country cuisine, swimming pool.

$$ Turnberry Boutique Hotel
130 St John St, T044-279 3268,
www.turnberryhotel.co.za.
Centrally located town hotel with 21 neat
rooms, restaurant with outside patio, friendly
tavern-style pub that's a focal point in town,
and a courtyard splash pool. Short walk to
sights on Baron von Rheede St.

$$-$ Karoo Soul
1 Adderley St, T044-272 0330,
www.karoosoul.com.
Good-value budget lodge set in a mock-
Tudor house with wide veranda and good
views across town, doubles/twins, dorms
and camping plus separate self-catering
cottages sleeping 4, thatched bar, meals
available. A peaceful option for families.

$ Backpacker's Paradise
148 Baron van Rheede St, T044-272 3436,
www.backpackersparadise.hostel.com.
Well-run lodge set over 4 houses, mix of
dorms and en suite doubles, camping,
volleyball court, kitchen, pub with pool
table, nightly ostrich braais, splash pool,
Wi-Fi, within walking distance of shops, free
pickup from the **Baz Bus** in George. Plenty
of activities can be organized from here
including bike hire (see page 170).

Restaurants

$$$ Colony
Queen's Hotel, see Where to stay, above.
Open 1800-2300.
Excellent restaurant set in this historic hotel,
local dishes include Karoo lamb, springbok
steak and ostrich. Balcony overlooking the
main street, good service, crisp white linen
and bar with fireplace.

$$ Bello Cibo
79 St Saviour St, just off Baron Van Reede
St, T044-242 3245, www.bellocibo.co.za.
Mon-Sat 1700-2230.
This friendly trattoria has generous portions
of all the Italian staples plus ostrich,
springbok, kudu and sometimes crocodile.
For something different try the ostrich
carpaccio, ostrich and vodka pasta or ostrich
saltimbocca. Bello Cibo means 'beautiful
food' in Italian.

$$ The Black Swan
109 Baron van Reede St, T044-272 0982,
www.blackswanoudtshoorn.co.za. Mon-Sat
1700-2200, Sun buffet lunch 1100-1500.
Restaurant and wine bar in a stocky
sandstone Oudtshoorn house, the menu is
short but has traditional dishes like oxtail,
ostrich fillet and Cape Malay curry, as well
as a good choice of seafood and pizza.

$$ Nostalgie
74 Baron van Reede St, T044-272 4085, www.
nostalgiebnb.co.za. Mon-Sat 0700-2200.

BACKGROUND

Oudtshoorn

In 1838 a small church was inaugurated on the Hartebeestrivier Farm to serve the farmers who had settled along the banks of the Olifants and Grobbelaars rivers. Nine years later the village of Oudtshoorn was founded when land was subdivided and sold by the surveyor J Ford. The town was named after Baron Van Rheede van Oudtshoorn, who died on his way to the Cape to take up the post of governor in 1773. In 1858 the first group of British immigrants settled in the village.

When visiting during the dry season it is easy to see how for many years the supply of water to the new settlement restricted its growth. A severe drought in 1865 persuaded many established farmers to move on and most made the long trek to the Transvaal. In its early days, water was brought to the town in barrels and then sold to households at sixpence a bucket. But the local farmers learnt to cope with this handicap and many of South Africa's early irrigation experts came from the region. When you cross the Grobbelaars River in the centre of town during the dry season, all the bridges and culverts seem redundant but they provide ample evidence of how much water can pass through when it rains. If you have time, walk across the Victorian **Suspension Bridge** where Church Street crosses the river; this is now a protected national monument.

It was the advent of two ostrich-feather booms (1865-1870 and 1900-1914) that truly established the town, and led to the erection of the fine sandstone buildings and 'ostrich palaces' that now line Oudtshoorn's streets. For a period of almost 40 years it was the most important settlement east of Cape Town. At the peak of its fortunes, ostrich feathers were selling for more than their weight in gold – little wonder that so many birds were bred. While ostrich farming no longer brings in as much wealth, it remains an important business in the Karoo. Today, it is the production of specialized agricultural seed which contributes most to the region's wealth.

In a lovely old house with fireplace and stoep overlooking the main street, a great place to try traditional home-cooked South African food and the warm hospitality that the Karoo is known for. Dinners include bobotie, ostrich, and Karoo lamb, and also serves breakfasts, light lunches and afternoon teas and has some B&B rooms.

Cafés

Café Brûlée
Queen's Hotel, see Where to stay, opposite.
Open 0700-1700.

Airy and elegant café with outside tables among potted palms, serving breakfasts, delicious and beautifully presented cakes. Wed-Fri there is a lunchtime table buffet priced by weight, the deli sells freshly baked bread, olive oil, jams and cook books.

Shopping

Baron van Rheede St is lined with curio shops selling every ostrich by-product imaginable, from expensive leather purses to feather dusters and tacky enamelled eggs.
ArtKaroo, *107 Baron van Reede St, T044-279 1093, www.artkaroo.co.za.* Talented

local artists are represented here in fine paintings and sculpture. Also organizes artists workshops and field trips, film and book nights.

What to do

Mountain biking

Mountain biking trips to the Swartberg Pass are run by **Backpacker's Paradise** *(www. backpackersparadise.hostel.com, see Where to stay, page 168)*. They leave daily at 0830; you are driven to the top and enjoy the 15-km long ride downhill. On the way back to Oudtshoorn, you can stop at the Cango Caves and all the other attractions along the R328. They also organize plenty of other activities as well as bus transfers to the Cango Caves and ostrich farms.

Transport

Oudtshoorn is 55 km north of **George** and the junction with the N2 coastal road. The quickest route from the Garden Route is to drive from George and head north over the Outeniqua Pass (N12), but another route goes from **Mossel Bay** (93 km) over the Robinson Pass (R328). Alternatively, **Cape Town** is roughly 450 km from Oudtshoorn via the scenic Route 62 east to Worcester and then the N1. **Greyhound** and **Intercape** buses stop at Oudtshoorn daily on the route between Mossel Bay and Johannesburg via Bloemfontein.

Around Oudtshoorn

working ostrich farms where tourists can learn all about this curious bird

Visiting an ostrich farm in the area can be great fun, although the appeal of riding ostriches, feeding ostriches, buying ostrich eggs and leather, or eating ostrich-egg omelette can fade quickly. To keep visitors for longer, some farms have introduced different species. Visiting the farms or the Cango Caves without your own transport can be surprisingly tricky. There are no tour companies that organize daily trips, although it is possible to find a guide through the tourist office in Oudtshoorn. Otherwise, you might want to hire a car for the day.

Safari Ostrich Farm

6 km from Oudtshoorn off the R328 towards Mossel Bay road, T044-272 7311, www.safariostrich. co.za, 0800-1600, R110, children (under 14) R55, 1-hr tours depart every hour, on the hour.

As well as the usual array of ostrich rides, educational exhibits and curio shops, there is also a smart homestead known as Welgeluk. The house was built in 1910, and is a perfectly preserved example of an ostrich palace. There are roof tiles from Belgium, teak from Burma and expanses of marble floors, proof of the wealth and influence the short-lived boom brought to Oudtshoorn families. Unfortunately, the house is closed to visitors; the closest you can get is the main gate.

Highgate Ostrich Farm

10 km from Oudtshoorn off the R328 towards Mossel Bay, T044-272 7115, www.highgate. co.za, 0800-1700, R125, children (under 16) R75, 1½-hr tours depart every hour, on the hour.

A very popular show farm named after the London suburb, Highgate has been owned by the Hooper family since the 1850s and opened its gates to visitors in 1938. You will learn everything there is to know about the bird, and can then try your hand at riding (or even racing) them. Snacks and drinks are served on the porch of the homestead.

Cango Wildlife Ranch

Shoemanshoek Valley along the R328 towards Cango Caves, 3 km from Oudtshoorn, T044-272 5593, www.cango.co.za, 0800-1700, R145, children (4-13) R90, under 4s free,

The ranch provokes mixed opinions as it is, in effect, a zoo which stocks animals including white lions, leopards, cheetahs and, oddly, jaguars, pumas and rare white Bengal tigers. There is even an albino python. However, the ranch is a leading player in conservation and breeding, particularly with cheetah and wild dog, and the enclosures are very spacious. After walking safely above the animals, you have the choice of paying a little more to pet a cheetah, or you can visit the restaurant. One of the most impressive attractions here is the **Valley of the Ancients**, a well-forested string of lakes and enclosures connected by boardwalks that are home to a number of unusual animals. The pools are home to Nile crocodiles, pygmy hippos, monitor lizards and otters, while birds include flamingos and marabou storks. You can watch the crocodiles being fed by hand and this is probably the only place in the world that offers cage diving with crocodiles (R340; children must be over 14).

Schoemanshoek

Following the R328 north, the road passes several ostrich farms and then follows the Grobbelaars River Valley towards the Cango Caves (see below). The little village of Schoemanshoek, 15 km from Oudtshoorn, is in a lush valley with small farms and homesteads and has some good places to stay.

Cango Ostrich Farm

Shoemanshoek Valley along the R328 towards Cango Caves, 14 km from Oudtshoorn, T044-272 4623, www.cangoostrich.co.za, 0800-1630, R85, children R50, 45-min tours depart every 20 mins.

One of several attractions on the way to Cango Caves, the farm attractions are also within walking distance of each other. You can interact directly with the birds, sit on or ride them, buy local curios and sample Karoo wines and cheeses.

Wilgewandel Holiday Farm

Shoemanshoek Valley along the R328 towards Cango Caves, 25 km from Oudtshoorn, T044-272 0878, www.wilgewandel.co.za, 0800-1500, camel rides R50, children (3-13) R30, other activities R10-30 per person.

A pleasant change from all the ostriches, this farm offers you the chance to ride a camel. There are also lots of attractions for children such as farmyard animals, a pet area, trampolines, waterslides, bumper boats, donkey cart rides, and a restaurant serving anything from tea and scones to crocodile and ostrich steaks.

Listings Around Oudtshoorn

Where to stay

$$$ Altes Landhaus
13 km north of Oudtshoorn towards the Cango Caves, T044-272 6112, www.alteslandhaus.co.za.

Award-winning guesthouse in a Cape Dutch homestead that used to be a rectory, 10 spacious rooms, each has its own special character, evening meals with fine wines, salt pool in garden with pool bar.

$$ Oue Werf
13 km north of Oudtshoorn off the
road to Cango Caves, T044-272 8712,
www.ouewerf.co.za.
Old 1857 homestead with 13 comfortable
B&B rooms in the farm house or in cottages
decorated with antiques, and some have
original reed ceilings. Pleasant gardens with
pool and the **Orchard Deli and Coffee Shop**
(Tue-Sun, 0800-1600) which also offers
4-course evening meals on request.

Cango Caves

impressive subterranean wonderland of caverns and stalagmites

Tucked away in the foothills of the Swartberg Mountains 29 km from Oudtshoorn, the Cango Caves are a magnificent network of calcite caves, recognized as among the world's finest dripstone caverns. In 1938 they were made a national monument. Despite being seriously hyped and very touristy, they are well worth a visit. Allow a morning for a round trip if based locally; if you have a car it is possible to visit them and Oudtshoorn on a day trip from towns along the Garden Route such as Mossel Bay, George and Wilderness.

The only access to the caves is on a guided tour. The standard one-hour tour is a good introduction to the caves and allows you to see the most impressive formations. It is, however, aimed at tour groups, so visitors with a special interest may find it rather simplistic. During the tour, each section is lit up and the guide points out interesting formations and their given names. Although one small chamber is lit in gaudy colours, the rest are illuminated with white light to best show off the formations. These are turned off behind you as you progress further into the system as research has shown that continued exposure to light causes damage to the caves. The adventure tour lasts for 1½ hours, is over 1 km long and there are over 400 stairs. This can be disturbing for some people, since it involves crawling along narrow tunnels, and at the very end climbing up the Devil's Chimney, a narrow vertical shaft. It leads up for 3.5 m and is only 45 cm wide in parts – definitely not for broad people. If at any stage you feel you can't go on, inform the guide who will arrange for you to be led out. Although strenuous, this tour allows you to see most of the caves, and gives a real feeling of exploration. The caves are usually around 20°C, so a T-shirt and shorts will be fine. Wear shoes with reasonable grip, as after rain the floors can become a little slippery. During the holidays it gets very crowded and nearly 200,000 people pass through the caves each year. Each tour has a maximum

Essential Cango Vaves

Cave information

On the R328 29 km north of Oudtshoorn, T044-272 7410, www.cangocaves.co.za. 0900-1700, standard one-hour tour departs every hour on the hour last tour 1600, R80, children (5-15) R45, under 5s free, 1½-hour adventure tour, half past every hour 0930-1530, R100, children (6-15; minimum age is six) R60, curio shop.

$$-$ Cango Caves Restaurant
T044-272 7313. Open 0900-1700.
Caters for tour groups but surprisingly good food and has terrace tables with views of the Swartberg Mountains. Breakfasts, light lunches, teas, the menu has a distinctive ostrich flavour – burgers, kebabs, steaks, or try the ostrich *potjie* with ginger and wild herbs or ostrich tempura with noodles.

BACKGROUND

Wilderness

The first European to settle in the district was a farmer, Van der Bergh, who built himself a simple farmhouse in the 1850s. But it was in 1877 that the name was first used, when a young man from Cape Town, George Bennet, was granted the hand of his sweetheart only on condition that he took her to live in the wilderness. He purchased some land where the present-day **Wilderness Hotel** stands and promptly named it 'wilderness' (of dense bush and forest) to appease his new father-in-law. At this time the only road access was from the Seven Passes Road between George and Knysna, and Bennet cut a track from this road to his new farmhouse. In 1905 the homestead was converted it into a boarding house, and when the property changed hands in 1921, the farmhouse/boarding house underwent further alterations and the Wilderness Hotel came into being.

number of people, so you may have to wait an hour or more. It's a good idea to get here early in the morning to avoid queues, or alternatively pre-book.

Wilderness and around
peaceful base with good hiking, indigenous forests and placid lagoons

This appealing little town is an ideal base for exploring the Garden Route and has a superb swathe of sandy beach. Check locally for demarcated areas for swimming and surfing. Children should be supervised in the sea as there are strong rip currents. One of the safest spots for swimming is in the Touw River mouth. Except for the few hectic weeks at Christmas and New Year, Wilderness is generally very relaxed and has an excellent range of accommodation. The highlight is the Wilderness Section of the Garden Route National Park, a quiet, well-managed area of the park, with three levels of self-catering accommodation and a campsite.

The town itself doesn't have much of a centre, but stretches instead up the lush foothills of the Outeniqua Mountains and along leafy streets by the lake and river. The supermarket, restaurants, post office and tourist office are by the petrol station, where the N2 crosses the Serpentine channel.

Garden Route National Park (Wilderness Section)
Off the N2, 4 km east of Wilderness, reception, T044-877 1197, www.sanparks.org, 0700-2000, R112, children (2-11) R56. There are 2 rest camps and the nearest supermarkets and restaurants are in Wilderness.

This section of the Garden Route National Park stretches from the Touw Rivermouth to the Swartvlei Estuary, covers 2612 ha and incorporates five rivers and four lakes as well as a 28-km stretch of the coastline. The four lakes are known as Island, Langvlei, Rondevlei and Swartvlei, and are situated between the Outeniqua foothills and sand dunes which back onto a beautiful, long sandy beach. The main attractions are the dense hardwood forest, the water and the birdlife in the reed beds affording the opportunity to encounter the brilliantly coloured Knysna lourie, or one of the five kingfisher species that occur here.

During spring, a carpet of flowers on the forest floor further enhances the verdant beauty of the park.

There are two ways in which to enjoy the surroundings; on foot or in a canoe. You can cover more ground by walking, but canoeing is ideal for seeing birds. There are five walking trails in the park from 2 km to 10 km. The most popular is the **Half-collared & Giant Kingfisher Trail**, a 7-km circular route, which can be completed in three or four hours and goes through forest and along the riverbank where there are picnic spots. The other walks are also forest walks, except for the 3-km **Dune Molerat Trail**, which takes you through dune fynbos where you may see proteas in flower in season. Maps are available at reception.

Eden Adventures (see below), who have an office at the Fairy Knowe Hotel, hires out canoes with waterproof containers for picnics and cameras and a map. One of the more interesting short routes is to paddle up the Touw River past the Ebb and Flow Camps. This quickly becomes a narrow stream and you have to leave your canoe. A path continues along the bank of the stream through some beautiful riverine forest and a 2-km boardwalk takes you to a waterfall where you can swim. Eden Adventures also organizes abseiling and kloofing.

Listings Wilderness and around *map p150*

Tourist information

Wilderness Tourism
Leila's Lane, T044-877 0045, www. wildernessinfo.org, Mon-Fri 0800-1700, Sat 0900-1300.
A very helpful office, especially when it comes to finding good-value accommodation during the peak season.

Where to stay

$$$ Dolphin Dunes
Buxton Close, approaching from George, turn right off the N2, 2.5 km after the Caltex petrol station T044-877 0204, www.dolphindunes.co.za.
A fine upmarket purpose-built guesthouse with 9 tasteful rooms with ocean views, minibar and DSTV, some with wheelchair access, splash pool, private access to the beach on a boardwalk.

$$ Fairy Knowe
Dumbleton Rd, T044-877 1100, www.fairyknowe.co.za.
A historic old hotel with 42 riverside rooms, restaurant and bar with wooden deck, in a beautiful and peaceful forested location on the Touw River. Birdwatchers will enjoy regular visits from the Knysna lourie and there are a couple of resident Cape spotted eagle owls.

$$ Moontide Guest Lodge
Southside Rd, T044-877 0361, www.moontide.co.za.
Award-winning guesthouse set under milkwood trees in a beautiful and tranquil garden right on the edge of the lagoon, with 8 delightful thatched cottages, one of them a honeymoon suite, each with tasteful decor with kilims and fine furniture. Easy access to the hiking trails in the national park, a short walk from the beach and a good spot for birdwatchers.

$$ Palms Wilderness Retreat
Waterside Rd, T044-877 1420, www.palms-wilderness.com.
Thatched guesthouse with 11 spacious a/c rooms, lounge and bar, spa, swimming pool in intriguing garden with nooks and crannies under milkwood trees that are full of birds, gallery selling some carefully chosen African artifacts.

$ Fairy Knowe Backpackers
Dumbleton Rd, just off Waterside Rd, T044-877 1285, www.wildernessbackpackers.com.
A great set-up in a farmhouse dating to 1874 with tight staircases and creaking wooden floors surrounded by gardens, spotless dorms and doubles, camping space, bar, great breakfasts, nightly camp fires and braais. Can organize all activities. A very relaxing place to rest up for a few days. **Baz Bus** stops here.

Garden Route National Park (Wilderness Section)

$$-$ Ebb and Flow
Turn right in the village to reception, reservations through SANParks, T012-428 9111, www.sanparks.org, for reservations under 72 hrs or cancellations contact the park reception directly, T044-877 1197.
Accommodation is laid out in 2 camps (North and South) divided by the railway and the Touw River. Both have self-catering units sleeping up to 4 in cottages, log cabins, or cheaper forest cabins with shared kitchens, some with views of the river and reed beds. The nearest shop is in the village.

Camping
Both campsites are in beautiful locations on the banks of the river and have plenty of grass and shade, wash block, no communal kitchen but braais, some sites have electric points.

Restaurants

$$$-$$ The Girls Restaurant
1 George St, next to the Caltex petrol station at the N2 turn-off, T044-877 1648, www.thegirls.co.za. Tue-Sun 1800-2200.
A simple brick building, but surprisingly warm and inviting inside and owners/chefs entertain in the open kitchen. Dinner only and expect Knysna oysters, prawns cooked in more than a dozen ways, excellent steaks and curries, and inventive vegetarian dishes.

$$-$ Pomodoro
George St, T044-877 1403, www.pomodoro.co.za. Open 0730-2230.
Traditional Italian trattoria (look out for the big red tomato signs) with generous portions of antipasto, pastas, grills and seafood, specials like venison and tuna, classic desserts. Also serves breakfasts and has outside tables among ferns.

$ Zucchini
At the Timberlake Organic Village (see Shopping, below), on the N2, 7 km from both Wilderness and Sedgefield, T044-882 1240, www.zucchini.co.za. Tue-Sun 1100-2100, closes at 1700 on Tue.
Wooden cabin decorated with local art, sunny outside deck, serving tasty organic light meals such as gourmet salads and sandwiches using free-range beef and poultry, milk and dairy products from local farms and home-grown produce.

Shopping

Food and drink
Timberlake Organic Village, *off the N2 midway between Wilderness and Sedgefield, 7 km to both, www.timberlake organic.co.za. Open 0900-1700.* A collection of charming wooden cabins including a deli, cheese, wine and health-food shops, a café (great for cheesecake and chocolate cupcakes), a shack selling oysters and other seafood snacks, and the **Zucchini** restaurant (see above). All produce is organic, locally sourced, and the vegetables are grown in the on-site garden. Children will enjoy the jungle gym and trampoline, and exploring the enchanting Fairy Garden.

What to do

Garden Route National Park (Wilderness Section)
Tour operators
Eden Adventures, *at the Fairy Knowe Hotel, T044-877 0179, www.eden.co.za (also see page 174).* Offer canoeing, kloofing, abseiling

and walking tours. The guides are very knowledgeable about the environment and are happy to answer endless questions.

Transport

Bus
Translux, Greyhound and Intercape stop at the Caltex garage in Wilderness, 20 mins before or after **George**. Towards **Cape Town** the **Baz Bus** arrives in Wilderness 1330-1345; towards **Port Elizabeth**, 1545-1600, and drops off at **Fairy Knowe Backpackers** (page 175). For more information, see page 207.

Sedgefield and around

sleepy village surrounded by lakes, estuaries and sand dunes

Between Wilderness and Knysna, Sedgefield is a long village strung along the N2 which was founded in 1929 by local farmers. It is surrounded by a magnificent coastal lake-system and five sandy beaches.

Since 2010 Sedgefield has adapted a 'slow town' ethos affiliated to 'Cittaslow International' (www.slowtown.co.za), founded in Italy in the 1990s. Its goals include improving the quality of life in towns by slowing down its overall pace, promoting sustainable living and encouraging local enterprize. In Sedgefield this ethos is reflected in (among other things) the village motto of being a place where 'the tortoise sets the pace' (look out for the tortoise sculptures), the markets selling fresh produce and local crafts produced by the close-knit farming and artisan community, and the **Slow Festival** every Easter (see page 177). Additionally the countryside around the village is spectacular and very peaceful. Between the main road and the beach is the **Swartvlei Lagoon**, South Africa's largest natural inland saltwater lake, most of which lies on the inland side of the N2. The lake is a popular spot for birdwatching, and look out for the secretive starred robin, the blue mantle flycatcher, the difficult-to-see Victorian warbler and the rare African finfoot.

Goukamma Nature Reserve
Turn off the N2 at the Buffalo Bay signpost where the N2 crosses the Goukamma River, follow road for 8 km and turn right, T044-802 5310, www.capenature.co.za, 0800-1800, R40, children (2-13) R20. For information on accommodation, see page 177.

On the Knysna side of Sedgefield is another lake, Groenvlei or Lake Pleasant, a freshwater lake lying within the Goukamma Nature Reserve. It was established to protect 2230 ha of the hinterland between Sedgefield and Buffalo Bay and a 13-km sandy beach with some magnificent sand dunes covered in fynbos and patches of forest containing milkwood trees. The **Goukamma River** estuary in the eastern part of the reserve has been cut off from the sea by the large sand dunes. The lake is now fed by natural drainage and springs, and is surrounded by reed beds which are excellent for birdwatching; more than 220 species have been identified including the rare African black oystercatcher. There are six hiking trails within the reserve from 4.2 km to 15 km and maps are available at the office. The circular 6.5-km **Bush Pig Trail** starts from the office and takes about two or three hours. It runs along a fynbos-covered ridge of dunes, with fine views of the ocean and lakes, and returns via a milkwood forest. Other trails follow the beach. On any of the walks in the reserve, always carry plenty of drinking water and keep an eye out for snakes, especially among the sand dunes.

Tourist information

Sedgefield Tourism
*30 Main Rd, T044-343 2658, www.
visitsedgefield.com, Mon-Fri 0800-1700,
Sat 0830-1300.*
Has good information on local events and
accommodation.

Where to stay

$$$ Lake Pleasant
*East of Sedgefield on the edge of
Groenvlei, follow the Buffalo Bay
signs from the N2, T044-349 2400,
www.lakepleasantliving.co.za.*
Comfortable country hotel set right on the
lake, 36 rooms opening onto gardens, cigar
bar, restaurant, pool, tennis court, gym and
spa. Rowing boats for hire and hides by the
lake for birdwatching.

$$ Lake Pleasant Chalets and Lodges
*Follow the Buffalo Bay signs from the N2,
T044-343 1985, www.lake-pleasant.co.za.*
Self-catering timber chalets sleeping 2-6,
with plenty of shade from milkwood trees.
Peaceful location overlooking the lake,
swimming pool, pub/restaurant, rents out
mountain bikes, canoes and fishing tackle.

$$ Sedgefield Arms
*3 Pelican Lane, off the N2 in the village centre,
T044-343 1417, www.sedgefieldarms.co.za.*
Mix of self-catering cottages suitable for
2-6 people with patio and braai, or B&B.
Attached restaurant and lively English theme
pub, good spot for lunch on the lawn, pool,
all set in leafy gardens.

Goukamma Nature Reserve
*For reservations, T021-659 3500,
www.capenature.org.za.*

Self-catering houses
There are 4 very comfortable self-catering
houses (**$$**) each sleeping 4, dotted around
the reserve, plus the **Muvubu Bushcamp**
which is a thatched house hidden away in
a milkwood forest sleeping up to 8. Each
house has a kitchen and braai area and is
a short walk from the lake, where you can
swim; canoes are available at each house.

Festivals

Easter **Slow Festival**, www.slowfestival.
co.za. Celebrating Sedgefield's community
spirit, this weekend of events and includes
food and beer stalls, cooking demos, live
entertainment, children's activities, fun runs,
raft races and a 'slow' bike race–competitors
ride as slowly as possible without falling off
and the winner is the one that comes last.

Shopping

Arts and crafts
Scarab Art and Craft Village, *on the N2
next to the Engen petrol station, T044-343
2455, www.scarabvillage.co.za. Open 0900-
1700.* Well worth a stop for the interesting
craft shops and stalls including one that
demonstrates making handmade paper, and
refreshments at the **Windpomp Diner** and
Sedgefield Craft Brewery. Also here is the
Wild Oats Market, www.wildoatsmarket.
co.za, a Sat-morning farmer's market.

What to do

Paragliding
FlyTime Paragliding, *T072-612 8168, www.
flytimeparagliding.com.* There are many
thermic sites around Sedgefield and
Wilderness, which are perfect for paragliding
with amazing beach and lake views. Tandem
flights cost R550 for 10 mins; R950/20 mins,
DVDs and photos extra, can arrange pickups
from accommodation between George
and Knysna.

Transport

Bus

Greyhound, **Intercape** and **Translux**

services stop at the Shell garage, 15 mins before or after **Knysna** (see below). The **Baz Bus** stops in Sedgefield on request.

★Knysna and around

lively upmarket holiday town famous for its oysters, waterfront and views of the Knysna Heads

Knysna (the 'K' is silent) is the self-proclaimed heart of the Garden Route and lies on the N2 (which goes through town as Main Road). It is no longer the sleepy lagoon-side village it once was – far from it – but is nevertheless a pleasant spot to spend a day or two. The town itself is fully geared up for tourists, which means a lot of choice in accommodation and restaurants, as well as overcrowding and high prices. It remains quite an arty place, though, and many of the craftspeople who have gravitated to the region display their products in craft shops and galleries. Nevertheless, development is continually booming and has set the pace for Knysna to become the Garden Route's most popular residential and lifestyle destination. A number of years ago a slick waterfront complex complete with glitzy shops and restaurants known as the **Knysna Quays** was developed around the old harbour, while more recently an extensive marina has been built on Thesen's Island with apartments and hotels, man-made beaches, sports fields and other recreational activities and is linked to the mainland by a causeway. If you're trying to choose between Knysna and Plettenberg Bay as a base, Knysna offers more amenities and activities, while Plett is far more relaxed and has the better beach. Both get very busy during high season. The centre of town is compact and it is easy to find your way about on foot, but you'll need transport to see the outlying sights.

Sights

Although there are a couple of sights and museums in the town, Knysna's highlights are its natural attractions. The **Knysna National Lakes**, a broad largely undefined region of protected areas, is wonderful to explore, comprising lakes, islands, seashore and beach.

Along with Wilderness and Tsitsikamma, the area is now administered by SANParks as part of the Garden Route National Park, and is now referred to as the **Knysna Lakes Section**. The most accessible area, and the main feature of the town is the **lagoon** around which much of Knysna life revolves. **The Heads**, the rocky promontories that lead from the lagoon to the open sea, are quite stunning. More than 280 species of bird are listed in the area and the tidal lagoon and open estuary of the Knysna River provides an excellent place to view waders in the summer months, and plovers, gulls, cormorants and sandpipers are common. Large species like African fish eagle and osprey should also be watched out for.

The area also incorporates the remaining tract of Knysna forests on the southern slopes of the Outeniqua Mountains behind Knysna, which first attracted white settlers to the region. No longer a single expanse, the patches go under a variety of names and include Goudveld Forest (see page 182) and Diepwalle Forest (see page 187). They are noteworthy for the variety of birdlife and their magnificent trees. Species of special interest include the yellowwood, assegai, stinkwood, red alder, white alder and the Cape chestnut. A variety of short walks has been laid out in the forests. In some areas horse riding and mountain biking is allowed.

The **Knysna Museum** ⓘ *Queen St, T044-302 6320, Mon-Fri 0930-1630, Sat 0930-1230, free but donations accepted*, is housed in the Old Gaol – the first public building erected by the colonial government in the 1870s. Most of the collection focuses on fishing methods used along the coast, with a variety of nets and tackle on display. Unless you are a devoted angler this is not going to take up too much of your time. The highlight is in fact a fish, or to be more precise, a coelacanth. This is a prehistoric fish that was believed to be extinct, but a live specimen was famously caught by a fisherman in 1938. There is also an art gallery, tearoom and gift shop.

Millwood House ⓘ *T044-302 6320, Mon-Fri 0930-1630, Sat 0930-1230, free but donations accepted*, is a single-storey wooden building similar to those that once made up the gold-mining community of Millwood (see page 182). The house was originally built in sections and re-erected here. It is now a national monument and houses the local history museum, including a display depicting the goldrush days. Next door is **Parkes Cottage**, a similar wooden house, which was moved three times before arriving at its present site. Originally erected in Millwood village, it was moved into Knysna when the gold ran out. In 1905 it was moved to Rawson Street, and then finally in 1992 it was moved to its present site.

1 **Knysna**

➡ **Knysna maps**
1 Knysna, page 179
2 Knysna lagoon, page 180

Where to stay	
Jembjos Knysna Lodge 1	
Knysna Backpackers 2	
Protea Knysna Quays 3	
Rex 4	
Wayside Inn 13	
Yellowwood Lodge 14	

Restaurants	
34' South 9	
Anchorage 1	
Cruise Café 4	
Freshline Fisheries 5	
JJ's 2	
Mon Petit Pain 3	

Thai Kitchen 8

Bars & clubs
Zanzibar 2

There are two **St George's** churches in Knysna, the old and the new. Both ran into financial difficulties during construction. To complete the old church the Bishop of the Cape Colony, Robert Gray, persuaded six local businessmen to come up with the necessary £150. The church was consecrated in October 1855. The interior has a timbered ceiling and a fine yellowwood floor. In the 1920s it was decided that a second church needed to be built to accommodate the local congregation. It was 11 years between the foundation stone being laid and the church being consecrated by Bishop Gwyer of George in April 1937. Construction had been delayed due to lack of funds. The community was very proud of the fact that all the materials used in the construction were local – the stone for the walls was quarried from the other side of the lagoon in the Brenton hills. Most of the interior fittings are made from stinkwood, and commemorate local worthies.

Featherbed Nature Reserve

T044-382 1693, www.knysnafeatherbed.com, daily 1000, R540, children (11-15) R255 (4-10) R120, under 4s free (including lunch), 1430, R380/130/60 (without lunch), additional times in season.

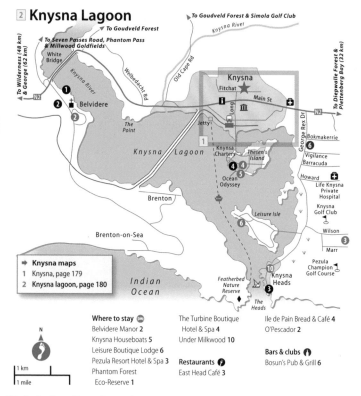

② Knysna Lagoon

Where to stay 🛏
Belvidere Manor **2**
Knysna Houseboats **5**
Leisure Boutique Lodge **6**
Pezula Resort Hotel & Spa **3**
Phantom Forest
  Eco-Reserve **1**
The Turbine Boutique
  Hotel & Spa **4**
Under Milkwood **10**

Restaurants 🍴
East Head Café **3**
Ile de Pain Bread & Café **4**
O'Pescador **2**

Bars & clubs 🍸
Bosun's Pub & Grill **6**

➡ **Knysna maps**
1 Knysna, page 179
2 Knysna lagoon, page 180

BACKGROUND
Knysna

The Hottentots named a local river in the area by a word that sounded like Knysna to the early Europeans, and it's generally believed to mean a place of wood or leaves. In 1804 George Rex, a timber merchant, purchased the farm Melkhoutkraal, effectively taking ownership of all the land surrounding the lagoon. It was rumoured he was the first and illegitimate son of England's King George III. By 1817 the Knysna Lagoon was being used by ships to bring in supplies, and later to take away timber. The vast, indigenous forests just outside Knysna became an invaluable source of timber for buildings, ships and wagons. In 1870, Arnt Leonard Thesen and his family moved from Norway to Knysna and set up the first trading store and counting house, and by 1881 the settlements of Melville and Newhaven united to form the new town of Knysna. The timber industry continued well into the 20th century and unfortunately wiped out much of the natural forest on the coast, so whilst there are still tracts of Knysna forest with yellowwoods and stinkwoods towering over forest ferns, much of the region has been given over to pine plantations and looks very different to what it did 150 years ago.

This private nature reserve, in the unspoilt western side of the **Knysna Heads**, can only be reached by the **Featherbed Co** ferry, which runs from the John Benn Jetty, at the Knysna Quays. The reserve is home to South Africa's largest breeding herd of blue duiker (*Cephalophus monticola*), an endangered species. Also of interest is a cave once inhabited by the Khoi, which has been declared a national heritage site. This four-hour excursion includes return ferry trip, 4WD vehicle ride up the western promontory of the Knysna Heads and an optional 2-km guided nature walk through the forest, onto the cliffs, into the caves and along the spectacular coastline. It ends with a buffet lunch under some milkwood trees before returning to Knysna. This is an excellent family excursion. The **Featherbed Co** also offers 1½-hour cruises around the lagoon on the double-storey *John Benn* (which has a cash bar) at 1230 and 1800 (1700 in winter) for R165, children (4-15) R75, and on a paddle cruiser at 1230 for R205, children (4-15) R100, or a dinner cruise at 1800 (1700 in winter), which includes a three-course buffet dinner, R465, children (11-15) R235 (4-10) R130. In addition, they run the **Cruise Café** at the boat departure point at the Knysna Quays (see Restaurants, page 184).

Belvidere, Brenton and Brenton-on-Sea
These villages, 12-14 km from town on the western shores of the lagoon, are now smart suburbs of Knysna. Belvidere lies on the banks of the river where it enters the lagoon, and the small village church, **Belvidere Church**, is a miniature replica of a Norman church. It was built in 1855 from local stone and timber, with picturesque stained-glass windows and stinkwood fittings. The rose window on the west side was installed in 1955. Further along the road is the seaside resort of Brenton-on-Sea, where the great attraction is the nearest sandy beach to Knysna, making it very popular during the school holidays. There is a fine hotel and a limited selection of seaside cottages.

Goudveld Forest

About 30 km northwest of Knysna, in the **Goudveld Forest**, are the remains of an old mining town, **Millwood** ⓘ *R40, children (2-11) R20, open sunrise-sunset*. Take the Phantom Pass road out of Knysna, just before the village of Rheenendal take a right turn, signposted to Millwood, and pass through the SANParks boom gate into the forest. This was the site of a minor goldrush in the 1880s, just before the gold was discovered at Pilgrim's Rest and Johannesburg. The first gold was discovered here in 1876 when a local farmer picked up a nugget in the Karatara River. This triggered the usual manic influx, and by 1887 Millwood had a court building, three banks, 32 stores, six hotels and three newspapers. By 1900 most people had left as the reefs became too difficult to mine. Today only one building survives, along with some mining machinery which has remained untouched for over 60 years. There are a few picnic spots and short paths leading into the forest; you only have to walk a few metres before being completely enveloped by trees.

Listings Knysna and around *maps p150, p179 and p180*

Tourist information

Knysna Tourism
40 Main St, T044-382 5510, www.visitknysna. co.za, Mon-Fri 0800-1700, Sat 0830-1300, hours extended in high season.
A helpful and professional office, well clued-up on the region, and can make reservations for accommodation, tours and public transport.

Where to stay

$$$$ Pezula Resort Hotel & Spa
Lagoon View Drive, T044-302 3410, www.pezularesort.com.
The Garden Route's most prestigious luxury resort with 83 suites spread across the clifftop overlooking the ocean, Knysna Heads or championship golf course (see page 186). **Zachary's** for gourmet food, cigar, champagne and whisky bars, award-winning spa, indoor and outdoor heated pools, and numerous sporting facilities. A shuttle bus takes guests to nearby Noetzie Beach.

$$$$-$$$ Phantom Forest Eco-Reserve
7 km from Knysna on Phantom Pass Rd, T044-386 0046, www.phantomforest.com.
Ultra-stylish accommodation in 14 luxurious and eco-friendly 'tree suites' connected by walkways, set in the forest high above the lagoon. Each has private terrace and luxurious bathroom – the showers and double baths are open to the trees, excellent restaurant, bar, spa and stunning pool on the edge of a wooden deck. The perfect place to experience the Knysna forest.

$$$ Knysna Houseboats
34 Long St, Thesen's Island, T044-382 2802, www.knysnahouseboats.com.
For something different, and especially recommended for families, self-catering houseboats are available for hire on the Knysna Lagoon. All eating and sleeping equipment is included, 'valet parking' and room service from local restaurants is on offer from the mooring on Thesen's Island, and you can hire fishing tackle. They are very easy to operate and allow you to explore the lagoon at leisure, and you do not need to have any nautical experience, though potential 'captains' need to go through a navigational briefing first.

$$$ Leisure Isle Lodge
87 Bayswater Drive, Leisure Isle, T044-384 0462, www.leisureislelodge.co.za.
Award-winning luxury guesthouse, 10 spacious rooms with all-white luxurious decor and views across the lagoon, heated pool, spa, superb food in the elegant

Daniela's restaurant, canoes and mountain bikes available.

$$$ Protea Hotel Knysna Quays
Knysna Quays, T044-382 5005,
www.proteahotels.com.
Large state-of-the-art hotel, with 123 comfortable a/c rooms, pay more for views over the lagoon, cocktail bar, heated swimming pool. Great location next to the Knysna Quays where hotel guests can sign for meals to be charged to their room account.

$$$ The Rex Hotel
8 Grey St, T044-302 5900,
www.rexhotel.co.za.
Super stylish in an architectural gem of a modern building, with 30 spacious luxury rooms, in muted browns and creams, with kitchenettes and balconies. Breakfast included and it's a short walk to restaurants in the Knysna Quays.

$$$ The Turbine Boutique Hotel & Spa
36 Sawtooth Lane, Thesen's island,
T044-302 5745, www.turbinehotel.co.za.
Hip and quirky, this luxury boutique hotel is built around an old power station and its turbines and has fantastic art hanging throughout. The 25 rooms have all mod cons and designer contemporary furnishings, most with lagoon views, and there's a tapas restaurant, café/bar and rim-flow pool.

$$$-$$ Under Milkwood
At the end of George Rex Drive,
T044-384 0745, www.milkwood.co.za.
16 self-catering log chalets sleeping 2-6 at Knysna Heads set in a grove of milkwood trees, though not all have views of the lagoon. Also has comfortable B&B rooms in the main building. Dec-Jan rates see a significant hike, as they do elsewhere in Knysna.

$$ Yellowwood Lodge
18 Handel St, T044-382 5906,
www.yellowwoodlodge.co.za.
Attractive guesthouse in one of Knysna's older houses built in 1897, with 10 rooms, the upstairs ones have relaxing balconies with views of the lagoon and Heads. Generous buffet breakfasts, and immaculate garden with swimming pool.

$$-$ Wayside Inn
48 Main St, T044-382 6012,
www.knysnawayside.co.za.
Simple, friendly and one of the best-value B&Bs in Knysna in a cottage right in the centre of town, with 15 neat rooms, some have doors opening onto a French balcony. Breakfast is served and there are restaurants close by in Pledge Square.

$ Jembjos Knysna Lodge
4 Queen St, T T044-382 2658, www.jembjosknysnalodge.co.za.
Well-located budget/backpacker accommodation in a modern house just a 2-min walk from Knysna Quays. Dorms and double/twin/triple/family rooms, self-catering kitchen, free breakfasts, lounge, braai area, bike hire, activity bookings and **Baz Bus** stop.

$ Knysna Backpackers
42 Queen St, T044-382 2554,
www.knysnabackpackers.co.za.
Large dorms and some doubles, TV room, kitchen, all meals on request, travel centre, set in a large rambling Victorian mansion in established gardens with space for camping and views across the lagoon, an easy stroll from the town centre. **Baz Bus** stop.

Belvidere

$$$ Belvidere Manor
169 Duthie Drive, Belvidere, T044-387 1055, www.belvidere.co.za.
Quiet location with 38 1- to 3-bed cottages, some self-catering, arranged around a pool in shady gardens. The manor house, from 1834, houses the elegant dining room, and The Bell pub is in an old farm cottage where you can see the wine cellar through a glass floor.

Restaurants

$$$ Anchorage
11 Grey St, T044-382 2230, www.anchoragerestaurant.co.za. Open 1830-late, from 1200 in season.
Established old-style seafood restaurant for platters and oysters, plus aged Angus steaks and a good choice for vegetarians, all accompanied by fine wines and excellent draught Mitchell's beer (to visit the brewery, see page 185).

$$$-$$ Cruise Café
400 m west of the Knysna Quays, T044-382 1693. Mon-Sat 0800-2300, Sun 0800-1700.
Great views of fishing boats on the lagoon, best known for seafood, plus good breakfasts and simple lunches such as fish and chips; more sophisticated and pricier menu in the evening such as prawn and crab risotto or roast duck; long wine and cocktail list.

$$ 34' South
Knysna Quays, T044-382 7268, www.34south.biz. Open 0830-2330.
Snacks and meals daily in a deli-style seafood restaurant, try the sushi, seafood platter or paella, make up a meal from the packed fridges or buy takeaway items, including cookbooks, wine and home-made goodies, laid-back sunny deck overlooking the quays.

$$ JJ's
Knysna Quays, T044-382 3359, www.jjsrestaurant.co.za. Tue-Sun 1130-1530, daily 1830-late.
Another good option at the Quays, still plenty of seafood but also game meat including crocodile, ostrich and kudu, and there's impromptu singing from the Xhosa staff. Look out for the framed money collection on the wall, which includes a Zimbabwe 100-trillion dollar note and a 50-year-old British fiver.

$$ Tapas & Oysters
Thesen's Island, T044-382 7196, www.tapasknysna.co.za. Open 1100-2300.
This seafood restaurant with views over the lagoon is perhaps the best place to try a dozen of Knysna's famous raw or cooked oysters washed down with a glass of fizz – a Kynsna must-do. Also consider the grilled sardines and calamari, smoked snoek and creamy mussels.

$ Freshline Fisheries Restaurant
Railway Siding Dockyard, corner Long St and Waterfront Drive, T044-382 313, www.freshlinefisheries.co.za. Mon-Sat 0900-1700.
For fresh seafood straight off the boats head to this casual place in the corner of the harbour. The fish and chips (snoek, sole, gurnard, tuna, kingklip, Cape salmon, among many others), crayfish and giant prawns are superb, and next door is a rib and steak outlet and a fish shop.

$ Thai Kitchen
4 Memorial Sq, Main St, T044-382 1396. Mon-Sat 1100-2130.
Cheap and cheerful, order at the counter, but delicious and authentic dishes, and you can watch the furiously sizzling woks in the open kitchen. The phad thai and tom yum soup are exceptional. Not licensed but BYO.

Cafés

East Head Café
25 George Rex Drive, T044-384 0933, www.eastheadcafe.co.za. Open 0800-1600.
Simple shack perched above the crashing waves, and you couldn't get a better view of The Heads unless you were on the water. Breakfasts, gourmet burgers, fish and chips (the battered hake is excellent) and, if the mood takes, washed down with a Pimm's or Bloody Mary.

Ile de Pain Bread & Café
The Boatshed, Thesen's Island, T044-302 5707, www.iledepain.co.za. Tue-Sat 0800-1500, Sun 0900-1330.
Superb bakery and café emitting lovely warm smells of freshly baked goodies, such as croissants and pastries; they start baking at 0200. Excellent spot for brunch or light

lunch and the baby chocolate brownies are to die for. **Mon Petit Pain**, Mon-Fri 0730-1500, Sat 0730-1300, is another outlet on the corner of Gordon St and Grey St.

Belvidere

$$$-$$ O'Pescador
Brenton Rd, Belvidere, T044-386 0036. Mon-Sat 1830-2230.
Long-established and popular Portuguese restaurant, traditional cosy decor, Mozambique prawns or try the spicy fish dishes, peri-peri chicken or grilled sardines. Portuguese wines, brandy and port.

Bars and clubs

Bosun's Pub & Grill
George Rex Drive, T044-382 6276, www. bosuns.co.za. Mon-Sat 1100-late, Sun 1100-1600.
English-style pub serving ales on tap from Knysna's own **Mitchell's Brewery** including Bosun's Bitter (bitter is hard to come by in South Africa). Pub grub like traditional bangers and mash or liver and onions, and a roast lunch on Sun. Hosts regular quiz nights and is a favourite spot for watching rugby and football.

Zanzibar
5 Mellville Centre, Main Rd, T044-382 0386, www.zanzibarknysna.com. Open 1900-0200, 1200-0200 in season.
Set in a converted theatre, with terraces overlooking Main Rd, dance floor and pool tables, tribal decor, occasional DJs, comedy and live music, and upstairs is a quieter cocktail lounge.

Festival

Apr/May Pink Loerie Mardi Gras & Arts Festival, *www.pinkloerie.co.za.* A gay festival with parade and 4 days of non-stop entertainment for anyone who enjoys a party. Most of Cape Town's gay community gravitates to Knysna for the weekend.

Jul Knysna Oyster Festival, *www. oysterfestival.co.za.* Oyster braais, oyster tasting, oyster-eating competitions and other molluscular activities; there's live entertainment and lots of sporting events – cycling, running, canoeing, downhill racing and sailing.

Shopping

Arts and crafts
Keeping in tune with Knysna's reputation as a cultural arts and crafts centre are a number of galleries and craft shops. Check at the tourist office for special exhibitions. There is a good **African craft market** on the side of the road as you enter Knysna on the N2 from George, with an extensive range of carvings, baskets, drums and curios. There is also a cluster of expensive curio shops and a daily fleamarket at the **Knysna Quays**.

Shopping malls
Knysna Mall, *Main Rd, opposite Knysna Tourism, T044 382 4574, www.knysnamall. co.za. Mon-Fri 0900-1730, Sat-Sun 0900-1400.* The town's newest mall with more than 60 shops including the main South African chain stores and the anchor supermarket is **SuperSpar**.
Woodmill Lane Centre, *corner Main and Long Sts, T044-382 3045, www.woodmillane. co.za. Mon-Fri 0830-1700, Sat 0830-1400, Sun 0900-1300.* Knysna's nicest mall, this is built around a restored Victorian timber mill constructed in 1919, for Geo Parkes & Sons, a Birmingham tool manufacturer, who was the first exporter of Knysna wood to England for the making of bobbins for the Midlands textile industry. They also manufactured wagon parts and a variety of tool handles. Today the centre has 75 shops, fountains and trees in the squares, and regular performing artists and buskers. There are several boutiques and arts and crafts shops and a branch of **Pick 'n' Pay** supermarket.

What to do

Boat trips

For details of the hugely popular ferry excursion to the Knysna Heads and Featherbed Nature Reserve, see page 180.

Knysna Charters, *Thesen's Island, jetty at Quay Four restaurant, T082-892 0469, www. knysnacharters.co*m. 75-min cruise to see **The Heads** with a little bit of commentary about Knysna; 0900, 1030 and 1200, R250, children (4-12) R80, under 3s free, and 1½-hr sunset cruises with drinks; departs Dec-Jan 1700, Feb-Apr and Oct-Nov 1600, May-Sep 1500, R370, children (4-12) R120, under 3s free. The 1½-hr **Knysna Lagoon Oyster Tour** also cruises to **The Heads** and includes oyster-tasting (wild and cultivated) and a glass of white wine; 1400, R520, children (4-12) R145, under 3s free. Also rents out single and double kayaks with life jackets and dry bags for a paddle around the lagoon from R100 per hr.

Ocean Odyssey, *Thesen's Island, jetty adjacent to The Turbine Boutique Hotel & Spa, T044-382 0321, www.oceanodyssey. co.za*. Cruises through The Heads and out into the ocean and the only permit-holder for whale-watching in Knysna (allowing boats to approach whales within 50 m). 2-hr whale-watching trips, 1000, 1200 and 1500 during whale season (usually Jun-Nov), R750, children (under 12) R550; the same cruise runs outside of whale season for slightly less to see seals, dolphins and marine birds. Also rents out standup paddle boards for 'SUPing' on the lagoon from R150 per hr.

Springtide Charters, *Knysna Quays, T082-470 6022, www.springtide.co.za*. 3-hr sunset cruises on a 50-ft sailing boat including a stop for a swim, departs Dec-Jan 1700, Feb-Apr and Oct-Nov 1600, May-Sep 1500, R795 including sushi and seafood snacks and champagne. Can also arrange 4-hr lunch excursions for R920 and the boat is available to charter overnight for honeymooners to stay in the lovely master cabin.

Diving

The 460-ton German ship, the *Paquita* struck the Knysna Heads in 1903. The anchors are still visible and the iron plates on the wreck act as an artificial reef and make an unusual dive.

Pro-Dive, *in the Beacon Island Hotel in Plettenberg Bay (see page 192)*, can also organize dives at Knysna.

Golf

Knysna is the most popular golfing destination on the Garden Route and 3 magnificent courses are within 6 km of the town centre.

Knysna Golf Club, *George Rex Drive, T044-384 1150, www.knysnagolfclub.com*. 18-hole, par-73 course with good views of The Heads.

Pezula Champion Golf Course, *at the Pezula Resort Hotel & Spa (see Where to stay, page 182), T044-302 5310, www.pezulagolf.co.za*. Immaculate 18-hole, par 72 championship course covering 254 ha of Knysna's cliff-tops with sweeping ocean views, considered the most scenic in South Africa.

Simola Golf Club, at Simola Golf and Country Estate, 1 Old Cape Rd, T044-302 9677, www.simola.co.za. Set high up in the hills above Knysna with lovely views across the Knysna Lagoon, an 18-hole. Par 72 course designed by Jack Nicklaus. For non-golfers, the spa here is open to day visitors.

Tour operators

Knysna Forest Tours, *T044-382 6130, www. knysnaforesttours.co.za*. Half- and full-day guided hiking, from R350 per person in the forests around Knysna and local nature reserves, on trails of varied difficulty 3-16 km long, plus canoeing on the Goukamma River, which is great for birdwatching.

Mountain Biking Africa, *T082-783 8392, www.mountainbikingafrica.co.za*. Guided mountain-bike trails around the forests in the area, easy rides, lots of downhills, bikes and refreshments included.

Transport

It's 500 km to Cape Town, 61 km to **George**, 1350 km to **Johannesburg**, 100 km to **Mossel Bay**, 120 km to **Outdshoorn**, 32 km to **Plettenberg Bay**, 260 km to Port Elizabeth, 90 km to **Tsitsikamma**.

Bus
Buses stop at Knysna daily on the route between Cape Town and Durban outside the old railway station near the Knysna Quays. **Greyhound**, **Intercape** and **Translux** run daily to **Cape Town** (8 hrs), **Port Elizabeth** (3½ hrs), and **Durban** (18 hrs). **Intercape** and **Translux** also have a daily service between Knysna and **Tshwane** (**Pretoria**) and **Johannesburg** (14 hrs), via **Bloemfontein** (11 hrs).

Baz Bus has a daily service between Cape Town and Port Elizabeth, from where it continues to **Durban** 5 times a week. Heading towards **Cape Town** the **Baz Bus** leaves at 1245-1300; towards **Port Elizabeth** at 1630-1645. It drops and picks up at all the hostels.

For more information, see Getting around, page 207.

East of Knysna

forest walks among giant trees and close encounters with elephants

Diepwalle Forest and Elephant Trail
From Knysna, follow the N2 towards Plettenberg Bay, after 7 km turn onto the R339 and the Diepwalle forest station is about 16 km on a gravel road. The R339 passes through the middle of the forest en route to Uniondale via the Prince Alfred's Pass. Open 0600-1800, no charge but you must sign in at the forest station where maps are on offer.

Starting from the Diepwalle forest station is the 20-km **Elephant Walk**, an easy-going, level hike that gives a clear insight into the forest environment. The trail is marked by elephant silhouettes and takes around seven hours to complete. The hike is made up of three loops, but it is possible to shorten the walk by completing only one or two loops. The three paths are simply known as Routes I, II and III, and are 9, 8 and 6 km long, respectively. Apart from the (very slim) possibility of spying the rare Knysna elephant (see box, page 188), the main attractions are the giant forest trees, particularly the Outeniqua yellowwood. There are eight such trees along the full trail – the largest, at 46 m, is known as the **King Edward VII Tree**, and stands just off the R339 by the Diepwalle picnic spot at the end of Route I and the start of Route II. The end of the **Outeniqua Trail** meets with Route III.

Knysna Elephant Park
On the N2, 20 km from Knysna and 10 km before Plettenberg Bay, T044-532 7732, www.knysnaelephantpark.co.za, 0830-1630, 1-hr tours depart every 30 mins, R260, children (5-12) R120, under 5s free, bookings not required; elephant riding 0730 and 1600, R925, children (5-12) R425, children under 5 not permitted, booking essential. **Elephant Lodge** *($$$) 5 twin rooms and 1 large family flat sleeping 6 over the boma where the elephants sleep, so you can fall asleep to their nightly sounds (and smells!), and see them when they are out and about. Modern and comfortable with DSTV, a spacious thatched lounge with large picture windows for viewing. Dinner on request.*

This small park is a refuge for orphaned elephants. Visitors are taken on tours around the forest area and are allowed to touch and play with the little elephants. Although the animals are 'free range' they are very used to human contact, making it a wonderful experience for children. Longer walks with the elephants can also be arranged and the

ON THE ROAD

Invisible elephants

No guide to Knysna would be complete without a mention of the fabled Knysna elephants. Their rumoured existence has come to represent the last stand of wildlife against man in the region. Reputedly the elephants live deep in the forest but few people have ever seen them, and little is known about their numbers or their characteristics. In 1876, several hundred elephants were recorded in the region, but under heavy pressure of ivory hunters they were reduced to 20 to 30 individuals by 1908. In 1970 the Knysna elephant population was estimated at 11, and by 1994, only one Knysna elephant was known to survive, an elderly female. In the same year, two young elephants from the Kruger National Park were introduced into the range of the elderly female in an effort to increase numbers. But they only joined up with the elderly female for short periods before choosing to spend 80% of their time in mountainous fynbos habitat beyond the Knysna forest. In 1999 they were recaptured and relocated to a private game reserve in the Eastern Cape. Since then, and although researchers claimed to have found spoor in 2007, no elephants have been seen. But the myth continues, so happy hiking – you may just see more than the Knysna lourie.

elephant riding is a two-hour excursion through the bush ending with refreshments. Sleeping with the elephants is also on offer, and six rooms have been built above the elephants' boma where they sleep at night (see page 187). This is also the only realistic chance you'll have of seeing elephants in the area – the fabled indigenous ones are far too elusive (see box, above). The restaurant serves breakfast, light lunches and afternoon teas. There's another similar elephant experience at **The Elephant Sanctuary** further along the N2 at The Crags, 19 km east of Plettenberg Bay (see page 196).

The Heath

On the N2, 4 km beyond the Knysna Elephant Park and 7 km before Plettenberg Bay, T044-532 7724, www.theheath.co.za, 0830-1700, 1800 in summer.

Another interesting diversion when driving along the N2, with a clutch of quality craft and decor shops, a pretty garden with a kids' jungle gym and merry-go-round, a farm shop for excellent home-made bakes, organic produc1e, pickles and preserves, and a café for great coffee and more substantial meals.

Also here is **Radical Raptors**, ① T044-532 7537, www.radicalraptors.co.za, Tue-Sun 0830-1700, R80, children (4-12) R60, under 3s free, a bird of prey rehabilitation centre which offers 45-minute free-flight/falconry shows at 1100, 1300 and 1500. Birds in residence may include owls, buzzards, kestrels and eagles.

If you are passing by on a Saturday, also stop at the **Harkerville Market** ① 18 km after Knysna and 2 km before the Knysna Elephant Park, www.harkervillemarket.co.za, Sat 0800-1200, one of the largest farmers', food, art and craft markets on the Garden Route.

classy holiday resort with beautiful beaches and lots of activities on offer

Plettenberg Bay, or 'Plett', as it is commonly known, is one of the most appealing resorts on the Garden Route. Although it is modern and has little of historical interest, the compact centre is attractive and the main beach beautiful. Plett has now become fashionable and, during the Christmas season, the town is transformed. Wealthy families descend from Johannesburg and the pace can get quite frenetic – expect busy beaches and long queues for restaurant tables. For the rest of the year it is calmer and the resort becomes just another sleepy seaside town. There are three beaches that are good for swimming, and a number of attractions along the N2 to the east of 'Plett', particularly around the settlement of The Crags, where visitors could easily spend a full day visiting the wildlife sancturies.

Sights

While there are a few old buildings still standing which represent a little of the town's earlier history, including the remains of the Old Timber Store (1787), the Old Rectory (1776) and the Dutch Reformed Church (1834), most of the buildings were destroyed in a fire in 1914, and today the main streets are just a collection of modern shopping malls and restaurants. The real attraction of this area is the sea and the outdoors. Aside from the three beaches, **Robberg**, **Central** and **Lookout**, there is excellent deep-sea fishing and, in season, good opportunities to spot whales and dolphins, particularly southern right whales from June to October. Plett climbs up a fairly steep hill; there are many elevated land-based vantage points as well as regular boat tours offering closer encounters with the marine life. The nearby **Keurbooms River lagoon** is a safe area for bathing and other watersports, and the dunes around the lagoon are now part of the **Keurbooms River Nature Reserve** (see page 195).

The **Milkwood Trail** is a 3-km circular trail in and around the town. Follow the yellow footprints. You can start the walk anywhere along the route and it takes you via Piesangs River lagoon, Central Beach, and Lookout Rocks, and in the centre of town, past some of the historic buildings.

There are also some recommended walks in the **Robberg Nature Reserve** ① *8 km south from Plett on Robberg Rd, T044-533 2125, www.capenature.co.za, Feb-Nov 0700-1700, Dec and Jan 0700-2000, R40, children (2-13) R20.* There are three possibilities ranging from 2-9 km on this loop along the Robberg Peninsula which forms the western boundary of Plettenberg Bay. Follow the 'seal' markers. Walking is easy thanks to boardwalks, and there are plenty of prominent viewpoints from which it is possible to see whales, seals and dolphins in the bay, but beware of freak waves along the coastal paths. Allow at least four hours for the full route. Also in the reserve is the **Cape Seal Lighthouse** which was built in 1950. It's nothing special to look at, but at 146 m above the sea, it's the highest navigational light on the South African coast.

Plettenberg Bay Game Reserve

12 km north of Plett, leave town on the N2 east and turn on the R340 to Uplands, T044-535 0000, www.plettenbergbaygamereserve.com, 2-hr game drives May-Sep 1100 and 1500, Oct-Apr 0830, 1000, 1100, 1230, 1500 and 1600, R425 per person 2-hr horse safaris 1000 and 1500, R425 per person (no children under 12).

Plettenberg Bay

To N2, Keurboom River Nature Reserve, Nature's Valley & Garden Route National Park
(Tsitsikamma Section), Goose Valley Golf Club & Plettenberg Bay Game Reserve

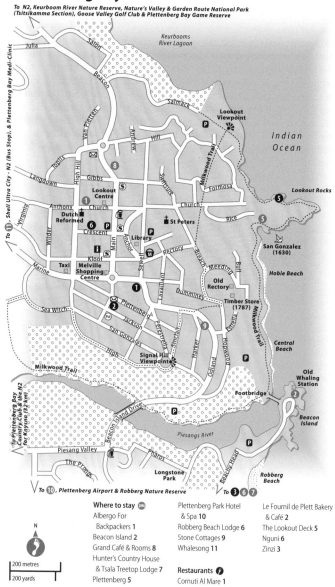

Where to stay
Albergo For
 Backpackers 1
Beacon Island 2
Grand Café & Rooms 8
Hunter's Country House
 & Tsala Treetop Lodge 7
Plettenberg 5

Plettenberg Park Hotel
 & Spa 10
Robberg Beach Lodge 6
Stone Cottages 9
Whalesong 11

Restaurants
Cornuti Al Mare 1

Le Fournil de Plett Bakery
 & Café 2
The Lookout Deck 5
Nguni 6
Zinzi 3

BACKGROUND
Plettenberg Bay

In 1630 a Portuguese vessel, the *San Gonzalez*, was wrecked in the bay. This was 20 years before Jan van Riebeeck's arrival at the Cape. The survivors stayed here for eight months, during which time they built two smaller boats out of the wreckage, and one of the boats managed to sail up the coast to Mozambique. The survivors were eventually returned home to Lisbon, but they left behind a sandstone plaque on which they had inscribed the name *Baia Formosa*. Today a replica can be seen in Plett in the same place that the first was left by the sailors. (The original is now on show in the South African Museum in Cape Town.) The Portuguese had a number of names for the bay, but none stuck for very long. Later the Dutch also gave the bay several different names, such as Content Bay and Pisang River Bay; it was only in 1778 when Governor Joachim van Plettenberg opened a timber post on the shores of the bay, and named it after himself, that a name stuck.

Plettenberg remained an important timber port until the early 1800s when the Dutch decided to move operations to Knysna since it was a safer harbour. For a period the bay became famous as a whaling station but all that remains is a blubber cauldron and slipway near the **Beacon Island Hotel**.

This private reserve is located on 2200 ha spread across the hills above the Garden Route coastline with good views of Plettenberg Bay and offers open 4WD safaris or guided horse-riding trails. The reserve boasts a diversity of natural biomes, including fynbos, grasslands and indigenous forests, and on the property is the natural confluence of the Keurbooms and Palmiet Rivers. The reserve has been stocked with over 35 species of game, including lion, white rhino, giraffe, hippo, crocodile, buffalo and a large variety of antelope, and 101 species of bird have been recorded. Accommodation is in a luxury lodge (see Where to stay, page 193) or visit for a game drive/horse ride followed by a drink and light meal in the bar.

Listings Plettenberg Bay *maps p150 and p190*

Tourist information

Plett Tourism
Melville's Corner shopping centre, Main St, T044-533 4065, www.plett-tourism.co.za, Mon-Fri 0900-1700, Sat 0900-1300, longer hours during the summer season.
A helpful office with a detailed website and blog about what's on in Plett.

Where to stay

$$$$ Hunter's Country House and Tsala Treetop Lodge
Hunter's Estate, off the N2, the turning is 10 km towards Knysna, which is another 22 km, reservations T044-501 1111, www.hunterhotels.com.
Sharing the same property, these 2 exclusive luxury hotels are members of the **Relais & Chateaux group**. The **Country House** has 21 thatched cottages with fireplace, antique

furnishings and private patios in gardens full of wild flowers, while **Tsala** has 10 stunning wooden and glass suites with outdoor showers and splash pools built 6 m above ground in the tree canopy, plus 6 additional family villas. Each has swimming pools, restaurants, bars and shops, and gourmet picnics on the estate can be arranged.

$$$$ The Plettenberg
40 Church St, Lookout Rocks, T044-533 2030, www.collectionmcgrath.com.
A **Relais & Chateaux** property and everything you would expect of an exclusive top-class, 5-star hotel. Located on a headland overlooking the bay with 37 luxury a/c rooms with contemporary decor, though you pay much more for sea views, superb food and wine, rim-flow pool and spa.

$$$ Beacon Island
Beacon Island Cres, T044-533 1120, www.tsogosunhotels.com.
Dubbed 'BI' by holidaymakers from Johannesburg, a multi-storey building dominating the bay, right on the water between 2 beaches, with 200 rooms, and a full range of facilities including 3 excellent restaurants, pool, tennis courts and gym. A superb location but an eyesore on Plett's sweeping beach.

$$$ The Grand Café & Rooms
27 Main St, T044-533 3301, www.thegrand.co.za.
Small and chic boutique hotel on Plett's main street with good bay views from the terrace, 8 designer rooms with oversized beds and extras like DVD players. Bistro-style restaurant (see page 193), shop selling contemporary African-inspired decor items, small splash pool, no children under 16.

$$$ Plettenberg Park Hotel & Spa
Follow Robberg Rd from town and turn left after Robberg Nature Reserve, T044-533 9067, www.plettenbergpark.co.za.
In an outstanding location perched right on a cliff-edge between Robberg Nature

Reserve and the airport, and set in 200 ha with a private lake and network of walking trails, 10 spacious suites, 25-m infinity pool, restaurant and spa. Great for whale- and birdwatching but access to the beach is down the steep cliff.

$$$-$$ The Robberg Beach Lodge
89 Beachyhead Drive, T044-533 0369, www.therobberg.co.za.
A set of 4 upmarket guesthouses – **Beachy Head Villa**, **Robberg House**, **Cottage Pie** and **Cordovan Villa** – offering 29 stylish rooms in total. Shared facilities include 2 swimming pools, 2 lounges and bars, a rooftop viewing deck, and all are no more than 100 m from Robberg Beach.

$$$-$$ Whalesong Hotel
Marine Drive, at the junction of the N2, T044-533 5389, www.legendlodges.co.za.
Above the town centre but handy for a late stop on the N2 and with sweeping ocean views, 24 comfortable thatched rooms with wooden decks and African ethnic decor, restaurant, bar, pool with sundeck, spa, travel desk for booking activities and Xhosa craft shop.

$$ Stone Cottages
corner of Harker and Odland Streets, T044-533 1331, www.stonecottage.co.za.
Group of rustic self-catering restored 19th-century cottages sleeping 2-5, with high ceilings and gleaming wooden floors, antiques and old photographs, panoramic views of the ocean, deck with jacuzzi overlooking the main beach. A good option for families or friends travelling together.

$ Albergo For Backpackers
6 and 8 Church St, T044-533 4434, www.albergo.co.za.
Centrally located hostel in 2 houses with sea views. Dorms, double rooms and camping area, garden with hammocks and bonfires, 2 kitchens, travel centre, TV room, bar and pool table, surfboards for hire. **Baz Bus** stop.

Plettenberg Bay Game Reserve

$$$ Baroness Safari Lodge
See page 189.
Set in a restored homestead built in 1822, 10 spacious suites with verandas, antiques, 4-poster beds, and free-standing bathtubs with bush views, lounge and library, outside boma with fire, bar with a deck overlooking a waterhole, pool. Rates include meals and 1 game drive or horse ride.

Restaurants

$$$ Zinzi at Tsala Treetop Lodge
See Where to stay, page 191. Open 1230-1430, 1730-2230.
Excellent gourmet food served in exquisite interior-designed dining room featuring lizard-print fabrics, pewter chandeliers and giant suede sofas. Expect the likes of local venison and seafood, plus global dishes including Moroccan lamb, Persian chicken or Szechuan tuna. The cellar has more than 3000 wines to choose from. Pricey but recommended for special occasions.

$$$-$ Nguni
6 Crescent St, T044-533 6710, www.nguni-restaurant.co.za. Mon-Fri 1000-2200, Sat 1800-2200.
Set in one of the oldest houses in Plett decorated with Nguni (cow) hides and historical photos, with well-presented dishes of South African gourmet cuisine such as springbok carpaccio, rib-eye game steaks, Karoo lamb chops and seared tuna. Also on the property is **The White House**, a theatre and venue that occasionally hosts music recitals.

$$ Cornuti Al Mare
1 Perestrella St, T044-533 1277, www.cornuti.co.za. Open 1200-2200.
Stylish pizza restaurant with whitewashed walls and high ceilings, and busy cocktail and wine bar with ocean views. Unusual pizza toppings include tuna, ginger and wasabi or strawberries and chocolate sauce, plus standard Italian dishes and good grilled fish.

$$-$ The Grand Café & Rooms
See Where to stay, page 192. Open 0730-2200.
Restaurant at this boutique hotel with shabby-chic decor of mismatched furniture, candelabras and gilt mirrors and excellent sea views from the deck. Small but sophisticated menu including seafood, Durban-style (spicy) curries and gourmet burgers.

$$-$ The Lookout Deck
Perched on the Lookout Rocks, T044-533 1379, www.lookout.co.za. Open 0900-2300.
Popular family restaurant, excellent seafood, soups, salads and steaks, also has a busy bar, lively, bustling atmosphere. Perfect location; from the terrace you can watch surfers share a wave with a dolphin.

Cafés

Le Fournil de Plett Bakery and Café
Lookout Centre, Main St, T044-533 1390. Mon-Sat 0800-1600, Sun 0800-1300.
French-style café and bistro with tree-covered patio, serving excellent baguettes and croissants, breakfasts and light meals, including open sandwiches, quiches and filled vol-au-vents.

Shopping

Arts and crafts
Lookout Art Gallery, *Lookout Centre, Main St, T044-533 2210, www.lookout- art-gallery.co.za. Mon-Fri 0900-1700, Sat 0900-1330.* Established gallery with antiques and artwork from local artists including paintings, sculptures, glassware and ceramics, and they can arrange to ship overseas.
Old Nick Village, *N2, 3 km east of Plett, T044-533 1395, www.oldnickvillage. co.za. 1000-1700.* Group of galleries, craft workshops and studios, and a weaving museum with working antique looms, set in restored 19th-century farm buildings. The **Old Nick Shop** is housed in the former

Gansvlei General Dealers Store which traded from the 1890s to the 1960s – when its main (black) customer base was moved out of Plett to new townships during Apartheid. This is a pleasant stop with a restaurant, coffee shop and bakery with outside tables in the indigenous garden where vervet monkeys may be spotted in the yellowwood trees, and there's a jungle gym on the lawns for children.

What to do

Diving and snorkelling
There are not many tropical fish but due to an abundance of planktonic matter there is a colourful reef life, and there is a good chance of seeing parrotfish, ragged-tooth sharks and steenbras. For those who enjoy snorkelling, there is a popular spot in front of the Beacon Isle Hotel known as **Deep Blinders**; behind the reef is a sandy area where you might see stingrays.
Pro-Dive, *in the Beacon Island Hotel, T044-533 1158, www.prodive.co.za.* PADI dive centre, runs daily diving and snorkelling trips and rents out equipment.

Golf
Goose Valley Golf Club, *Goose Valley Rd, off the N2 east of Plett, T044-533 5082, www. goosevalleygolfclub.com.* A challenging par 72, 6000-m, 18-hole golf course on the banks of Keurbooms Lagoon designed by Gary Player with good ocean views.
Plettenberg Bay Country Club, *Piesang Valley Rd, T044-533 2132, www.plettgolf. co.za.* Lush 18-hole course in the middle of a private nature reserve, Piesang Valley. The Knysna loerie and woodpeckers are often seen on the course. Priority bookings for members Dec-Jan, visitors welcome the rest of the year.

Skydiving
SkyDive Plett, *at Plettenberg Airport, off Robberg Rd, T082-905 7440, www.skydive plett. com.* Tandem skydives with stunning coastal views, and if lucky, you may spot whales and dolphins from the air. After a briefing, flights over Plettenberg Bay take 20 mins, and the drop is from 3000 m with a 35-sec freefall; R2000, R400 for a DVD.

Surfing
Learn to Surf Plett, *T082-436 6410, www. learntosurfplett.co.za.* 2-hr surfing and standup paddle boarding (SUP) lessons from Plett's beaches, from R400 including boards and wetsuit. Also gear rental.

Whale and dolphin watching
Several companies organize whale-watching trips in season (Jul-Dec), about 2 hrs and cost around R700, children (under 12) R350. Both the companies below are permitted to get within 50 m of the whales. Out of season there are cheaper (R440, children under 12, R220) trips to see seals, dolphins and marine birds.
Ocean Blue Adventures, *T044-533 5083, www.oceanadventures.co.za.* Can also organize sea-kayaking.
Ocean Safaris, *T044-533 4963, www.ocean safaris.co.za.* One of the vessels is called *Fat Boy*, the local nickname for a southern right whale.

Transport

It's 525 km to **Cape Town**, 93 km to **George**, 32 km to **Knysna**, 171 km to **Mossel Bay**, 236 km to **Port Elizabeth**, 55 km to **Tsitsikamma**.

Bus
Baz Bus has a daily service between **Cape Town** and **Port Elizabeth**, from where it continues to **Durban** 5 times a week. Heading towards Cape Town the **Baz Bus** leaves at 1200-1215; towards Port Elizabeth at 1745-1800. It drops and picks up at all the hostels.
  Buses depart from the Shell Ultra City on the N2 out of town. Arrange a taxi with your hotel, but remember that some buses pass

through in the early hours. **Greyhound**, **Intercape** and **Translux** all stop here daily on the Cape Town–Durban route. **Cape Town** (8½ hrs) daily, **Durban** (17½ hrs) daily via **Port Elizabeth** (3½ hrs). **Intercape** has a service between Plettenberg Bay and **Tshwane** (**Pretoria**) and **Johannesburg** (14 hrs) daily via **Oudtshoorn** (2 hrs), and **Bloemfontein** (11 hrs).

For more information, see Getting around, page 207.

East of Plettenberg Bay

wildlife sanctuaries, nature reserves, river estuaries and a very high bungee jump

The N2 continues east from Plettenberg Bay, but don't expect to travel too fast as there are a number of attractions and sights in rapid succession that are worth stopping for.

Keurbooms River Nature Reserve

On the east side of the Keurbooms River Bridge on the N2, 7 km east of Plett, T044-533 2125, www.capenature.co.za, 0800-1800, R40, children (2-13) R20, double canoe hire R120 per day, if you just want to picnic next to the river at the reserve entrance near the bridge it's R5 per person.

First up is the 750-ha Keurbooms River Nature Reserve. The headwaters of the Keurbooms River come from the Langkloof, north of the main Tsitsikamma mountain range. Its gorge is spectacular and well worth a voyage upstream to enjoy the unspoilt, unpolluted beauty. A variety of habitats are conserved, including the relatively unspoilt riverine gorge, patches of Knysna forest along the flood banks and in protected kloofs, coastal fynbos, and dune fields. The reserve is named after the Western Keurboom (*Virgilia oroboides*) or choice tree, which grows in the coastal forest edges. The environment attracts a number of birds; look out for the Knysna lourie, malachite and giant kingfisher, Narina trogon fish eagle, white-breasted cormorant and various sunbirds. You can hire canoes for the day from the **Cape Nature Office**, and contact them for information about an overnight canoe trail up the river to **Whiskey Creek Cabin**, but taking a sailing trip upstream on the **Keurbooms River Ferry** (see What to do, page 199, for further details) is the best way to spend a few hours. You are ferried 5 km along the river through a spectacular gorge overhung by indigenous trees and other flora.

Monkeyland, Birds of Eden and Jukani Wildlife Sanctuary

Take the N2 from Plettenberg Bay for 15.5 km to the turn-off on the right to Jukani; Monkeyland and Birds of Eden is another 9 km at The Crags, turn-off at Forest Hall Rd, T044-534 8906, www.monkeyland.co.za, www.birdsofeden.co.za, www.jukani.co.za, 0900-1700, last tours depart at 1600, guides are multilingual, each attraction costs R175, children (3-12) R88, under 3s free; a combo ticket for all three is R368, children R184. Note that Jukani is 9 km before Monkeyland and Birds of Eden on the N2 if coming from the Plett direction but combo tickets for all three can be bought at each attraction.

This group of three award-winning wildlife attractions is well worth a stop and is great (and informative) for both adults and children. All are members of the **South African Animal Sanctuary Alliance** (www.saasa.org.za) whose aim is to maintain captive-bred wildlife populations in as near as possible to wild environments. Allow about four hours to visit all three and each has a restaurant/café. **Monkeyland** was the first of the three facilities to open (in 1998) and as the name suggests is a primate sanctuary where the animals are free to move about in the living indigenous forest. Most are rescued pets and it is home to over 550 primates including gibbons, howler monkeys, vervet monkeys, langurs, sakis, capuchins, squirrel monkeys, spider monkeys, ring-tailed lemurs and the critically endangered black and white ruffed lemurs. Visitors join a guided half-hour tour which takes in various waterholes in the forest, and guides have a keen eye for spotting the animals. One of the highlights here is the Indiana Jones-style rope bridge that spans 128 m across a canyon, offering glimpses of species that spend their entire lives in the upper reaches of the forest. The primates themselves also use this bridge (supposedly the longest of its kind in the world).

Birds of Eden is the largest single span free-flight aviary in the world, a 2.3-ha mesh dome spanning more of the same forest as Monkeyland with 2 km of walkways, 900 m of which is elevated, that go past waterfalls and dams. Along the same principal as Monkeyland and Jukani, previously caged birds have been released into a natural environment and its home to more than 3500 birds from some 200 species including several species of parrot, turaco, waterfowl, finches, cranes, hornbills and many more. Visitors are permitted to wander around without a guide.

The main focus of the **Jukani Wildlife Sanctuary** is the big cats, and lion, cheetah, leopard, caracal and serval are in residence as well as a few non-African species such as tigers (Siberian, Bengal and white), jaguars and pumas. Other predators include hyena, wild dog and jackal. Again it's a place of refuge from the hunting/pet trade. Unlike many other such sanctuaries in Africa, Jukani does not allow interaction with the animals – there is no 'having a photo taken with a cheetah' option here and they disapprove of the 'petting tourism' industry, believing that animals should not be used (or bred) for that purpose. Visitors are shown around on a one-hour tour.

The Elephant Sanctuary Plettenberg Bay
Directly adjacent to Monkeyland and Birds of Eden, T044-534 8145, www.elephantsanctuary. co.za, 0800-1530, 'trunk-in-hand' R500, children (4-14) R240, no under 4s, elephant ride R500, children (8-14) R370, no under 8s.

This offers a similar experience to the Knysna Elephant Park on the N2 west of Plettenberg Bay (see page 187). Guests can interact with the six tame elephants and ride them. There is no need to book for the one-hour 'trunk-in-hand' option, when guides explain about elephant behaviour and you can feed and walk with them. This is followed by an optional 10-minute ride, but booking ahead for this is recommended in high season.

Tenikwa Wildlife Awareness Centre
Take the same turning on to Forest Hall Rd for Monkeyland and Birds of Eden, and then follow signs left for 2 km, T044-534 8170, www.tenikwa.co.za, 1-hr Wildcat Experience; tours depart every 30 mins 0900-1630, R185, children (6-13) R95, under 6s free, bookings not required; 1½-hr Cheetah Walk; 0730 and 1630, R750 per person, no under 16s or under 1.5 m minimum height, booking essential.

At the same turn-off to Monkeyland and Birds of Eden is this centre for orphaned, abandoned and injured wildlife, which it endeavours to rehabilitate and return to the wild whenever possible. Many of the animals are brought to the centre by **Cape Nature** from their protected reserves along the Garden Route, and when released are returned to these sites, while some are introduced back into the wild on some of the private game reserves in the Eastern Cape. In accordance with Cape Nature's regulations, the public cannot interact with any of the animals scheduled to be rereleased as this would reduce their chances of rehabilitation. But the centre has some resident species which can be viewed at close quarters. The one-hour **Wildcat Experience** starts with a visit to the educational centre before a short walk to meet serval, caracal, leopard, African wildcat, black-footed cat and cheetah in enclosures. The 1½-hour **Cheetah Walk** takes visitors for a walk with semi-tame cheetahs at either sunrise or sunset when they are exercised. It can be combined with the Wildcat Experience (at a discounted rate). Other animals to see include meerkats and tortoises, and birds such as marabou storks and blue cranes (South Africa's national bird). African penguins can be seen through glass in the penguin pool; many of them have been washed ashore by strong currents from colonies on the islands along the Garden Route, and after they are stabilized, they are returned to sea. There's a pleasant tea garden on site.

Nature's Valley

If you are in a hurry, stay on the N2, but the more spectacular route is via the village of Nature's Valley along the old R102 that branches off the N2 just after The Crags, about 30 km east of Plettenberg Bay. This approach by road is particularly spectacular. The R102, dropping 223 m to sea level via the narrow **Kalanderkloof Gorge**, twij102sts and turns through lush green coastal forest. Look out for vervet monkeys and Knysna loeries in the trees. At the bottom is a lagoon formed by the sand dunes blocking the estuary of the **Groot River**, which is popular for swimming, sailing and canoeing. Beyond is the beach where there are several braai spots, but be warned that swimming in the sea is not safe. A right turn leads into the village, which is surrounded on three sides by the western section of the **Garden Route National Park (Tsitsikamma Section)** (see below), and is made up of a collection of holiday cottages and the **Nature's Valley Restaurant & Trading Store**, an all-in-one shop, restaurant, bar, takeaway and **tourist information bureau** ⓘ *T044-270 6833, www.natures-valley.com, 0830-1700.* Note that there are no banks in Nature's Valley. At the store, you can pick up a booklet with maps of local forest trails. The best (though steepest) is to **Pig's Head**, a rocky outcrop overlooking the lagoon. The views of the estuary, ocean, and on a clear day, as far as the Robberg Peninsula on the far side of Plettenberg Bay are magnificent.

Groot River and Bloukrans Passes

As the road starts to climb out of the Groot Valley on the Groot River Pass, built in 1880 by Thomas Bain, it passes the **Nature's Valley Rest Camp** on the right. This is the camp at the western end of the Garden Route National Park (Tsitsikamma Section) (see page 199 for details). Many visitors will find themselves here because it is one end of the Garden Route's most spectacular hiking trails, the **Otter Trail** (see box, page 200). From the top of the Groot River Pass the road continues for 6 km before crossing a second river valley, the Bloukrans Pass. Here it descends 183 m into the narrow gorge before crossing the river and climbing up again. The R102 rejoins the N2 highway 10 km further on and crosses the **Bloukrans Bridge**, built in 1984, 217 m above the Bloukrans River, and reputedly the highest single-span arch bridge in Africa, Just after the bridge is a turning to the left that leads to a viewpoint at the top of the Bloukrans Gorge.

   The main reason for stopping here is the **Bloukrans Bungee Jump** ⓘ *38 km from Plett, T042-281 1458, www.faceadrenalin.com, 0900-1700, booking not essential but recommended, bungee jump R850, which includes the bridge walk, bridge walk only R120, DVDs and T-shirts available, Cliffhanger Pub & Restaurant.* At 216 m this is the highest commercial bungee in the world. The first rebound is longer than the previous holder of the record, the 111-m bungee jump at Victoria Falls. It's a hugely exhilarating experience and the free fall once you've leapt from the bridge lasts seven seconds, travelling over 170 kph before you reach the maximum length of the bungee cord. The minimum age is 14 and there is no upper age limit; a 96-year-old has previously jumped. If you cannot muster the courage to jump, you can go on a guided bridge walk, which involves walking out to the bungee platform along the caged walkway underneath the road surface of the bridge, where a guide tells you how the bridge was built and a little bit about the surrounding area. This is not for anyone who suffers from vertigo, but if you want to support a mate who's doing a jump, it's a great way to feel some of the fear they are experiencing when standing on the lip of the bungee platform. Also at the top of the gorge is the **Tsitsikamma Forest Village Market**, a sustainable initiative to help local people make and sell curios to the many passing tourists. Shops are in a collection of attractive reed Khosian huts, and you can buy items such as candles or home-made paper.

Listings East of Plettenberg Bay *map p150*

$$$$ Hog Hollow Country Lodge
18 km east of Plettenberg Bay at The Crags off the N2, T044-534 8879, www.hog-hollow.com.
Set in a private nature reserve, with 15 suites, each with its own wooden deck with hammock overlooking the Matjies River gorge and Tsitsikamma Mountains. Good evening meals, swimming pool with stunning views, library/lounge, plenty of walks which are ideal for birdwatching,

$$$$-$$$ Kurland Hotel
19 km east of Plettenberg Bay at The Crags off the N2, T044-534 8082, www.kurland.co.za.
Set in expansive 1700-ha grounds, famous for its polo fields, with 12 Cape Dutch-style cottages, some with loft rooms for children, excellent food and wine, pool and spa, horse riding and quad-biking. Luxurious but family friendly with nannies and kids' activities.

$$ Forever Resorts Plettenberg
6 km east of Plett on the Keurbooms River, T044-535 9309, www.foreverplettenberg.co.za.
30 neat self-catering chalets nestled along the riverbank, plus 112 camping and caravan spots ($) with excellent facilities, swimming pool, canoes and pedalos for hire, good all-round family option but gets busy during school holidays.

Nature's Valley
SANPark's Nature's Valley Rest Camp in the Garden Route National Park (Tsitsikamma Section) is accessed from Nature's Valley; for details see page 197.

$$ Face Tranquility B&B
130 St Michaels Av, T044-531 6663, www.tranquilitylodge.co.za.
Lovely reed-and-timber lodge in pretty gardens, 7 small but comfortable rooms, nicely decorated throughout, good breakfasts and next door to **Nature's Valley Pub & Restaurant**, splash pool, kayaks to enjoy on the lagoon. Affiliated with Face Adrenalin who operates the Bloukrans Bungee Jump; guests get 10% off the jump or a free bridge walk.

$$ Lily Pond Country Lodge
on the R102 3 km from the turn-off on the N2, T044-534 8767, www.lilypond.co.za.
Set in 12 ha of lovely indigenous forest. 10 modern rooms with small patios, dining deck, and a jacuzzi and stunning black rim-flow pool surrounded by (as the name suggests) beautiful lily ponds which attract birds and butterflies.

Restaurants

$$ Bramon Wine Estate
N2 18 km from Plett, 2 km before The Crags, T044-534 8007, www.bramonwines.co.za. Open 1100-1700.
Close to the animal attractions at The Crags, this wine estate produces an award-winning Cap Classique sparkling wine and 'The Crags' Sauvignon Blanc. There's a tasting centre and the delightful restaurant offers outside tables that are placed at the start of each row of vines with views of the Tsitsikamma Mountains. To accompany a glass or 2 of bubbly, the menu is tapas-style (cheeses, oysters, cold meats, pâtés and the like) served with home-made bread and polished off with a decadent dessert. Set aside a few hours to enjoy the experience.

Cafés

Peppermill Café
N2, just before the turn-off to Monkeyland, T044-534 8997. Open 0800-1700.
At the Mill Centre Mohair Shop, serving breakfasts, light meals, including ploughman's lunch, cakes and fruit smoothies. The shop sells mohair blankets, scarves and luxurious soft socks, and there are a few Angora goats that children can pet.

Thyme and Again
N2, opposite the Keurboom River turning, T044-535 9432, www.thyme-and-again. co.za. Open 0800-1600.
Great farm stall with tables on a vine-covered stoep, serving breakfasts and a delicious selection of still-warm breads, pies and pastries. Try the home-made ginger beer.

What to do

Boat trip
Keurbooms River Ferries, *the ferry departs from the jetty on the east side of the Keurbooms River Bridge on the N2, 7 km from Plett, T083-254 3551, www.ferry.co.za.* 2½-hr boat trip plus walk and swim, 1100, 1400 and 1700, R140, children (3-12) R70, under 3 free, (plus Cape Nature entrance fees), there's a cash bar and you can bring your own picnic. This is a relaxing way to be introduced to the plants, sights and sounds of the Keurbooms River Nature Reserve, and the ferry goes upstream through a spectacular gorge. At the furthest point there is an optional 30-min guided walk; make sure you are wearing sturdy footwear.

Garden Route National Park (Tsitsikamma Section)
coastal bush, rocky shoreline and one of the country's best hiking trails

Tsitsikamma is a khoi word meaning 'place of abundant or sparkling water', and this section of the Garden Route National Park consists of a beautiful 80-km stretch of lush coastal forest between Nature's Valley and Oubosstrand. At the western end, where the Otter Trail (see box, page 200) reaches the Groot River estuary, the park boundary extends 3 km inland, but for most of its length it is no more than 500 m wide, though the park boundaries reach out to sea for more than 5 km in parts. The main administrative office is at Storms River Mouth Rest Camp, which is almost the midpoint of the park.

Visiting Garden Route National Park (Tsitsikamma Section)
The Tsitsikamma Section is 68 km from Plettenberg Bay and 195 km from Port Elizabeth. There are two access points into the park depending on which rest camp you are staying in, although day visitors generally enter through the Storms River Mouth entrance, where

Otter Trail

This is one of South Africa's best hiking trails, managed by **South African National Parks (SANParks)**, T012-426 5111, www.sanparks.org. The 42.5-km, five-day/four-night trail, marked with painted otter footprints and named after the Cape clawless otter that occurs in the region, runs between Storms River Mouth and Nature's Valley in the Tsitsikamma Section of the Garden Route National Park. Only 12 people can start the trail each day and groups must consist of a minimum of four, no under 12s and anyone over 65 needs a doctor's certificate to confirm fitness level. It costs R1000 per person, which includes four nights in the hiking huts as well as the permit. Due to its popularity, bookings are open up to 13 months in advance.

None of the sectors is that long, but it is still fairly strenuous in parts since you have to cross 11 rivers and there are steep ascents and descents at each river crossing. The Bloukrans River crossing presents the most problems. Check tide tables; you will at least have to wade, or even swim across. Waterproofing for your rucksack is vital. If you are unable to cross the river, you can take the escape route, which branches to the right of the trail, where it climbs steeply to the top of the plateau and leads to the N2. At each overnight stop there are two log huts, each sleeping six people in bunk beds; mattresses and firewood are provided. Each hut has a braai place with a sturdy steel grill but hikers need to provide their own pots for cooking. There are numerous streams and springs throughout the length of the Otter Trail that are suitable for drinking. However, it may be wise to use purification tablets.

The trail traverses some spectacular landscape and never strays far from the coastline. Vegetation varies from fynbos plateaux to densely forested valleys and in parts goes along rocky cliffs and boulder-strewn beaches. Apart from the natural beauty and the birdlife, the trail passes some fine waterfalls and Strandloper caves. Look out for the fine old hardwood trees which have escaped the dreaded axe, and in spring, an abundance of wild flowers.

there are better facilities for those on day trips. The turn-off for **Storms River Mouth Rest Camp** is on a straight stretch of the N2, about 20 km after Bloukrans Bridge, and 4 km before the Storms River Village. A surfaced road leads down to the reception centre on the coast. The last part of this drive is a beautiful, steep descent through lush rainforest, a marked contrast to the coniferous plantations along the N2.

The **Nature's Valley Rest Camp** is just outside the village of the same name 40 km west of Storms River Mouth and can only be reached from the R102; when approaching from Plett take the Nature's Valley turning at Kurland (see page 197).

Park information Gates 0600-1930, office 0730-1800, overnight visitors arriving after 1800 should arrange to pick up keys from the gate, T042-281 1607, www.sanparks.org, R180, children (2-11) R90. At the Storms River Mouth Rest Camp there's a shop, 0800-1800, which stocks gift items as well as groceries, wine and beer, and a restaurant, 0730-2130, and other facilities include a swimming pool, and short boat trips on the *Spirit of Tsitsikamma*, which runs every 45 minutes, 0900-1600, and goes up the Storms River Gorge from the jetty below the suspension bridge.

Vegetation and wildlife

A cross-section of the coastlands would reveal the Tsitsikamma Mountains (900-1600 m), whose slopes level off into a coastal plain or plateau at about 230 m, and then the forested cliffs which plunge 230 m into the ocean. The slope is only precipitous in a few places; elsewhere along the coast it is still very steep, but there is enough soil to support the rainforest which the park was in part created to protect. The rainforest is the last remnant of a forest which was once found right along this coast between the ocean and the mountains. The canopy ranges between 18 m and 30 m and is closed, which makes the paths nice and shady. The most common species of tree are milkwood, real yellowwood, stinkwood, Cape blackwood, forest elder, white pear and candlewood, plus the famous Outeniqua yellowwood, a forest giant. All are magnificent trees which combine with climbers such as wild grape, red saffron and milky rope to create an outstandingly beautiful forest.

The mammal species that live in the park include caracal, bushbuck, blue duiker, grysbok, bushpig and the Cape clawless otter, but given the steep slopes and dense forest, sightings are very rare. Birdwatching, however, is very rewarding, and over 220 bird species have been identified. The most colourful bird in the forest is the Knysna lourie (*Tauraco corythaix*). Its call is a korr korr korr, and in flight it has a flash of deep red in its wings, with a green body and distinctive crest. In the vicinity of the Storms River and Groot River estuaries you will see an entirely different selection of birds: over 40 species of seabird have been recorded here. The most satisfying sighting is the rare African black oystercatcher, with its black plumage and red eyes, beak and legs.

Hiking

There are four trails in the vicinity of the Storms River Mouth Rest Camp. The most popular is the 2-km **Mouth Trail,** which goes along a raised boardwalk from the restaurant to the mouth of the Storms River, the *Spirit of Tsitsikamma* boat jetty, and the suspension bridge (which appears in many pictures promoting the Garden Route). Allow about 40 minutes for the walk to the bridge and back, or the path continues on the other side of the bridge where you can climb the hill for superb views. The other trails are the **Lourie Trail,** 1 km through the forested slopes behind the camp; the **Blue Duiker Trail,** 3.7 km further into the forest; and the **Waterfall Trail,** a 6-km walk along the first part of the Otter Trail (see box, page 200); hikers without a permit have to turn back at the waterfall.

In addition to the Otter Trail managed by SANParks is the **Dolphin Trail** ① *T042-280 3588, www.dolphintrail.co.za,* a three-day guided trail to the east of Storms River Rest Camp. This is a more 'upmarket' hike – luggage is transported from one night stop to the next, accommodation is in luxurious lodges, all meals are included (pre-packed picnics for lunch), and the hike is professionally guided. This trail is R5500 per person for three days (no children under 12). For those without transport, transfers can be arranged from George or Port Elizabeth.

Storms River Village

Surrounded by the **Tsitsikamma Forest,** Storms River Village is 23 km from Bloukrans and 4 km east from the entrance to the Garden Route National Park (Tsitsikamma Section), and 1 km south of the N2. Administratively, this is the first settlement in the Eastern Cape Province, but it is also regarded as the first and last town along the Garden Route, hence its inclusion here. This small village of around 40 houses, some of them restored historical woodcutters cottages, has several accommodation options catering for visitors to the park, and hikers wishing to head for the inland mountains. It's also a stop-off for the **Baz Bus** and the starting point for many of the adventure activities in the region. The small supermarket and liquor store are useful for those self-catering at Tsitsikamma. Note that the village is nowhere near the sea and is not to be confused with Storms River Mouth which is in the park. Another 5 km east of the village along the N2 is the **Petroport Tsitsikamma** next to the 120-m-high bridge that spans the Storms River Gorge (again inland from the actual river mouth). A service station has been here since the bridge was built in 1956, and it remains a popular stopover with petrol pumps, curio shops, a restaurant and takeaways, and there's a viewing platform to look down into the river gorge. It's also an official stop for the mainline buses that travel along the Garden Route. From the Petroport, the N2 continues for another 165 km to Port Elizabeth.

Listings Garden Route National Park (Tsitsikamma Section) *map p150*

Where to stay

Reservations, through **SANParks**, T012-428 9111, www.sanparks.org, for cancellations and reservations under 72 hrs contact **Storms River Mouth Rest Camp** directly, T042-281 1607.

$$-$ Storms River Mouth Rest Camp
Off the N2 between the Storms River Bridge and Storms River village.
This is the main camp on a narrow strip of land between the ocean and forested hills, and is one of the most beautiful settings of all the national parks. It's a real thrill to watch the waves crashing on the rocks right in front of you but it is exposed when the wind blows. There are a number of wooden fully equipped self-catering chalets sleeping up to 6, and basic forest cabins sleeping 2 and sharing communal kitchen and ablutions with campers. Swimming pool, shop selling some groceries and restaurant.

$ Nature's Valley Rest Camp
40 km west of Storms River Mouth Rest Camp and accessed from Nature's Valley (page 197).
Set in an indigenous forest on the banks of the Groot River, with simple forest huts with 2 beds and electricity and campsites. There's no shop or restaurant, but there are these in the village, 3 km away. There are several day walks from the camp, and canoes can

be hired from reception for paddles to the Groot River mouth.

Storms River Village

$$$-$$ Tsitsikamma Lodge
2 km east of the village along the N2, T042-280 3802, www.riverhotels.co.za.
Country resort set in forested grounds with 32 log cabins each with spa bath (perfect after a long hike) and braais, some with fireplaces and extra lofts for children. Restaurant serving buffet breakfasts and dinners, packed lunches available, swimming pool, can arrange transport to the start and from the end of the Otter Trail (see page 200).

$$ Tsitsikamma Village Inn
Darnell St, T042-281 1711, www.tsitsikammahotel.co.za.
Central original Cape Dutch homestead dating from 1845 with 49 rooms in the gardens in recreated colonial-style buildings: terraced Georgian cottages, woodcutter's log cabins, or a Drostdy (magistrate's house), for example. All have comfortable furnishings, many with brass beds and private stoeps. Good restaurant and the **Hunter's Pub** is the focal point of the village.

$ Tube 'n Axe

Corner of Darnell and Saffron Streets, T042-281 1757, www.tubenaxe.co.za.
4-bed dorms, doubles and A-frame log cabins sleeping up to 4, set in a forested garden with plenty of room for camping and vehicles. The rustic bar has a pool table and braai pit. Breakfast and dinner available or self-catering kitchen. Shuttles to the Bloukrans Bridge Bungee, they rent out quad bikes and mountain bikes, and operate the popular **Blackwater Tubing** (see right). **Baz Bus** stop.

What to do

Untouched Adventures, *office at the Storms River Mouth Rest Camp, T078-871 1952, www. untouchedadventures.com.* Can organize a number of activities in the park including snorkelling among the rocks in front of the restaurant, from R180, scuba diving including wetsuits, etc, from R500, and 2- to 3-hr combo trips for R400 of kayaking and kloofing which involves kayaking from the suspension bridge at Storms River Mouth as far as it's possible before alighting for a scramble over the rocks in the gorge.

Storms River Village
Tour operators

Blackwater Tubing, *Tube 'n Axe, see Where to stay, left, T042-281 1757, www. blackwatertubing.net.* This starts with a briefing at Tube 'n Axe, before a short a drive through the Tsitsikamma forest, then a steep descent by rope ladder to the Storms River gorge followed by a float on a giant inner tube to the suspension bridge within the Garden Route National Park (Tsitsikamma Section). The 'blackwater' refers to a stretch of river where you float under 2 overhangs of rock so close together, it's like floating through a cave. The excursion takes 4-5 hrs and costs R850.

Tsitikamma Canopy Tour, *the office is on Darnell St in the middle of the village, T042-281 1836, www.canopytour.co.za.* This is the original canopy tour, although there are now several others around South Africa. It is a fantastic way to see the forest from a different angle, which involves climbing up into the giant yellowwood trees and gliding between 10 different 30-m-high platforms on a steel rope, the longest of which is 100 m. Excellent for birdwatching, and the Knysna loerie may be spotted. Suitable for all ages from 7 years old. Departures every 45 mins Sep-May 0700-1600, Jun-Aug 0800-1530, the excursion lasts around 3 hrs, costs R495 and includes light refreshments. DVDs and photos available.

Practicalities
Cape Town &
Garden Route

Getting there

Air

The three main international airports in South Africa are: **OR Tambo International Airport** in Johannesburg, **Cape Town International Airport** in Cape Town, see page 73, and **King Shaka International Airport** in Durban. Johannesburg is the regional hub with numerous daily flights to and from Europe, North America, Asia and Australia. Although most flights arrive in Johannesburg, a fair number of international carriers also fly directly to Cape Town, and a couple directly to Durban.

With a huge choice of routes and flights, you need to book well in advance for the best fares, especially over the Christmas and New Year period which is the peak summer holiday season in South Africa.

For live flight information visit the **Airport Company of South Africa**'s website, www.acsa.co.za, or phone T0867-277888.

Jet lag is not an issue if flying from Europe to South Africa as there is only a minimal time difference.

Getting around

South Africa has an efficient transport network linking its towns and cities, making travelling the considerable distances a straightforward experience. Affordable domestic flights link the cities, a sophisticated army of private coaches criss-crosses the country, and the train system, although painfully slow, offers another way of getting from A to B. City transport is improving all the time, and new transport systems are being developed at a rapid pace, while existing ones are being upgraded. Nevertheless, having your own transport on a visit to South Africa remains the most flexible option.

Air

There are numerous daily flights linking the cities, and Johannesburg and Durban are no more than two hours' flying time to Cape Town. There are also flights from Johannesburg to George on the Garden Route and Port Elizabeth in the Eastern Cape, the nearest airport to the eastern end of the Garden Route.

Airlines

By booking early online, good deals can be found with all the airlines. You can either book directly or through the national booking agency **Computicket**; online at www.computicket.com, or in South Africa, at any of their kiosks in the shopping malls or any branch of **Checkers** and **Shoprite** supermarkets.

British Airways Comair T011-441 8600, www.britishairways.com, has daily flights between Johannesburg, Cape Town, Durban, Nelspruit and Port Elizabeth, as well as regional flights between Johannesburg and Mauritius, Windhoek, Livingstone, Victoria Falls and Harare.

FlySafair T0871-351 351 (in South Africa), T011-928 0000 (from overseas), www.flysafair.co.za, is a no-frills airline with daily services between Cape Town, Johannesburg, Port Elizabeth and George.

Kulula T0861-585 852 (in South Africa), T011-921 0111 (from overseas), www.kulula.com, is British Airways no-frills airline with daily services between Cape Town, Durban, Johannesburg, Port Elizabeth, Nelspruit, East London and George. They also fly to Mauritius, Maputo, Windhoek, Victoria Falls, Livingstone and Harare on a code-share agreement with BA.

Mango T0861-162 646 (in South Africa), T011-359 1222 (from overseas), www.flymango.com, another no-frills operator, has daily flights between Johannesburg, Cape Town, Durban, George and Bloemfontein.

South African Airways (SAA), T0861-359 722 (in South Africa), T011-978 1111 (from overseas), www.flysaa.com, cover all the country's major centres and have flights to most southern African cities, in conjunction with both their subsidiaries SA Airlink and SA Express.

Rail

Most of the major cities are linked by rail and, while this is a comfortable and relaxing way to travel, it is very slow. The trains are run by **Shosholoza Meyl**, part of the national network **Spoornet**, T0860-008 888 (in South Africa), T011-774 4555 (from overseas), www.shosholozameyl.co.za. There are services between Johannesburg and Cape Town (27 hours) and Johannesburg and Port Elizabeth (20 hours); timetables and fares can be found on the website. All the trains travel overnight, so they arrive at some stations en route at inconvenient times, but they have dining cars and sleeping carriages with coupés that sleep two or four people.

Spoornet also operate a more upmarket service, the **Premier Classe**, T011-774 5247, www.premierclasse.co.za, between Johannesburg and Cape Town (25 hours), twice a week. A lot nicer than the regular train, the two-bed coupés have extras like dressing gowns, toiletries and 'room service', and there's a good restaurant car serving breakfast, high tea and dinner; fares include all meals. The train has an additional 'spa-car' for pampering, and vehicles can be taken on the trains, which gives the option of taking the train in one direction and driving in the other.

Luxury trains

If the journey is more important than the destination, then old-fashioned luxury trains operate much like five-star hotels on wheels. The **Blue Train**, T021-334 8459, www.bluetrain.co.za, is considered to be southern Africa's premier luxury train. The wood-panelled coaches feature luxury coupés with en suite bathrooms, elegant lounge cars and fine dining in the restaurant car. It runs between Johannesburg and Cape Town and takes one day and one night. **Rovos Rail**, T012-315 8242, www.rovos.co.za, is a similar luxury train that runs between Tshwane (Pretoria) and Cape Town. Check out the websites for schedules and prices.

Road

Bus and coach

Baz Bus The **Baz Bus** (T021-422 5202, www.bazbus.com), a hop-on, hop-off bus that collects and drops off passengers at their chosen backpacker hostel, remains one of the most popular ways of seeing the country on a budget. There are a few exceptions such as Hermanus, where the bus will drop you off at the closest point on the main road, and the hostels will then meet you for an extra charge. The Baz Bus route is **Cape Town–Durban** along the coast, and **Durban–Tshwane (Pretoria)** via the Drakensberg. Tickets are priced per segment, for example from Cape Town to Port Elizabeth, and you can hop on and off as many times as you like in the given segment, but must not backtrack. Visit the website for the full timetable.

Intercity coaches **Greyhound**, T083-915 9000 (in South Africa), T011-276 8550 (from overseas), www.greyhound.co.za; **Intercape**, T0861-287 287 (in South Africa), T012-380 4400 (from overseas), www.intercape.co.za; and **Translux**, T0861-589 282 (in South Africa), T011-774 3333 (from overseas), www.translux.co.za, are the three major long-distance bus companies that run between towns and popular destinations, and to some cities in South Africa's neighbouring countries. All bus tickets can be booked directly with the companies or through the national booking agency, **Computicket**; online at www.computicket.com, or at any of their kiosks in the shopping malls or any branch of Checkers and Shoprite supermarkets in South Africa. The coaches are air conditioned and have a toilet; some sell refreshments and show videos. They will stop at least every three to four hours to change drivers and give the passengers a chance to stretch their legs. Note that long-distance buses are more than twice as fast as the trains.

Car

Hiring a car for part, or all, of your journey is undoubtedly the best way to see South Africa; you get to travel at your own leisurely pace and explore more out-of-the-way regions without being tied to a tour or a timetable. Driving isn't challenging; the roads are generally in excellent condition and, away from the major urban centres, there is little traffic. Fuel is available 24 hours a day at the fuel stations in the cities and along the national highways. Driving is on the left side of the road and speed limits are 60 kph in built-up areas, 80 kph on minor roads and 120 kph on highways.

There is a range of vehicles to choose from, from basic hatchbacks and saloon cars, to camper vans and fully equipped 4WD vehicles. Costs for car hire vary considerably and depend on days of the week, season, type of vehicle and terms (insurance, excess, mileage, etc). A compact car starts from as little as R200-250 per day; a fully equipped 4WD or camper van with tents and equipment from R800-1300 per day.

The minimum age to rent a car is usually 23. A driver's licence (with a translation if it's not in English) and a credit card are essential. Tourist offices usually recommend large international organizations such as **Avis** or **Budget**, but there are a number of reliable local companies and it is worth asking at hotels for recommended local car hire companies. Most of the large companies have kiosks at the airport and partner with the airlines, so it's also possible to book a car online with your flight. For car hire companies see Cape Town Transport, page 75.

In the event of an accident, call your car hire company's emergency number. For emergency breakdown and traffic update information contact the **Automobile Association of South Africa**, T083-84322, www.aa.co.za.

Hitchhiking

This is not common in South Africa and is not recommended as it can be very dangerous. Women should never hitch, under any circumstances, even in a group. If you have to hitch, say if your vehicle has broken down, be very wary of who you are accepting a lift from, and a car with a family or couple is usually the best option.

Taxi

Except in the major cities there are few taxi ranks in South African towns so it's generally a better idea to order a taxi in advance. Any hotel or restaurant will make a booking for you. Taxis are metered and charge around R11-14 per kilometre. Groups should request a larger vehicle if available as these can carry up to seven people. Some can also accommodate wheelchairs.

Minibus taxi The majority of South Africa's commuters travel by minibus taxis. However, the accident rate of such vehicles is notoriously high, with speeding, overcrowding and lack of maintenance being the main causes. There is also the problem of possible robbery, especially at the crowded taxi ranks, so you should exercise caution and always ask people in the know before using them. In Cape Town, the better option is to use the larger public buses.

Essentials A-Z

Accident and emergency

Police, T10111; **Medical**, T10177; **Fire**, T10111. All emergencies from a cell phone, T112.

Disabled travellers

Facilities are generally of a high standard and the airports are fully wheelchair accessible and can provide transport for less mobile travellers. Modern hotels have specially adapted rooms, but it is worth enquiring in advance at older hotels or more remote places. Almost all shopping malls, museums and tourist attractions have ramps or lifts and disabled parking right by the entrance. The more modern transport – for example **City Sightseeing Cape Town** and **MyCiTi** buses – are accessible for wheelchairs. With notice, the larger car hire companies like **Avis**, **Budget** and **Hertz**, can organize cars with hand controls.

Electricity

220/230 volts AC at 50 Hz. Most plugs and appliances are 3-point round-pin (1 10-mm and 2 8-mm prongs). Hotels usually have 2-pin sockets for razors and chargers.

Embassies and consulates

For embassies and consulates of South Africa, see www.embassiesabroad.com.

Health

Before you travel

See your GP or travel clinic at least 6 weeks before departure for general advice on travel risks and vaccinations. Make sure you have sufficient medical travel insurance, get a dental check, know your own blood group and, if you suffer a long-term condition such as diabetes, epilepsy or a serious allergy, obtain a Medic Alert bracelet/necklace (www.medicalert.co.uk). If you wear glasses, take a copy of your prescription.

Vaccinations

Confirm your primary courses and boosters are up to date. Courses or boosters usually advised: diphtheria; tetanus; poliomyelitis; hepatitis A. Vaccines sometimes advised: tuberculosis; hepatitis B; rabies; cholera; typhoid. The final decision, however, should be based on a consultation with your doctor or travel clinic.

Health risks

Diarrhoea Symptoms should be relatively short lived but if they persist beyond 2 weeks specialist medical attention should be sought. Also seek medical help if there is blood in the stools and/or fever. Adults can use an antidiarrhoeal medication to control the symptoms but only for up to 24 hrs. In addition keep well hydrated by drinking plenty of fluids and eat bland foods. Oral rehydration sachets taken after each loose stool are a useful way to keep well hydrated. These should always be used when treating children and the elderly.

The standard advice to prevent problems is to be careful with water and food. If you have any doubts drink bottled water, and be wary of salads, re-heated foods or food that has been left out in the sun. On the positive side, very few people experience stomach problems in South Africa.

HIV Southern Africa has one of the highest rates of HIV in the world. Visitors should be aware of the dangers of infection and take the necessary precautions with sex, needles, medical treatment and in the case of a blood tranfusion.

Malaria South Africa only has a very low seasonal (Dec-Apr) risk of malaria in the extreme east of the country along the Mozambique border. This includes part of Kruger National Park, so if you are travelling there from the Western Cape, consult your doctor or travel clinic about taking anti-malarials and ensure you finish the recommended course.

Sun Protect yourself adequately against the sun. Apply a high-factor sunscreen (greater than SPF15) and also make sure it screens against UVB. Prevent heat exhaustion and heatstroke by drinking enough fluids throughout the day. Use rehydration salts mixed with water to replenish fluids and salts and find somewhere cool and shady to recover.

If you get sick

There are plenty of private hospitals in South Africa, which have 24-hr emergency departments and pharmacies, run by **Medi-Clinic** (www.mediclinic.co.za) or **Netcare** (www.netcare.co.za). It is essential to have travel insurance as hospital bills need to be paid at the time of admittance, so keep all paperwork to make a claim.

Cape Town

The most central hospitals in Cape Town are:
Cape Town Medi-Clinic, *21 Hof St, Gardens, T021-464 5500, www.mediclinic.co.za.*
Christiaan Barnard Memorial Hospital, *181 Longmarket St, T021-480 6111, www.netcare.co.za.*
Netcare Travel Clinic, *11th floor, Picbel Parkade, Strand St, T021-419 3172, www.travelclinic.co.za*, if you need to have a vaccination or buy anti-malaria medication while in South Africa.

Winelands

Medi-Clinic, *Main Rd, Somerset West, T021-850 9000, www.mediclinic.co.za.*
Medi-Clinic, *corner of Saffraan and Rokewood avenues, off the R44 south*

of town, Stellenbosch, T021-861 2095, www.mediclinic.co.za.
Medi-Clinic, *Berlyn St, Paarl North, Paarl, T021-807 8000, www.mediclinic.co.za.*

Whale Coast

Hermanus Medi-Clinic, *Hospital St, Hermanus, T028-313 0168, www.mediclinic.co.za.*

Garden Route

Life Bay View Private Hospital, *Alhof St, Mossel Bay, T044-691 3718, www.lifehealthcare.co.za.*
George Medi-Clinic, *corner of Gloucester and York streets, George, T044- 803 2000, www.mediclinic.co.za.*
Klein Karoo MediClinic, *185 Church St, Oudtshoorn, T044-272 0111, www.mediclinic.co.za.*
Life Knysna Private Hospital, *Hunters Drive, Knysna, T044-384 1083, www.lifehealthcare.co.za.*
Plettenberg Bay Medi-Clinic, *Muller St, Plettenberg Bay, T044-501 5100, www.mediclinic.co.za.*

Insurance

We strongly recommend that you invest in a good insurance policy that covers you for theft or loss of possessions and money, the cost of medical and dental treatment, cancellation of flights, delays in travel arrangements, accidents, missed departures, lost baggage and lost passport. Be sure to check on inclusion of 'dangerous activities' if you plan on doing any. These generally include climbing, diving, skiing, horse riding, parachuting, even trekking. You should always read the small print carefully. Not all policies cover ambulance, helicopter rescue or emergency flights home.

There are a variety of policies to choose from, so it's best to shop around. Your travel agent can advise on the best deals available. Reputable student travel organizations often offer good-value policies. Travellers from North America can try the **International**

Student Insurance Service (ISIS), which is available through STA, T800-7814040, www.statravel.com. Companies worth trying in Britain include Direct Line Insurance, T0845-246 8704, www.directline.com, and the Flexicover Group, T0800-093 9495, www.flexicover.net. Some companies will not cover those over 65. The best policies for older travellers are through Age UK, T0845-600 3348, www.ageuk.org.uk.

Money

Exchange rates: £1 = R19.95, US$1 = R12.75, €1 = R14.29 (August 2015).

Currency

The South African currency is the **rand** (R) which is divided into 100 **cents** (c). Notes are in 200, 100, 50, 20 and 10 rand, and coins are in 5, 2, 1 rand and 50, 20 and 10 cents. You can carry your funds in currency cards, credit cards, rand, US dollars, euros or pounds sterling.

Banks and changing money

South Africa's main banks are ABSA, First National, Nedbank and Standard Bank. All have foreign exchange services. You can also change money at Bidvest, www.bidvestbank.co.za, Master Currency, www.mastercurrency.co.za, and Travelex, www.travelex.co.za, which have bureaux de change at the main airports and large shopping malls in the cities. These have longer hours than the banks and are open on Sun and public holidays.

ATMS, currency and credit cards

You can get all the way around South Africa with a **credit** or **debit card**. Not only are they a convenient method of covering major expenses but they offer some of the most competitive exchange rates when withdrawing cash from ATMs, and you can only hire a car with a credit (not debit) card. The chip and pin system is common, though not yet universal in South Africa. **ATMs** are everywhere: Plus, Cirrus, Visa, MasterCard, American Express and Diners Club are all accepted. The amount you can withdraw varies between systems and cards, but you should be able to take out at least R2000 a day. Note that theft during or immediately after a withdrawal is not unknown, so never accept a stranger's help at an ATM and avoid using street-side ATMs. Instead, go into a bank or shopping mall, where guards are often on duty.

If you don't want to carry lots of cash, prepaid **currency cards** allow you to preload money from your bank account, fixed at the day's exchange rate. They look like a credit or debit card and are issued by specialist money changing companies, such as Travelex and Caxton FX. You can top up and check your balance by phone, online and sometimes by text.

Lost or stolen cards American Express, T0800-110929; Diners Club, T0800-112017; MasterCard, T0800- 990418; Visa, T0800-990475.

Public holidays

South African school holidays are mid-Dec to mid-Jan; mid-Apr to early May; early Aug to early Sep. During these times the price of accommodation in Cape Town and along the Garden Route is often higher and most of the popular destinations are fully booked. The government lists the exact dates for the school calendar on their website: www.gov.za. When a public holiday falls on a Sun, the following Mon becomes a holiday. Most businesses will close but shopping malls and large supermarkets in city centres remain open (public holidays are some of their busiest days). All tourist attractions are open on public holidays.

1 Jan New Year's Day
21 Mar Human Rights' Day
Mar/Apr Good Friday; Family Day
(Mon following Easter Sunday)
27 Apr Freedom Day
1 May Workers' Day

16 Jun **Youth Day**
9 Aug **National Women's Day**
24 Sep **Heritage Day** (also National Braai Day)
16 Dec **Day of Reconciliation**
25 Dec **Christmas Day**
26 Dec **Day of Goodwill**

Safety

Dangers facing tourists are on the whole limited to mugging or, on occasion, carjacking. You should be aware that your assailant may well be armed and any form of resistance could be fatal. South Africa has had more than its fair share of well-publicized crime problems but, despite the statistics, much of the serious, violent crime is gang-based and occurs in areas that tourists are unlikely to visit. The crime rate in the districts where most of the hotels, hostels, nightlife and shops are located has dropped significantly in recent decades, due mainly to an increase in security measures, and you should experience few problems in these areas. Nevertheless, listen to advice from locals about which areas to avoid, and as the likelihood of being mugged increases sharply after dark, take a taxi directly to and from your destination. Avoid driving after dark, and if you are going to be travelling alone in a car, it's a good idea to take a mobile phone in case of break down.

Taxes

Tourists can reclaim the 14% VAT on purchases bought in South Africa whose total value exceeds R250. You can do this when departing, at the VAT reclaim desks at airports in Johannesburg, Cape Town and Durban or at border posts. For more information visit www.taxrefunds.co.za.

Telephone *Country code: +27*

International direct dialling code 00; directory enquires T1023; international enquires T1025.

You must dial the full 3-digit regional code for every number in South Africa, even when you are calling from within that region.

The telephone service is very efficient and public coin and card phones can be found in shopping malls, airports and post offices. However, note that they are gradually being decommissioned given that almost everyone in South Africa carries a mobile phone. Overseas visitors should be able to use their mobiles on international roaming. Alternatively, you can buy a local SIM card and start-up pack from any of the phone shops and at the 3 international airports, which also offer phone and SIM hire.

Time

South Africa has only 1 time zone: GMT +2 hrs (+1 during UK Summer Time Mar-Oct).

Tipping

Waiters, hotel porters, chambermaids and tour guides should be tipped 10-15%. When leaving a tip make sure it goes to the intended person. It is common practice to tip petrol pump attendants, depending on their service – around R5 for a fill up, oil and water check and comprehensive windscreen clean. It is also customary to tip car guards R2-5 if parking on the street. They are usually identified by a work vest or badge. On safari you are expected to tip guides. If in any doubt, ask the company that you booked with for advice on how much to tip.

Tourist information

South African Tourism (SATOUR), *T011-895 3000, www.southafrica.net*, has a very useful website with information on special interest travel, maps, latest travel news, airlines, accommodation and national parks. The website is published in 15 languages and each version provides specific information for people coming from specific countries. SATOUR also has offices around the world. Regional and local tourism authorities are some of the best sources of information once in the country; even the smallest town will have a tourist office with details of local sights and accommodation. Local tourist offices are listed under individual towns.

Visas and immigration

Most nationalities, including EU nationals and citizens from the USA, Canada, Australia and New Zealand, don't need visas to enter South Africa. On arrival, visitors from these countries are granted a 90-day **visitors' permit**. You must have a valid return ticket or voucher for onward travel and at least 3 empty pages in your passport to get a permit. It is possible to apply for an extension to the permit at the office of the **Department of Home Affairs**, T021-462 4970 (Cape Town), www.home-affairs.gov.za.

Citizens of countries other than those listed above should consult the South African embassy or consulate in their country for information on visa requirements. See www.home-affairs.gov.za, to find the nearest office.

Note...

As of June 2015, children under 18 need to produce an unabridged birth certificate as well as a passport. If both parents' names are entered on the unabridged birth certificate, but only one is travelling with children, consent is required from the other parent. If children are travelling with guardians, these adults are required to produce consent from parents proving permission for the children to travel.

Weights and measures

The metric system is used in South Africa.

Index

Entries in bold refer to maps

FOOTPRINT

Features

Credits

Footprint credits

Editor: Nicola Gibbs
Production and layout: Patrick Dawson
Maps: Kevin Feeney
Colour section: Angus Dawson

Publisher: Patrick Dawson
Managing Editor: Felicity Laughton
Administration: Elizabeth Taylor
Advertising sales and marketing:
John Sadler, Kirsty Holmes
Business Development: Debbie Wylde

Photography credits

Front cover: Gimas/Shutterstock.com
Back cover: Top: Pocholo Calapre/
Shutterstock.com. Bottom: PhotoSky/
Shutterstock.com.

Colour section

Inside front cover: imageBROKER/
SuperStock.com; Gallo Images/SuperStock.
com; LOOK-foto/SuperStock.com. **Page
1**: Ollyy/Shutterstock.com. **Page 2**:
Dietmar Temps/Shutterstock.com. **Page
4**: InnaFelker/Shutterstock.com; Quality
Master/Shutterstock.com. **Page 5**: Robert
Harding Picture Library/SuperStock.
com; Watchtheworld/Shutterstock.
com; Quality Master/Shutterstock.com;
Hoberman Collection/SuperStock.com;
Travel Pictures Ltd/SuperStock.com. **Page
6**: Ken C Moore/Shutterstock.com. **Page 7**:
michaeljung/Shutterstock.com. **Page 8**:
Etienne Oosthuizen/Shutterstock.com.
Duotone Page 22: Pocholo Calapre/
Shutterstock.com. **Page 102**: David Steele/
Shutterstock.com. **Page 132**: Ken C Moore/
Shutterstock.com. **Page 148**: Dominique
de La Croix/Shutterstock.com.

Printed in Spain by GraphyCems

Publishing information

Footprint Cape Town & Garden Route
2nd edition
© Footprint Handbooks Ltd
September 2015

ISBN: 978 1 910120 53 8
CIP DATA: A catalogue record for this book
is available from the British Library

® Footprint Handbooks and the
Footprint mark are a registered
trademark of Footprint Handbooks Ltd

Published by Footprint
6 Riverside Court
Lower Bristol Road
Bath BA2 3DZ, UK
T +44 (0)1225 469141
F +44 (0)1225 469461
footprinttravelguides.com

Distributed in the USA by
National Book Network, Inc.

Every effort has been made to ensure that
the facts in this guidebook are accurate.
However, travellers should still obtain
advice from consulates, airlines, etc about
travel and visa requirements before
travelling. The authors and publishers
cannot accept responsibility for any loss,
injury or inconvenience however caused.